Ungodly
Fear

*This book is dedicated to all
who have been hurt as the
result of Christian ministry*

Stephen Parsons

Ungodly Fear

*Fundamentalist
Christianity
and the Abuse
of Power*

A LION BOOK

Published by
Lion Publishing plc
Sandy Lane West, Oxford, England
www.lion-publishing.co.uk
ISBN 0 7459 4288 1

First edition 2000
10 9 8 7 6 5 4 3 2 1 0

A catalogue record for this book is available
from the British Library

Typeset in 13/17 Berkeley Oldstyle

Printed and bound in Great Britain by
Biddles Ltd, Guildford and King's Lynn

Contents

Foreword

This is a very disturbing book, which needs to be read by many people. Over the centuries some members of the church have engaged in activities that, by their very nature, are contrary to the gospel, but done in Christ's name. But the gospel has to influence the way in which they practise their faith, as well as what is said. Too much that goes under the name of 'evangelism' is in fact proselytism. That is, using means inimical to the gospel to preach the gospel. This has always been the case and should be a cause of much repentance and apology. Those who have become the victims of such practices have every reason for rejecting Christianity because of the way they have been mistreated or abused. It is surprising that so many stay within the faith.

Many pastors will be aware of casualties. This book should help them to understand what people have been through. It is deplorable that church leaders seem to be so unwilling to tackle these issues.

Stephen Parsons deserves the gratitude of many for his careful research, his charitable understanding and his courage in laying these matters firmly before us.

Robert Jeffery
Christ Church, Oxford

Preface

In writing any book there are acknowledgments that should be made, but are too numerous to mention or remember. This book has been nurtured over many years by conversations with other people, both those agreeable to my point of view and those against it.

I should first of all mention the participants and speakers at a two-day conference on harmful religion at King's College, London, in 1995, where some robust and controversial sentiments about the damaging side of Christianity were uttered. Another inspiring conference was one held at St James's, Piccadilly, in 1996, where the same theme was addressed in the aftermath of the Sheffield Nine O'Clock Service.

Two particular individuals have helped to guide the reading behind this study. In the first place I should mention Martyn Percy, formerly chaplain of Christ's College, Cambridge, and now of the Lincoln Institute in Sheffield, who has encouraged my interest in this area for a number of years. Latterly I have been guided by Harriet Harris of Exeter University whose own research has been an invaluable source of inspiration.

I should also mention, with gratitude, the help of Maurice Lyon of Lion Publishing who has overseen the manuscript from the time when it was simply an idea to its completion. St Deiniol's residential library in Hawarden, where much of the writing was done, has provided a happy environment for reading and study over a number of years, and I am deeply appreciative of all that I have received from there.

Much of the material in chapter six was found on the

official Anglican web pages on the Internet, and I am grateful for the technology of the World Wide Web, which has revolutionized the collecting of information and access to obscure and little-known publications.

Next I should mention the real 'heroes' of this book: the individuals whose stories have provoked me into writing. Some have allowed me to record their stories, others have been listened to. All the stories have indicated to me that the narrative of abused people within the church needs to be heard and understood by as many as possible.

I must also thank my wife Frances for her patience in allowing me to use days off and holidays for writing, particularly over the past nine or ten months.

Finally I must mention Andrew Kirk, whose careful scrutiny of the completed manuscript saved me from a number of errors.

December 1999

Introduction

This has not been an easy book to write. The difficulty was not that it took several years to produce, or that I had to make numerous false starts. The problem was that the book is about suffering, and that the writing of it might possibly cause others further pain. Within the book are five stories involving four individuals and one married couple who have been through difficult times and may find themselves, through reading this book, revisiting that stage in their lives once more. Further distress may be caused through the use I make of those stories: to critique and question treasured beliefs held by sincere Christian people. Has the task of stirring up memories of suffering with the possible result of creating upset in others been worth the effort? Perhaps the answer to that question lies with you, the reader. From my point of view, the book was written in a firm belief that facing up to pain, which has been endured unjustly or unnecessarily, will have the effect of making that suffering slightly less likely to happen in the future. It is an attempt to bring something that has gone on in secret – the damaging of Christians by Christians – out into the open; to examine it and ask why it happens. When people are forced to face up to such things, they have to form an opinion about them and possibly be forced to act.

The harming of Christians by other Christians is too serious a matter to ignore. If the discussion was about the moral failing of particular Christian individuals, then this matter could be left to the disciplining bodies of the churches or the courts. This book, however, while touching on such moral failings, is more concerned with institutional abuse. By this I mean abuse that is made possible because of the teaching and theological understanding of particular church bodies. In short, the book claims that Christians are, on occasion, being harmed by beliefs and doctrines held by sincere Christian people.

I am well aware of the acute sensitivity of these matters, but I decided to press ahead with this study because it is important in itself and touches on issues in my own personal history. I have a need to make sense of things that have happened to me over the years. My relationship with those that I shall call here 'fundamentalist Christians' has, sometimes, been a source of puzzlement, but also friendship. It is only fairly recently that my concern for the health of Christianity as a whole has led me to this study and its uncomfortable questions. To explain where I am and where I come from, I need to set out part of my story.

The initial interest in the subject matter of this book probably resulted from events of some thirty-five years ago, when I was an undergraduate at university. There, for the first time, I encountered the distinctive expression of Christian Protestantism that many describe as biblical fundamentalism. Intelligent students felt compelled to argue for beliefs about the Bible which seemed very strange. They believed, for example, that the book of Isaiah was written by one man in around 710 BC, even though the second part mentions the name of a Persian king, Cyrus, who only came to the throne some 170 years later. His name was apparently revealed to the writer by direct inspiration from God, which certain conservative interpreters believed to be part of the process of prophetic insight. Daniel and the events in the book bearing his name were understood to be from historical records, and his visions were believed in some cases to foretell events happening in our own day. Jonah really spent three days and nights in a whale because that is the plain meaning of the biblical text.

I did not then understand the appeal of such beliefs about scripture, which seemed to create so many more problems than they solved. Giving accurate and detailed predictions about the future was not what I understood the Old Testament prophets to have been engaged in anyway. According to the consensus of those expounding the Bible for the benefit of theological students and ordinands like myself, the prophets were in the business of interpreting the events of their age and discerning the will of God within these events for their contemporaries. Sometimes there was, among the classical prophets, a passing interest in the distant future, but anyone who suggested that this was the main focus of their concern could be thought never to have read them properly.

Such understandings of the Bible seemed to be placing scripture into a straightjacket which fitted it very badly. All the fascination to be found in studying scripture, particularly the Old Testament, using the tools of textual and linguistic analysis, archaeological and historical research, would have been lost by this apparently arbitrary imposition of dogmatic ideas of divine authorship. Because God was in some sense the author of scripture, only a very narrow range of interpretations for any passage was deemed acceptable. This form of interpretation seemed, in comparison with the incredibly interesting fruits of 200 years of scholarly research, somewhat dull. The scholars who were not tied down by such dogmatic considerations were able to change their minds about what a

passage meant, and the continuing process of debate and
scholarly research was always capable of throwing up new ideas
about, and fresh insights into, the Bible. By contrast the
popular conservative scholarship being offered to my fellow
students was committed to defending a fixed position about
the interpretation of a passage – fixed in accordance with
certain dogmatic ideas. They were never allowed to consider
the possibility of error either in the text or in their
interpretation. I remember once trying out an argument with a
conservative Christian which went something like this.

Suppose the conservative interpreters were right in arguing for
the literal accuracy of the Bible in nine cases, but the scholars
arguing from a non-conservative position were right in one,
would that change things, given the fact that few people can be
right about everything all of the time? No, was the reply, the Bible
was true in all that it affirmed and they would point to many
books they trusted, which argued with great conviction for these
conservative positions. If the Bible is not true at every point, then
how do we know what is true? I then began to recognize that this
was an expression of Christianity which, while trying to set forth
the truths and the teachings of the Bible, was doing it in a way
that could not allow alternative perspectives to be entertained or
even heard. In short, fundamentalist Christianity was to be
understood as a belief system which proclaimed certain beliefs
about God and the Bible, but did so in a militant almost
aggressive way to protect its own convictions from compromise
or questioning. For me, fundamentalists were simply those
Christians who could not, or would not, listen.

It was while I was still a student that I encountered, in Greece,
another manifestation of Christianity that dealt in certainties and

thus was able to give support to ultra right-wing political views. This was the Christianity of a group of army officers who seized power in Greece in 1967. I arrived in the country a few months after the colonels' coup on a year's travelling scholarship to study the Orthodox Church. Amid the protestations of religious faith by those in power, I watched the gradual erosion of open debate in favour of a narrow pietistic nationalism which dictated what was to be said and thought in all areas of public life. From the top downwards all public discussion was enveloped in a miasma of platitudes and religious and nationalistic slogans. All the individuals that I naturally respected for an independence of spirit were the objects of persecution and harassment. I felt with them and for them a real anger at a system which invoked the name of God to stifle free discussion and debate, not only about politics, but also about any subject which directly or indirectly touched on it.

One fact that is not widely known is that the religious impulse within the ideology formulated by the Greek colonels came from a splinter group within Orthodoxy known as Zoe, or Life. Zoe was far more indebted to Western pietistic, puritan models than to mainstream Eastern Orthodoxy. Greece taught me to be angry at religiously supported and inspired tyranny, in very much the same way, one imagines, as Christians in the old South Africa.

The negative experiences of my student days were, to a considerable extent, softened by a series of more positive experiences with those of Christian conservative beliefs. In particular, I was impressed by the way that many who accepted a conservative view of scripture were also caught up in what became known as the charismatic movement and had a lively sense of the way that God could be active in day-to-day experience. Miracles were no problem to them and that expectancy seemed to make healings actually happen among them.

For a time from around 1972 I became intrigued and fascinated by this movement, which fitted well into aspects of Eastern Orthodoxy that I had studied in Greece. In particular, charismatic spirituality seemed to transcend mere words and focus on a wordless contemplation of God – not far from traditions of Eastern Christian spirituality. In the late 1960s and early 1970s the movement attracted many people from a wide variety of traditions and spiritualities. For a time it looked as if there might be a move towards Christian unity which was based on a sense of spiritual oneness far deeper than the formulae of denominational confessions.

For many Christians in Britain touched by charismatic worship and teaching, there have been lasting effects. One is an appreciation of lively worship. Secondly, there comes an acknowledgment of the power of group prayer and the way that the intensity of such groups is able to kindle within the participants a lively sense of the divine presence. Thirdly, many people have discovered within the charismatic movement a greater openness to fellowship, even intimacy, than they had previously experienced in their churches. Just as the High Church Oxford Movement in the nineteenth century gave to Anglican worship a new dignity, so the charismatic movement has given to the whole church a new appreciation of vibrancy and informality in worship.

An openness towards charismatic Christianity allowed my wife and I to participate in non-denominational Pentecostal worship when seeking healing for her rheumatoid arthritis.

The experience that she had in the Shire Hall, Hereford, in February 1983 led to many things: considerable physical relief from her illness, a new spiritual awareness and, in due course, a healing ministry for the two of us. Out of these events came a book, *The Challenge of Christian Healing*, which was an attempt by me to understand the nature of Christian healing and the implications it had for the Christian faith.

I was, at that time, as appreciative of the charismatic dimension as I ever had been. When, however, the book came out towards the end of 1986, there was a sour note which perhaps symbolized the fact that I, as an individual, would never be acceptable to this strand of Christianity. In the city of Hereford there were two religious bookshops, the first being the cathedral bookshop, which stocked predominantly mainstream Christian books. There was also, not far off, a Christian bookshop which limited itself to mainly evangelical Christian books. On the day of my book's publication, quite a number of people in Hereford went to both bookshops to buy their copies. The evangelical bookshop had five copies and these sold out on the first day. Friends from the Free and Pentecostal Churches began to ring me up and ask why my book was not on sale in the Christian bookshop, the only one they had dealings with. I eventually tackled the manager, but could get no satisfactory answer as to why he had failed to reorder. In the end I concluded that, somewhere in the chain of command, someone had put a block on the shop stocking my book because the information on the back cover revealed that I was an ecumenical officer. In some circles, 'ecumenical' is a code word to describe a woolly Christian who does not know what he believes, or worse still is prepared to talk to Roman Catholics!

This incident was, in many ways, a symbol of how something that in itself was life-giving, joyous and freeing was in retrospect being quietly, but inexorably, stifled by the tentacles of a fundamentalist, controlling form of religion. That process had been going on steadily within much of charismatic Christianity over most of the previous fourteen years that I had known it and it continues right up to this day. From the time of open communication across the mainstream denominations, which I had noticed in 1972, there had been a gradual 'ghettoization' of the charismatic style of Christianity in many places. In short, what seemed to be happening was that instead of the free joyous styles of worship and church life that marked the early conferences being sustained, there was a gradual descent into authoritarian structures and rigid belief systems, and an adoption of fundamentalist expressions of faith. People like myself who had regarded themselves as friends now found themselves excluded by an increasing harshness of tone.

What was happening? The first thing was that the very freedom that had marked the charismatic movement in its early days could not be sustained. The process of sensing a tremendous sense of liberation in their inner experience of worship had meant that many Christians began to regard denominational ties as unimportant. Later the focus of the movement shifted from fellowships within the denominational churches to independent house churches, and these, through the latter part of the 1970s and into the 1980s, appeared to be where the action was liveliest. These house churches, often beginning with meetings in the homes of individuals, gradually blossomed into full-blown denominational structures, with networks of leaders and organization stretching right across Britain. The older denominations were, to a considerable extent, being rejected in this process. A definitive and sympathetic account of this movement of independent house churches is given by Andrew Walker in his book, *Restoring the Kingdom*. The history of these churches is not, however, the concern of this study. What is of concern is the way that the very independence of these fellowships led to their increasing dependence on the only system of authority and organization available to them: the authority of their leadership and biblical authority as filtered through these same leaders. In short, the charismatic impulse was being overtaken by fundamentalist structures and ideas. The weakness of an appeal to the Bible was that those who search the scriptures for models of church life find very much what they wish to find there.

My more recent exposure to the charismatic/fundamentalist world has been marked, not by direct association, but by my attempt to help individuals who have been touched by that world in a negative way. Like many other people I was aware of a number of stories in the press about high-profile situations of Christian abuse, such as that in Sheffield surrounding the Nine O'Clock Service. In that particular episode, which made headlines in Britain in August 1995, an Anglican church leader, Chris Brain, was found to have manipulated and abused a considerable segment of his congregation. The comparative ease with which Brain obtained a hold over those he abused alerted many people to the real power that a religious leader can exert. Brain, by the time his abuse was exposed, had moved beyond the charismatic culture which provided the setting for his own formation as a Christian. He had embraced a distinctive theological emphasis known as creation spirituality, but the charismatic structures of church life that gave him enormous unquestioned authority were still intact. One lasting effect of Sheffield has been a growing awareness of the existence of religious abuse in other settings and contexts, though to my knowledge there has been little detailed study of the issues raised by that event. It has especially become apparent that relationships and ideas which exist in certain manifestations of the charismatic/fundamentalist culture are sometimes the cause of pain and hurt. I started to meet people who needed to talk through the fear and bewilderment that they had experienced through a traumatic encounter with a conservative Christian individual or institution. Thus it can be said that this present study arises out of my own need to make sense of the trauma suffered by individuals I have met, as well as understand an important issue within the life of the wider church.

Having made a decision to write about abusive Christianity I found myself, during 1998, acquiring some extremely vivid stories which illustrated well the power of ideas to inflict damage on individuals. These stories reached me in a variety of ways. I found that once I had told people about my study they often seemed to know someone, often far away, who had had an experience of Christian abuse. One story reached me through a cult-watch organization. Another story was given to me over lunch at a conference on Christian healing. Yet another was telephoned to me by someone who knew nothing of my research, but had heard that I was a 'safe' person with whom to share their story. Two stories became six and I realized that, without having searched it out, I had a wealth of material which needed to be collected together and made the backbone of my presentation of this theme.

The stories were mostly recorded on tape while I was on a writing break from the parish in January 1999. As the reader will discern, the gathering of such personal information was not without its problems. As a clergyman I am well used to hearing personal information of all kinds, but it is never gathered for the purpose of dissemination and comment. There was also a tension between hearing the story as part of a piece of research to raise issues in a book and facing individuals in human need. Most of my stories have no neat fairy-tale ending. In some cases the continuing pain is all too obvious. Walking out with a tape of an individual's personal life story felt wrong. The pastoral person was in conflict with the researcher/writer with a crusade.

Of the six stories recorded and edited, five appear in the book. The sixth was left out because the individual, having lived with her transcript for a month, was unable to let it go. The experience of catharsis achieved by telling of her tribulations was followed by a sense that she would have no peace if it appeared in print, however heavily disguised. All the other stories have been changed in their details to spare the tellers as much as possible any further pain. I hope they may feel that the effort and pain of sharing their stories has not been wasted if, as a result, the reader is made more aware about victims of certain conservative Christian ideas. When terrible things are done in secret, they often have no name and no one is held accountable. Once they are in the open and discussed everyone becomes aware of and alert to their occurrence.

A further problem in listening to and recording the stories of individuals who report harmful incidents is that there is no opportunity to interview the churches or people that have allegedly caused the abuse. Such an attempt to present the other point of view was impossible, not only because of the elapse of time, but also because the victims in most cases would not have allowed me to do it. A victim retains a sense of powerlessness towards his or her abuser even after the passage of years. Any suggestion that some dialogue is possible, even indirectly, is probably unrealistic. So I have been left with one-sided accounts which I have attempted very hard to interpret fairly. The stories remain, nevertheless, allegations. As an observer I have, generally speaking, given all the stories a high degree of credibility even though I am aware that some of my readers may wish to question their total veracity. For my part their credibility lies in the fact that they fit into a wider picture of damaging ministry that I have become aware of over several years. The stories thus represent and typify other accounts not recorded in this book. It was listening to these other earlier unrecorded stories of abuse that gave me the context as well as the motivation to do this study.

This book, then, attempts to understand and, at the same time, provide a critique of, the form of Christianity that is variously described as charismatic/fundamentalist, particularly in its capacity to harm those it seeks to serve. The book would not, of course, claim that this is an inevitable consequence of this type of Christianity. It would also not claim that abuse is only confined to this manifestation of the Christian faith. The longer this study has continued the more I have become aware of the way that the whole church has a problem with power and its abuse. But it is, I believe, right to focus on fundamentalist Christianity, and this branch of the faith will always have a distinctive problem with power in the claims that it makes for itself, namely that it possesses a book containing God's very word, preserved without error. To know or possess without ambiguity God's word, and thus to know his will, is to have an object containing irresistible power for those who share this belief. By definition, if we have something that is infallibly true, everything which does not agree with it is wrong. Any human power that is exercised will be the stronger and less able to be resisted when it is backed up by an authority which cannot be challenged. Opposition to this authority will be treated as opposition to God himself, and the need to discredit it or even destroy it becomes paramount. In the final chapters there will be cause to ponder further on this characteristic of militancy, which is such a prominent feature of what I would regard as a fundamentalist position. Resistance to challenges to the system is an important part of the way that the influence and honour of the system are upheld. It is when such resistance begins to use unacceptable violence that areas of danger can be seen, both for the individuals caught up in the system and for the integrity of the Christian faith itself.

The energy and power that surround an infallible belief system are not unattractive, particularly to those who lack power in society: the poor and disadvantaged. By being identified with a powerful expression of Christianity their own morale and self-esteem are raised. Others who come under its influence, by seeking help as sick or needy people, will also feel the enormous power claimed by this belief system. Who can argue with or contradict God's will? The only realistic response is to submit to this power, and trust that it is indeed the power of God it claims to be. Unfortunately, where power

over people's hearts and minds is claimed, there will always be
the potential for those who enjoy wielding power to use it
corruptly. So the doctrine of a Bible without error may easily
become the opportunity for individuals and groups to wield
considerable power, with all the opportunities for damage to
other people that such power affords. This book's subtitle is
'Fundamentalist Christianity and the Abuse of Power',
because the possibility of abuse is one real danger for this form
of Christianity. While there is, of course, no inevitable
connection between a Bible without error and harmful
incidents, there will always be a need for those who have such
a belief system to realize how easily such ideas can do damage.
Five stories of abuse do not, of course, prove that in one
particular manifestation of Christianity abusive power is a
problem. Nevertheless, I believe the stories do indicate at the
very least that conservative Protestant Christianity will always
need to examine its structures to ward off a constant
temptation to use the particular power that is given to it by its
own theology harmfully and abusively. This is a task that it
shares with the whole church.

This book is written both for victims and for perpetrators. By
perpetrators I am not suggesting that any reader of this book who
holds conservative views about scripture is necessarily guilty of
the malpractice or abuse revealed by my case studies. Far from it.
But I do challenge all conservative Christians to look at the
environment of their fellowships, churches or healing centres to
ensure that abuses of the kind recounted in this book cannot
happen. It is not simply a matter of making sure that a particular
congregation or fellowship is not playing power games or
indulging in abusive practices. That can happen in churches of

any tradition. It is recognizing that the belief systems, and the fashions of ideas that people may attach themselves to, need to be constantly reviewed. Even if I am not the person creating any harm, I may be indirectly helping the abusers by sharing in the same belief system in an uncritical way.

All those in this book who appear to victimize individuals by rigid application of fundamentalist principles found in the Bible are surrounded by fellowships and congregations who collude with them in the beliefs that are being acted out in an abusive way. Without that collusion of many people both within and across congregations, the ideas that are responsible for the harm could never have taken root and achieved their power to hurt. The ideas that lay behind the treatment of Kathleen in chapter two were fashionable and widespread in the early 1990s. It was the wide, uncritical acceptance of those ideas that gave the counsellors their power to interpret Kathleen's life in a particular way. When those ideas went out of fashion, did anyone mark the event by apologizing for having been so obsessed with them as a way of explaining the advent of illness? Did anyone take responsibility for the damage caused by these once-fashionable ideas?

For an individual not to apologize or feel shame for past and present mistakes by individuals in their fellowship, or in the wider body with which they identify, is, to a greater or lesser extent, to collude with them. The level of blame to be apportioned to an individual will, of course, vary enormously, but the attitudes people have – their racism, their class prejudices and their intolerance – will always in some way give comfort to those who act out those attitudes in deeds of violence or abuse. The Stephen Lawrence episode in all its horror was not only a violent racist murder of an individual, but also a symptom of a wider racism in society. Without this widespread intolerance being held, the murderous intentions of the perpetrators could never have been nourished and sustained. In the same way, prejudice and assumptions in churches about women, for example, will occasionally be acted out by an individual in a deed of cruelty or humiliation against a particular woman. The mindset that creates abuse in a church setting will always have its roots in the wider institution and the attitudes and assumptions that have been nurtured there.

This book is, however, written against a background of hope. I would never have been able to talk to the individuals in it, and write their stories, unless I believed that there was a higher and better expression of Christianity to be found. If a story about abuse of power is to be told without making the reader feel overwhelmed by his own powerlessness, there needs to be a counterblast of hope. That counterblast is to be found in the attitude of Jesus himself, who, as chapter nine will show, was passionate about condemning the abuse of power and about the need to stand up for the weak and vulnerable against the self-justification of the abusers. It is this deep concern of Jesus that lies in the pages of the gospels, always available for rediscovery by Christians in each generation. It is always there to challenge those guilty of using their power wrongfully and inappropriately. Above all the attitudes of Jesus show that at the heart of the Christian faith and the God who inspires it, there is a new way, a fresh way, to deal with power, the abuse of which has been so frequently and so predictably a feature of human history, both Christian and secular.

If Shirley was downstairs and wanted something, she would say, 'Go and fetch this for me upstairs. Run.' They were treating you like a child.

Chapter One

The Church as a Family – Promise and Disillusionment

Of all the promises that are offered by the church, one of the most attractive is that it will act for its members as a substitute family. This is particularly appealing to those who live alone or whose experience of early family life has been traumatic or incomplete. The offer of community life, of involvement within a close family structure, was one that held great appeal for a couple in their early forties struggling to cope with problems of family life. The church appeared to offer a solution. This is how the reality of that promise turned out for John and Rachel.

The story now to be recounted can be summarized in a few sentences. After eight years as members of a large, successful charismatic church in an English city, John and Rachel left to become members of a community church which was run by an American pastor and his wife. Within a short time they had handed over £78,000 to the church, the proceeds from the sale of their house, hoping in that way to become founding members of a group living in community. The reality was very different. After a couple of years they found their position so impossible that they left, even though in doing so they became temporarily homeless and penniless. John and Rachel are now members of no particular church, but they are able to look back over their experiences without bitterness, with their faith still intact.

In my first meeting with John and Rachel, having heard the outline of their story, I shared with them, during the taped interview, the thought that their Christian experience up to the point where they had handed over all their money had predisposed them to passivity and dependence on individuals in positions of authority. They told me about their experiences at St Philip's (the large charismatic church) as way of responding to this question.

In 1980 Rachel, a divorced mother with two boys, visited her doctor with depression:

> My doctor brought me to St Philip's. He drew a diagram on his prescription pad. 'Life with Jesus at the centre and life with you at the centre. You don't need a psychiatrist, you need the Lord. I'll ask my wife to come and see you.' 'What will she do?' 'Oh she'll probably pray with you. Will that be all right?' And I thought OK. She came round and she said, 'Bring the boys to church on Sunday.' And I started going to church at St Philip's. That was in 1980 and I met John in August 1980 when he answered my advert in the local free newspaper to join a concert-going group. We then joined the same home group towards the end of 1980.

They moved in together a few months later and soon Rachel became pregnant. This did not fit well with their membership of St Philip's and soon the home-group leader visited them. As

Rachel put it, 'They came hot-foot and said you must commit to each other and you must commit to Jesus. So we said, "OK then."' They were married in the summer of 1981 with the home group giving them a great deal of welcome love and support.

A year or two into their marriage, when their son Luke was, in his mother's words, 'an angry controlling toddler', Rachel went to a new couple in the church for counselling. She went for an hour, week after week, and she revelled in the attention that she received, something that she had never had when she was a child. She recognized how dependent she became on them:

> Maybe God used it to a degree, but I think [John and I] both agree that we never actually got conviction of sin. It exalted self, it was about me, it was an hour, hour and a half, every week talking about me. The great I am, delving into my childhood and all that – there is plenty of muck in my childhood which does make you the way you are partly. To a degree it was helpful but it was superficial.

John explained how he also came into counselling after his marriage to Rachel:

> I had gone from being a 37-year-old bachelor to being a father of three sons; there was no transition time. I was ill-fitted for the task. I liked children, but it is the problem of any people living together that you become aware of each other's sin in a way that you don't when you're alone. Alone you can be as self-centred as you like and nobody cares. Then with someone else you have demands made on you and the other people's

needs. The home-group leader came and rescued us from a battle we were having. We used to cry for help. We were drowning in it because we were angry with each other. But I believe now that it is the responsibility of the mediators and pastors to show the sheep where to feed. So that they can feed themselves. That wasn't really happening.

John and Rachel eventually moved from being helped by the home-group leader to being counselled by the vicar's wife. There had been considerable problems in their relationship, problems connected with drink and domestic violence. The church as a whole was moving into family therapy, and Rachel and John agreed to act as guinea pigs. Rachel's older boys, now thirteen and fifteen, loathed these sessions when everyone was encouraged to talk about their individual pain and the effect of their stepfather's violence and drink problems. Rachel, moreover, allowed herself to see the vicar's wife as a surrogate mother, but she recognized even then that this dependence was in no way contributing to the building up of her relationship with John.

At this point John made an observation about the dynamics of St Philip's. 'Within the charismatic churches there are two sorts of people: those who say, "Daddy, Daddy, help!" and those who want to be leaders and therefore want to be Daddy. They need to be needed.' The church was very good at attracting needy people with a variety of problems, both spiritual and emotional. The sheer weight of this need meant that everyone was drawn to help in some way, even if they were inexperienced and vulnerable themselves. John and

Rachel found that in no time they were being asked to lead a group. Later, they were asked to form part of a church plant to another area in the parish. John had some musical abilities and became part of a music group. Both were asked to preach from time to time. They also took part in street marches, until these were stopped after local people objected to the press that they did not wish to be woken up on a Sunday morning by the sound of a drumbeat! By this stage, although they were locked into the church by their emotional dependence on those who were counselling them, they began to feel a little disquieted at the way leadership was exercised. John explained, 'There was a worship leader, a very lovely guy, and one day the PCC decided they didn't need him and just fired him. Utterly ruthless. I was utterly shocked by it. Perhaps he had seen some things were wrong and spoken out.'

A further problem they can now identify was the way in which they were not only dependent on individual counsellors, but also on the institution for their identity. Theologically they now criticize the teaching of the church because it laid no emphasis on the need of the individual to take responsibility for their own sin. John expressed the dilemma in this way:

The church was creating dependency without responsibility. I was getting my identity from the church. I was
fleeing from family responsibility by going to all these
meetings. I shudder now to think of all the damage done.
The status we had was from the organization, not one
under God. We propped up the organization. We were
being offered palliatives without ever being offered a path
to responsibility. We both had very low self-esteem. Give

me more comfort was the message. You're sold the wrong
stuff. We ended up worse off in the end.

John and Rachel also recognize now that they were being
sucked into a church system that, partly under the influence of
John Wimber, the American evangelist, was seeking to solve
problems by offering more and more in the way of power. Like
many Christians in this tradition they were becoming chasers
after sensation and novelty, always expecting a new Christian
guru around the corner to solve their problems in a stroke.
After their years at St Philip's searching for healing, they went
one stage further, seeking healing through spiritual deliverance.
Such a specialized form of ministry was not on offer locally, so
they travelled to Ellel Grange in Lancashire to find it. Rachel
continued,

> We were aware of our shortcomings and we were des-
> perate to get healing. And when it didn't happen, we
> looked for the power thing with deliverance. We went
> to Ellel Grange for some weekends away. I was impressed
> by that and I went praying, 'Lord, sort me out.' And the
> first evening we went there was such a sense of unity
> there. And during the worship I had this picture of my
> father trying to strangle me. And when I told Peter
> Horrobin [a minister at Ellel Grange] that, he and his
> friends were administering deliverance until way after
> midnight. And that was a good release, but I can see that
> we embraced the deliverance thing... because we sensed
> we needed more power and the Word of Faith teaching
> offers you more power. I see why we were hooked into

that. It was actually psychological, it was carnal; there wasn't actually much of the power of God in it. We knew we were lacking that. And that predisposed us to go for a still more powerful kind of teaching.

John and Rachel left St Philip's around 1990 after accepting total-immersion baptism at another church. It marked an end to their association, as they knew that the church would not accept this action. Leaving was no simple matter, as Rachel explained, 'The full-immersion baptism was a cut-off point. It was awful after we left. People in the street would literally just ignore me. People were so suspicious of you for having left the best church ever.' Perhaps the chief reason for leaving was that they had had a surfeit of triumphant Christianity when their own needs were still unmet. John added his comment,

You go wanting to be uplifted and you come back feeling totally depressed. Lust is wanting to be satisfied, but the goodies were not on offer. Lust is never satisfied. Christianity à la John Wimber says that Christianity is going to be one continuous joyride or party. When the party stops, disillusion starts. You get to a point where you're sick of it. You throw up.

Both John and Rachel still had a continuing need for healing. This was in addition to the educational needs of their young son Luke who was unhappy at school and had been educated at home for a time. Now unemployed through redundancy, John and his family travelled 100 miles to another city to visit a church with a school attached. The church was one belonging to the Word of Faith family, an American church group with distinctive ideas about prosperity and health being God's will for his people as long as they have sufficient faith. Their first experience of walking into the school was overwhelming. Although there were only seventeen children, the sense of order, discipline, efficiency and love captivated them. 'We looked and thought, This is the place for our son.'

The school solved various problems for John and Rachel simultaneously. As well as providing a place for Luke, it also offered work, albeit unpaid, to both parents. John's musical abilities as well as his previous experience as a teacher were going to be used, and Rachel was also given a role. In the light of what happened later, however, John could see what was really happening:

> I can see that I was looking spiritually again to pass the buck. Spiritually it is the responsibility of the father to bring up the child, but we were looking for an excuse to offload a responsibility we didn't want. I wanted the school to discipline Luke because I wasn't able to do it properly or lovingly. The convicting thing is that I wanted to pass the hot potato on to someone else. We were attracted to this dynamic organization, full of vision; they were full of good humour, energy and joy.

Having accepted a place for Luke, the family found a rented house nearby, and both parents went off on a week's course at the national headquarters for the organization that supplies material from the United States to all the Christian schools in the network. The training was far from conventional:

The training consisted of going through a series of books, listening to tapes with headphones, filling in the gaps. It was supposed to indoctrinate you or get you acquainted with the philosophy behind ACE (Accelerated Christian Education), and also allow you to identify with the children filling in the gaps. It's very mechanical. The whole thing depends on the administration of the system. We sat with our headphones on, going through all these workbooks. It was horrendously difficult. Lots of people found it very hard among the adults. The bait was that if you got enough marks you became supervisors. Then you'd be well in. We both got good marks.

John was, however, not accepted as a teacher, because the school, still young, had never had a man on the staff.

I asked Rachel what were her duties at the school:

I was a monitor, not a supervisor. It was quite stressful really. You went round and checked all the children's homework, that each individual's work had been done. They were in individual desks with sides. They weren't allowed to leave their desks unless they put their flag up. There was no talking. You answered the flag. Everything had to be referred to June the supervisor. Everything. The children marked their own work. They'd fill in the gaps in the workbook in the core subjects and then they would go to the scoring station. You had to check their scoring, check that they were scoring properly. There was no classroom teaching in the morning, but in the afternoon they did various things; the art teacher did art, the music teacher did music and the cookery teacher did cookery.

Things, however, that are supposed to run like clockwork do not necessarily suit the flexible needs of real human beings. Rachel felt real anger on behalf of a child that she felt was being crushed by the system. The supervisor, however, took a very different view of her insubordination. 'She took me into the office and really laid into me. "You have to set a good example to these children. How dare you trample on the blood of Jesus." I think I picked up the total lack of compassion. There was an absolute rule from the top and no flexibility.' I enquired further about the discipline in the school, and Rachel first of all spoke about Luke's experience:

Luke was paddled a few times, whacked as other children were, and we thought it was good. Sometimes we thought we saw good come from it. He was paddled for mocking. Also he would get into trouble because of his attitude. They were also very hard on cheating, deceiving, lying or covering up. They tried to encourage you to walk openly and be honest. That was good, but it was a regime of being ruled by fear. I think he grew in confidence, it did him some good.

But Rachel recounted another method of control, control through shaming:

June had Luke up in front of the whole school. He had been mocking and she didn't know how to stop it. So she

made it public and I was on duty that day. I remember
fighting back the tears. My little boy stood up in front
of the whole school and she did it in the name of
Christian love. She said to all the children, 'Luke needs
your help. He can't stop mocking and using his tongue
as a weapon to hurt people. And so I want you all to
go up to him and tell him you love him.' It was very
moving in one sense, but later I thought, Was that
right? Was that of God? To make a public spectacle of
him? It looked good, but when you went deeper it was
different.

How often did paddling happen? Quite frequently at the school.
Paddling consisted of being hit by a wooden spoon on the leg
above the knee (the boys all wore short trousers), and most days
at least one child would get the paddle. So on average each child
would get hit with a spoon at least once a month. The rule book
was enforced with great precision. A great deal of time, according
to Rachel, was spent explaining to them how they had sinned
with the intention of making them aware of the nature of their
sin. There was also a large amount of 'counselling'. I suggested
that another word for it might be 'intimidation'.

John then commented, 'The ACE system tends to produce
either robots or rebels.' Rachel went on,

The children used to spend the whole morning at the
books and even children of three-and-a-half years old
were subjected to that. This was something contrary
to any sense of education. In my last term I was in the
pre-school and we had to make the children – fifteen

kids we had – fill in colours within a strict time limit.
They had to use the correct colours to colour in. It was
mayhem. Yet some of the more difficult children did
grow and flourish, perhaps because of the individual
attention. There was a high pupil–teacher ratio and,
bear in mind, nearly all the children had a parent in
the school anyway. At the end we were burned out,
exhausted. Absolutely exhausted. The relentlessness of
the demands on us, the staff as well as the children, the
lack of freedom for the Holy Spirit. Sometimes I found
myself going round to the children and saying, 'You
know, even if you fail that test, God will still love you.'
I think I would have been condemned if they realized
I was going round saying this. June was paranoid once
towards the end of term: 'What if they don't finish
their paces [exercises]?' I was amazed and said, 'June, it
won't be the end of the world.' It was their life, it was
an obsession.

The ethos of authoritarianism from the top embraced both staff
and children. Peremptory orders were handed out: 'If Shirley
[the head] was downstairs and wanted something, she would
say, "Go and fetch this for me upstairs. Run." They were treating
you like a child. Every time I hit something like this I swallowed
it. I thought, "They've got to be right. It's me that's wrong."'
    Although Rachel was a volunteer and wanted to work
mornings only, so that she could be around for Luke when he
came home, this was soon stopped. 'They said you need to
come back in the afternoons to fill in all the paperwork. If
you've worked in the morning you have to finish off. So I was

on the trot the whole time. It was terrible. I got very tired and my legs were bad then.'

In spite of danger signals coming at them from all sides from the very beginning, John and Rachel made over to the church almost the entire proceeds of their house sale, totalling £78,000, in the summer of 1991. This was to enable the church to bid for a vandalized but roomy building that was coming onto the market at that time. It would, when restored, house both the school and the leaders of the church, as well as John and Rachel. They moved in at the end of 1991, when some basic repairs had been done.

Communal living was never to be a bed of roses. The flats were not divided from one another as they all led into one another:

And it so happened that when they had guests, that the only convenient loo for them was ours. One day June said, We are expecting so-and-so to be coming, we'll expect your loo to be cleaned up. Absolutely squeaky clean. The words came to my mind, but not to my mouth at that time, Is that a request or a command, June?

Rachel continued,

The stress levels went up big time in March with the county festival. All the children had to do the extra work to prepare for that. The choral verse-speaking was all right for the first year, but it got harsher. It seemed extraordinary to expect children as young as four-year-olds to keep going for hours with this choral speaking. But what got to me at the end was that here am I, supposedly worshipping a God who is not into performance orientation because I can't possibly do enough to earn God's love. He just gives it to me freely simply because I say, 'Help, Lord, please.' And yet here I am in a school that is obsessed with performance.

Apart from the sacrificial time given to the school, time had to be freely given to the church. John and Rachel recalled an instance when a huge mound of earth had to be cleared, and the church leaders demanded that everyone, including the children, muck in to shift it one Saturday, to save money on hiring earth-moving equipment. It was in the height of summer.

Sunday worship also began to become a gruelling ordeal: 'There was a worship practice for an hour from 8.30, then an hour of Bible study, then a two-hour service. So Luke aged ten would get up for half past eight and not get back till half past one.'

John, reflecting on his time at the Faith church, observed how many needy and previously abused people were attracted to the church. The vulnerable, people who had had their self-esteem damaged in childhood by various kinds of abuse, would flock to a church that promised to give them an experience of family. In return for absolute commitment to the leaders, such people were often re-abused and exploited. What finally drove John and Rachel away was the situation of Rachel contracting MS in early 1992, and the almost complete lack of compassion for her in her weakness. The worship leader did offer prayer for her at the beginning of worship practice each week, but little sympathy was forthcoming at the school, where she found herself less and less able to meet the demands of the head teacher and supervisors. The school day lasted from 7.45 till 5.30 or 6 p.m. When she finally gave her notice on grounds of illness, she was still 'persuaded' to work in the office every morning, and drive children around the place in the afternoon. On one particular afternoon, in a state of near exhaustion, she asked a friend to do the school run for her. This friend let her down and the pastor then telephoned to demand that she collect the children. Rachel, though terrified of disobeying a direct command, refused. This resulted in a confrontation between John and the leadership and John and Rachel finally moved out of the home that they had half paid for at the end of March 1993.

When I first met John and Rachel in the summer of 1998, they had passed through the stage of self-recrimination and guilt and were seeking, through legal means, to get back some or all of the money they had handed over. Although living on John's income from full-time care work, in a rented house, their marriage seemed stronger than at any time during the period they had described to me. The frenetic search for 'family' and a parental figure seemed to be over, as they were learning to live out of the resources of their own faith. For the time being they live outside a church institution, creating their own sacred space and their relationship with God, which does not demand of them subordination to, or indeed humiliation by, other human beings or any human institution.

Comment

The story of John and Rachel is not one of abuse from beginning to end. Rather, it appears to be about a couple who became, through membership of one church, predisposed to abuse by another. St Philip's, the Anglican charismatic church of which they were members from 1980 to 1990, gave them many things, but it seems from their account to have failed to encourage them in the maturity and independence of thought that would have enabled them to stand up to the abusive situation at the Faith church, at the next stage of their Christian journey. How had the Anglican church failed them?

John, in his taped interview, put his finger on two important issues during his assessment of his membership of the charismatic church. The first thing was the creation of a culture of dependency. In its enthusiastic embrace of the healing ideas propagated by John Wimber and his team in the 1980s, John's church set up structures designed to help individuals meet every need – physical, social, mental and spiritual – within the confines of the church. It is possible to believe that God has provided resources to meet every human need, but a problem will arise if that help is, for any reason, inadequate or incompetent. The help offered will also be beyond the checks and balances that officially guide secular therapeutic practice.

The way that John and Rachel responded to the apparent culture of dependency at St Philip's seems to have led to their taking on the role of grateful children within a substitute family. When a church operates in an individual's life as a substitute family, by responding to a conscious or unconscious need on the part of the member to be re-parented, various dangers arise. One is that the individual may well cease to be able to act independently. There was nothing apparently deliberately harmful in the way the family dynamic worked at St Philip's. The church appears to have operated at the benevolent end of the spectrum, eschewing abusive practice, but John claimed that even with this level of gentle control, their spiritual growth was hampered. He spoke about never having been brought to the foot of the cross, and this was his way of saying that neither he nor Rachel had ever been faced with full responsibility for their actions. This atmosphere of passive dependency is well described in a study of an American fundamentalist church by Nancy Ammerman. Joe Slavin is reported as saying, 'I love the absolutes... I'm glad I serve a living God that is absolute. He has all the answers. I don't have responsibility. He gives us all the answers. He makes the decisions for me and that's great.'

In this particular church there was little by way of an atmosphere of dialogue, openness and freedom through which the possibility of growth towards maturity might have been sought. In such a situation there is a stark choice to be made. Either one submits to the authority of the prevailing leadership and the total ethos of the church and remains dependent, or one breaks away. However benevolent St Philip's was, the issue of, albeit unwittingly, keeping members at the level of dependent children is a serious one which affects many churches, and not only those of a charismatic flavour.

The second issue which caused John and Rachel's final breakaway from St Philip's was the claim that ever greater and more wonderful blessings were constantly being offered to members. I have already spoken appreciatively of the spiritual environment, particularly within worship, that charismatic churches offer to their members. The problem, however, for the movement as a whole, is that sometimes the old no longer seems to satisfy, and thus there are frequent reinventions of the experience, or what are called 'new outpourings'. Any church which makes its name from introducing large numbers of people to exciting experiences of spiritual ecstasy has an almost impossible task to perform. Once a church has introduced its members to exotic psycho-spiritual experiences, there is a drawing away from the boring business of getting on with ordinary living into an exotic realm where all is new and constantly exciting. As John claimed, it is like a drug of which one can never have too much. A cynic might claim that such religious experience was a kind of reward for devoted subservience to the church and its constant demands, rather than any induction into spiritual maturity. The charge made by John that the religious exoticisms over ten years had not enabled them to grow spiritually is a serious one and, as far as I know, not properly addressed in the books about such experiences. So often these experiences, because they are apparently the work of the Holy Spirit, are treated as an end in themselves. Constant exposure to such experiences, whatever their source, means that the important business of growing up and out may simply cease to happen.

Both John and Rachel admit that their personal needs for themselves and for Luke made them blind to what was going on at the Faith church they joined after leaving St Philip's. Unlike St Philip's, the Faith church appears to have had a strong hierarchical controlling structure, wherein the interests of the leaders seem to have been more important than those of the membership. And yet it was the very power and confidence that flowed to the leaders as the result of all this obedience and quasi-militaristic functioning that was so attractive to John and Rachel. Having felt so dependent and passive for so long, they were grateful for the scraps of attention and care given to them by self-confident leaders.

The cult of power and personality that is often a feature of the charismatic environment means that idealization and hero-worship is not infrequently found in this style of church life. A powerful personality is easily presented as the consequence of being 'close to God', rather than of being placed high up in a human hierarchy. The disadvantaged and vulnerable long for this power for themselves, but have to make do with being merely close to their admired role models. The only power John possessed was that in the capital left over after selling the house. With that, he and Rachel sought to buy some of the power and self-esteem that their life histories and their experience of church life over the previous eleven years had denied them. What they obtained was a brief moment of civility and attention from the leadership before they were thrust back into being foot soldiers in the service of an army, in which they had very little idea of what they were fighting for.

Although the church they had joined was a Faith church, which stressed God's will for the health and prosperity of his servants, the main thrust of church teaching, as recalled by John and Rachel, seems to have been far more on control and obedience. Emphasis on instant compliance was what they remembered, from the organization of the school to the running of the Sunday services. Members seem to have bought into the idea that obedience to the leadership was obedience to God. To question the need for such obedience was to put their assurance of salvation in jeopardy.

What did the leadership have that allowed it to retain such control? The answer must lie in the fact that at the central act of the Faith community, the Sunday service, the word of God was preached. The pastor would have had a greater knowledge of scripture than his flock, and that knowledge, as well as ability in preaching and exposition, was a catalyst for all the power he exercised over the Faith community. Lip-service would have been given to the idea that God's word was dominant, but it is hard, from John and Rachel's account, to discern any way in which the power of the leaders was checked by an awareness of their own fallibility. Power of this magnitude bolstered, one imagines, by other personalities too vulnerable and lacking in self-esteem to question and to challenge, was simultaneously immensely attractive and abusive. It fascinated its subordinates, yet also damaged them and denied them the chance of finding their way back to their own power. Obedience to this power was made into a test of faith in God. When obedience was given by an individual, what was actually achieved was humiliation and a greater distance from their inherent self-respect.

John and Rachel wanted desperately to prove their faith by giving away their money. What also seems to have been happening was that they were looking for approval from a parental figure. At the same time they were trying to buy family life both for themselves and their son. In fact, community life, whether Christian or otherwise, will always meet difficulties when individuals bring their vulnerabilities and unconscious and unacknowledged needs into close proximity with others. The leadership, whether for reasons of naïvety or calculating deviousness, completely ignored the possibility or probability of the community not having a long-term future. No thought was apparently given to what would happen in that eventuality. They had seemingly no scruples about accepting this money from an unemployed couple and they were careful to ensure that a Deed of Waiver was signed. If the leadership genuinely saw no problem in accepting the money, as is possible, then they were also blind to the dynamics of power operating within their community. The fact that there was an obvious imbalance of power between John and Rachel and the leadership suggests that there was, in all probability, a cynical use of a position of influence for their own ends.

John and Rachel's story involves power. In both churches power belonging to God and the Holy Spirit would have been celebrated and acknowledged, but there would probably have been a lot of blindness, deliberate or otherwise, about how the power was operating at a human level. It is probable that the Faith church would fall apart if the power issues were honestly faced up to. Any outside observer would have been able to spot that the church was not only attracting vulnerable and needy people, but also, in different ways, using them through what I would describe as exploitative structures. The earth-moving incident recorded in John and Rachel's account reads more like an example of exploiting people for selfish ends than any exercise in community building. The leadership, on that occasion, simply gave the orders and the membership did the work.

Word of Faith churches

The Faith churches under the leadership of Kenneth Hagin will be given a more extensive scrutiny in chapter seven, particularly in connection with their far-reaching influence in the worldwide charismatic movement. Their essential message is simple: God wants all his people to be blessed physically and materially and such blessing is available to all who have faith. I noted in commenting on John and Rachel's account of their time at the Faith church that the main remembered focus of teaching was obedience rather than the blessings of faith. No doubt were I to have listened to actual sermons at their church I would have heard the attractive promises of this type of Christianity. Somehow, in the light of what happened to John and Rachel, such promises seemed a little out of place and were not remembered.

On the international scene Faith ideas have a prominent place. Figures that are quoted of Christians in Africa increasing by 15,000 to 20,000 daily relate to churches with a strong charismatic emphasis in which Faith ideas are important. Two things give Faith ideas a particular attractiveness to the African people. Firstly, the economic decline of Africa has been little short of catastrophic over the past thirty years, with incomes dropping by 40 per cent during the 1980s. The Faith gospel of a new access to wealth and material blessing is especially compelling in this situation. Secondly, many Africans are receptive to the wider aspects of charismatic Christianity, with its emphasis on demons and spiritual presences, as such teaching blends in well with traditional African demonology. It should also be mentioned that the vast bulk of missionary work throughout the continent is supported and paid for by American money and personnel. The greater part of this missionary effort comes from organizations that are outside the denominational structures. Such newer networks of Christians are particularly open to the 'modern' views of charismatic Christianity strongly influenced by Faith ideas, particularly when these are so obviously crowned with 'success'.

A few general remarks need to be added about this worldwide explosion of a Christianity that is wrapped up in the notion of individual achievement and success. Quite apart from the question of whether such teaching is in accordance with the spirit of Christ and traditional Christianity, there is the more important issue of the social effects that are to be felt. In the remarkable book, *Exporting the American Gospel* by Steve Brouwer and others, on which this short summary is based, the authors point out how little a Christianity based on wealth and success contributes to the economic and social betterment of society. The gospel that is heard and acted upon has quite a bit to do with helping to create a society of individual consumers who will be resistant to the blandishment of socialist ideals. For this reason this fundamentalist/charismatic export to the poorer countries is one of Americanism as much as, if not more than, one of Christianity. The case study of the situation in Guatemala, which is described in some detail in the book, is fairly chilling in its portrayal of how right-wing attitudes and charismatic Christianity are sometimes combined in the same people, thus, in this instance, preserving both American economic and political interests in the region. One would wish for the space to say more on this topic, but this would mean danger of straying far from the main concerns of the study.

Christian schools and Accelerated Christian Education

The organization, curriculum and aims of the Christian school that John and Rachel helped out at follow closely those of similar Christian schools in the United States. These schools are united in an association known as the AACS (American Association of Christian Schools). Affiliated schools subscribe 'without reservation' to a statement of faith, which is a statement of conservative Protestant doctrine including the inerrancy of the Bible, Christ's virgin birth and second coming, salvation only 'by grace through faith' and the necessity of the 'new birth'. The AACS neither has a centralized bureaucracy, nor prescribes standards for its member schools. Nevertheless it offers accreditation to member schools to ensure that 'proper biblical and academic standards are upheld'. In Britain there is a network of independent Christian schools which have a headquarters at Swindon in Wiltshire. I have no accurate figures as to how many belong to this network, but a perusal of school lists published in the press, along with exam statistics, suggests that there are several dozen up and down the country.

As has been described in the account of John and Rachel, learning in these Christian schools is based on very formal methods. Accelerated Christian Education is the name of the particular system or programme in use and it is widely employed in similar schools in the United States. As expected, the content of the curriculum is very conservative and children would be exposed to a fairly restricted choice of texts in, say, English literature. The Bible is taught without any critical ideas being entertained. The method used is based on the idea that each child will work on their own through a system of workbooks. It means that the school can operate with very few pupils over quite a wide age range. As was indicated in John and Rachel's story, such schools function on a fairly tight budget, using the goodwill of parents to a considerable extent.

Child-rearing practices

In the account of the Christian school it was noticed that physical punishment was used regularly. At the time of writing a group of Christian schools in Britain is appealing against an European Commission directive banning physical punishment in all schools as from 1 September 1999. Philip Greven, an American author, has written an important book, *Spare the Child*, which shows the links between the physical punishment of children and the rationale given to it by religious beliefs, especially those of Protestant Christianity. There is in this expression of Christianity a long tradition of rearing children according to 'biblical principles', a system that includes corporal punishment as a matter of routine. The Old Testament in particular is a quarry for proof texts to justify the administration of harsh physical discipline, especially by fathers towards their children. The model of Yahweh as a father chastising a son with a rod for his iniquity (2 Samuel 7:14–15) is carried over into the book of Proverbs, with its frequent references to the rod in the context of family discipline. Although the saying often quoted, 'Spare the rod, spoil the child,' is not found in scripture, the texts that are found there are equally chilling. 'A father who spares the rod hates his son, but one who loves him keeps him in order' (Proverbs 13:24) and, 'If you take the stick to him yourself, you will preserve him from the jaws of death' (Proverbs 23:14) are typical of the instructions in the book.

Another text that supports the idea of violence against the young is found in Deuteronomy 21:18–21 where the rebellious son is stoned to death at the request of his parents.

Those who quote such texts have failed to notice the changed concept of God that is found in the New Testament, and in particular the attitude of Jesus himself towards children. Jesus never gives any indication of a need to punish children physically, and indeed when speaking of children in one particularly striking passage his words suggest the opposite: 'But if a man is a cause of stumbling to one of these little ones who have faith in me, it would be better for him to have a millstone hung round his neck and be drowned in the depths of the sea' (Matthew 18:6). For me, this text appears to reach the heart of Christ's teaching far more than other frequently quoted texts from Hebrews 12:5–8 and Revelation 3:19.

A further aspect has been the tendency of generations of Protestant teachers to read into the New Testament a doctrine of atonement in terms of a wrathful Old Testament God requiring in some way the hideously cruel death of Jesus. However much the doctrine of substitutionary atonement is qualified and muted by modern writers, there are large numbers of Christians today who have a picture in their minds of God's fatherhood involving violence against his child. Also, when the summary teaching that 'Jesus died for my sins,' is unpacked, there still remains a picture of God as Father in some way requiring the punishment of one that he loves. It is small wonder that such teaching is sometimes carried over into violence against children in fundamentalist schools and families.

Behind the idea that harsh discipline towards children is in some way countenanced and even encouraged by scripture, is the wider issue of the threat of future punishment. In short, the Bible, especially the New Testament, teaches the existence of hell, a place of everlasting torment for those who have not been granted a place in heaven. For older generations the threat of an everlasting torment was seldom absent from their minds. In some cases a morbid fascination and horror about this state reduced individuals to depression and despair. To have heard one of the sermons of the eighteenth-century preacher Jonathan Edwards would have easily destroyed any sense of inherent self-worth in the presence of God. He proclaimed, 'in pain, in wailing and lamenting, groaning and shrieking, and gnashing your teeth; with your souls full of dreadful grief and amazement, with your bodies and every member full of racking torture, without any possibility of getting ease…' For the Calvinist such as Edwards, life was lived against the terrible continuing thought that in it there was no assurance that one had been truly converted and saved.

According to Philip Greven, a morbid fascination with hell and eternal punishment seems to be more a pathological state linked perhaps to a pre-vocal memory of parent neglect or abuse. As long as it exists, however, it forms the background to cruel treatment of children as parents battle to suppress the behaviour which they believe will lead to something far worse. Children need to be moulded and disciplined to save them from the pains of hell, and thus physical punishment can be justified to break their will and tendency to sin. There is in the Protestant literature about child rearing a great deal about the need for unquestioning obedience reinforced by recourse to physical terror and pain. The reasoning of a book, *The Christian Family*, by Larry Christenson, which is quoted by Philip Greven, suggests that just as God does not spare people pain as part of their discipleship, neither should we withhold pain from our children to obtain their obedience.

The recommended age when physical pain should start as part of the process of disciplining small children varies from author to author. Christenson recommends discipline beginning when the child is still in the cradle. Another book examined by Greven by an evangelical psychiatrist, Paul Meier, recommends spanking and slapping children when necessary between eighteen and thirty-six months. This effort to mould the will at this young age, however, is presumably not ultimately successful for Meier, as he recommends using 'spankings' with children right up to the time when they reach eleven or twelve. For the child enduring physical punishment, the literature recommends that the process should be ritualized. This will have the effect of increasing the fear and dread involved in the whole process. Parents are told, 'The ritual should be deliberate and last at least ten or fifteen minutes… It should be a ritual dreaded by the child.' After administration of punishment the child will be permitted to cry for a time, but further smacking will ensue if the child uses his or her tears as a form of protest or rage. In case any parent might feel squeamish about using such physical violence against their child, a writer quoted by Greven, Roy Lessin, assures them that the failure to use 'loving discipline through spanking is also a form of child abuse'. Both Lessin and Meier base their recommendation of using violence towards children on the words of Proverbs.

The use of violent punishment with young children is, of course, not without its critics. The most telling arguments against its use are put forward by Philip Greven in *Spare the*

Child. In one section he lists all the negative consequences of physical violence against children, showing without any shadow of doubt that any apparent gains obtained by the use of physical discipline are vastly outweighed by the negative destructive consequences. Not only are there some serious psychological implications, but also there are results in the way a child grows up to view God. The use of violence by a parent towards a small child will have the effect of creating enormous anger at a subconscious level. That anger may not come out against the perpetrator, but in future years may re-emerge to be taken out on society or a wife or child. In the absence of anger, which is in many ways a healthy response, there may well be an opposite reaction of depression and, in extreme cases, suicide. The reaction of depression to Puritan methods of upbringing over several centuries is traced by Julius Rubin in his book, *Religious Melancholy and Protestant Experience in America*. He chronicles, through the journals of Protestant writers, a tendency towards gloom and despair, fuelled by harsh discipline and what is described as 'soul-murder', the attempt to destroy the will and the separate identity of another person. It is hard to disagree with the charge that to seek to 'break the will' of another person, however young, is a form of spiritual murder, however apparently honourable the motives of the one doing it.

A further twist in Philip Greven's account is his description of the way that violence against children in the name of godly discipline creates a personality which is likely to repeat the treatment with another generation. In addition, an individual who has been taught to obey authority for fear of painful punishment will absorb the idea that dialogue and mutual consent have no place in the face of what is perceived to be a final authority. Here are the beginnings of an insight into the remarkable way that fundamentalist thinking is very often found combined with right-wing, even fascist, forms of thought. Alice Miller in her book, *For Your Own Good*, has traced the way that the harsh discipline towards children found in Germany in the early part of the last century prepared them for the totalitarian government of Hitler. It is no coincidence that the parties of the extreme Right in the United States combine beliefs in the inerrancy of scripture with fiercely held ones in white superiority, which advocate violence against other racial groups. A theme I will pick up in a later chapter, namely the submission of women to men, is also likely to trace itself back to patterns of family life in which family roles are strictly defined. According to another author quoted by Greven, Jack Hyles, 'she [the female child] should never be allowed to argue at all. She should be submissive and obedient. She must obey immediately… The parents who require this have done a big favour for their future son-in-law.'

The final connection that Greven makes between the violent punishment of children and fundamentalist belief systems is the most sinister and at the same time the most intriguing. He reminds the reader of the theme of apocalyptic destruction that is contained in the ideas about Armageddon which so fascinate a large segment of the fundamentalist constituency. As shall be seen in a later chapter, the book of Revelation, when read literally, promises a cataclysmic tribulation ushering in a millennium of peace under the lordship of Christ. Only 'true' Christians will survive the appalling events of the tribulation, having been snatched up out of it.

Millennial speculation is less visible in Britain than in the United States, but the fact is that there are, around the world, countless Christians contemplating with satisfaction the destruction of billions of their fellow beings in the millennial catastrophe. This is chilling to say the least. Greven speculates that this apocalyptic impulse in American Christianity comes out of the 'life history of pain and suffering, and is grounded in the assaults against the body, the will and the spirit of children that are rationalized as discipline'. Furthermore, 'the painful punishment of children creates the nuclear core of rage, resentment and aggression that fuels fantasies of the apocalyptic end of the world'. Alice Miller believes that a violence perpetrated against German children which denied their selfhood ultimately generated the Holocaust. According to Greven, an obsession with punishment as being a manifestation of God's will for a large segment of humanity is particularly attractive to those whose whole experience of life has been one of violence and abuse. He sees the book of Revelation as 'one of the most enduring sadomasochistic fantasies', which allows those who have experienced pain and abuse in this life to contemplate a place where it will cease. At the same time the anger and hatred that the pain has generated are redirected into pleasurable contemplation of cruelty and destruction for countless others.

This section on the physical punishment of children has summarized the arguments of two writers who are convinced that the cruel physical punishment of children, while apparently based on biblical texts, is a cultural and social aberration which has caused great suffering over the years.

When physical punishment of children is perpetuated in the name of obedience to the Bible, it has the effect of continuing the less attractive aspects of fundamentalist Christianity – the authoritarian, the vengeful and finally those which are destructive of life itself. It is small wonder that Greven, Miller and those who follow them plead for a new attitude towards the nurture of children, one that emphasizes compassion, gentleness and love.

Every time I went in it always
came up about witchcraft… it
didn't matter what I went in
there for, that is what always
came up.

Chapter Two

Christian Counselling and Abuse

Kathleen was in her mid-thirties when she became involved with the local healing centre in 1987. She was at a vulnerable point in her life; a series of misfortunes had befallen her. Her first marriage had failed eight years earlier, leaving her with two boys to bring up alone. At the time of her divorce she had contracted meningitis, which caused headaches and memory problems. Her family were not close either physically or emotionally and she suffered deeply from loneliness. The invitation to go and help decorate and clean a large building in a nearby town, which was going to be used as a healing centre, was an attempt by a friend to get her out of the house, to give her some focus beyond the family. The cleaning and decorating were punctuated by cups of coffee and periods of worship that she enjoyed, particularly for the new contacts that came her way.

She appreciated the services that took place every Thursday when the centre finally opened. They combined traditional Anglican worship with informal prayer and praise, and were quite different from those of the Anglican church near her home that she had tried and rejected. It didn't occur to her for some two years that the weekly invitations to go up for prayer and laying on of hands could apply to her. None of her physical problems were improving, and she had fallen victim to backache. Also, the behaviour of her eldest boy, then aged thirteen, was giving her a lot of anxiety. Prayer seemed to have some effect, but it did not lift the overall sense of physical and emotional malaise. Eventually, when one of those praying for her suggested that she needed more faith, she stopped going for a while.

Kathleen's physical condition reached a new trough with the onset of ME around 1990. She found herself caught up in a spiral of physical, emotional and mental troubles which all fed off one another. Although she had embarked on a second marriage with a 'new' Christian in 1992, stress still seemed to dominate her life. Soon after her wedding she was invited to go to the healing centre with her new husband for a week where her problems could be more directly addressed. The attitude of her husband Bill towards the centre was initially one of condescending amusement as the whole thing was quite outside his experience. It turned to irritation as Kathleen was counselled on her own for an hour and a half one afternoon and then came out of the session totally unable to share anything with him. Seven years later, the content of that fateful session was shared with another person in detail for the first time. In summary, what had happened was that during the counselling Kathleen had talked about her family and the problems of her relationships over the years. Then, towards the end of the session, the leader of the two counsellors with her had told her a whole series of 'facts' about her early childhood. These included the allegation that her father had sexually abused her, her mother had tried to

abort her and, though she had failed with her, there was a
twin brother who had been got rid of. I gently probed as to
where these ideas had come from and learned that, even
seven years later, she felt responsible for this diagnosis as the
'facts' were all connected to a picture she had shared with the
counsellors:

> I find this point difficult, but I still feel responsible for
> a lot of what came up and for a lot of what was said.
> Because if God hadn't shown the pictures he had shown
> me then they wouldn't have pursued the interpretation.
> I had a picture of what I thought was me in a cupboard
> under the stairs. I said I could see the shape of the stairs.
> And one of the counsellors said that's God's hand.
> 'That's God holding you in your mother's womb.' That
> was when all the other prayers were prayed and that's
> when I found out that supposedly I was one of twins.
> Because I was unwanted they were actually trying to
> abort me. They made that conclusion. And then God
> had held me back – that was the hand, which was the
> shape of the stair – but one baby, one foetus had been
> aborted, but God had held me in place. I couldn't
> understand why I should get a picture like that and
> that's when the counsellor turned and said that in
> actual fact it wasn't the stairs I could see, but the
> fingers of God's hand.
>   I came out of there absolutely exhausted. I know
> that. I couldn't get my mind round what had been
> going on. There were awful problems with Bill and we
> didn't speak for a week when we got home, because

I couldn't tell him and he wanted to know. I think
I was absolutely over the moon that one day I would
meet up with my brother. They told me it was a brother.
I had no doubt in my mind that afternoon that their
interpretation was right. It lasted about a week and
I saw them again, and then the stuff about witchcraft
came in. I actually started thinking, I just can't accept
this.

Kathleen was trapped by this session of counselling. On the
one hand she had severe doubts about the truth of what was
being revealed, but on the other hand the doubts were not
sufficiently articulate or strong for her to be able to test her
feelings with anyone else. The authority of the counsellors
also meant that she did not allow her doubts to challenge
them.

The next level of abuse to be 'revealed' was that of
witchcraft and Satanism. Kathleen had told me before that
the counsellors had suggested her mother was involved in
witchcraft, but I wasn't prepared for what came next.

Every time I went in it always came up about witchcraft.
And they talked about ancestors and it didn't matter
what I went in there for, that is what always came up.
Because I wasn't wanted, Mum and Dad had offered
me up for witchcraft. I had once a picture of skulls, a
stone wall, lights and flames, and then I saw a table,
a stone table and horrible figures around me. They said
that Mum and Dad had actually offered me up for
witchcraft. They'd physically done this and I had been

laid on that stone slab and I'd had a knife inserted in
me, which is what they do apparently to baby girls. I
was terrified. I believed them to start off with, but then
I started thinking while I was there, This can't be right.
I don't know how to accept these things. And they'd
always finish off with prayers at the end of it and leave
me to rest before I went home. I used to come home
and cry myself silly. I used to go and see my friend
Lydia, who was a staunch Christian, and cry with her
and say, 'I don't understand this. I can't take this on
board and I don't know what to do. Because these
Christians, who have been Christians a lot longer than
I have, are telling me this. I don't know how to cope
with it.' It still today bothers me. I would like to say no
100 per cent that I don't believe it. Rationally I know
that my parents wouldn't do it.

Although the counsellors made their 'discovery' that her
father had sexually abused her, Kathleen could not remember
how this diagnosis had arisen or what picture had prompted
it. She did, however, recall an incident that took place at the
healing centre during the week that she and her husband
were staying. She was attending one of the services and had
had to come out because of headaches:

I sat outside the building and they started singing a
song which I can't remember, and I burst into tears
and one of the staff came over and stood me over by
the wall. And a man came out, one of the chaps who
used to do some counselling, and said to me, 'You're

suffering,' or something like that, 'and I can see that you've got an armour, complete suit of black armour, and I can see that you're completely closed in by the enemy and there's no light at all shining from you. I am going to take this armour off you now, and we're going to enclose you with a fresh armour of God.' And that is what he proceeded to do. He said I would feel better after he had done it all. So he and another lady prayed every single piece of armour off my body and then prayed a new piece back on me again. They said now that I had got the armour of God back on I would feel better and lighter in myself. I did feel lighter in myself. I was completely taken aback by the diagnosis.

I asked Kathleen if she could remember anything else positive about the sessions, or if she could remember being built up at all by the counselling. She replied, 'I always got a couple of verses from the Bible given to me before I left, and I was to go away and think on them. But after all I'd been through for an hour a couple of verses from the Bible was not much.' At this point the irony of what she was saying broke through and she laughed, the only time humour entered our session together. 'I used to go away from there feeling absolutely drowned. It was awful. They never told me what they were aiming to do. It was weekly, but it became fortnightly because I wasn't coping; I was so shattered through the week. I can't remember the good things. I can remember the bad things.'

Kathleen summarized what she perceived to be the aim of the counselling as the placing of a wedge between her and her family, and that was not just her living family of parents and brothers and sisters, but also her family from the past, no longer alive. The counsellors were convinced that witchcraft was responsible for many of her problems, and that it had come into her family tree on her mother's side.

> There was the cutting-off part. They were not just talking about me, but they were saying, This is what we want to do for you. They were saying that they wanted to make sure that you don't get anything through from your father. So they'd talk about my dad and then cut me off, cut me free from him, and then they'd talk about Grandfather and cut me free from him. And then they would even pray about further back down the family, where the witchcraft came in, further down the line. The witchcraft came through my mother's side. I've no idea how it came through. I thought that these were such brilliant people who knew everything and I was a mere person who's got a very low opinion of themself, and these were people who'd come along to love me and take care, and so I accepted what was going on. You became the child. I felt that they knew better than I did.

Kathleen's problems were not being solved by these extreme measures. Her physical and mental problems were no better and by 1993 her ME was particularly bad. Her counsellors finally despaired of their ability to help and effectively dumped her. The way they did this was to inform her that she had spirits in her which were such that they did not have the ability to deal with them. They thought that someone else should handle them and Ellel Grange in Lancashire was mentioned. No one had mentioned spirits before in her counselling, and the implication of having spirits and its meaning was not explored. After that the counselling simply stopped. Kathleen had been taught to mistrust her family, believe that she was oppressed by witchcraft, and finally told that she had spirits who were beyond anything that normal prayer or counselling could deal with.

In spite of her level of despair, Kathleen struggled to attend some final services at the centre.

> I went over to the centre on the Tuesday evening. I was on a bed because I wasn't allowed to sit because of my back and my ME. I was basically ignored for two weeks and on the last night I went up for healing. I went up and Elizabeth [one of the counsellors] said to me, 'Do you want to be healed? I want you to be healed and I know God wants you to be healed. You are now healed. Go and pick up your bed and walk out of here.' And as I was walking out a man said to me, 'It's because of your lack of faith that you are not healed.' I was so upset that I never ever went back there again. I got the impression that they were absolutely fed up to the back teeth with me.

Kathleen's final comments to me revealed the depth of the way that, for her, counselling had been an exercise in being put down, blamed and humiliated:

> I never felt loved as a human being. At the centre I felt a nuisance. The counselling was never an exercise in

being affirmed; it always ended up with witchcraft or praying down the generations or something like that. Always. I was so unsure of myself anyway that I blamed myself for just about everything that was going on. I was blamed for the break-up of my first marriage; I was blamed for the way my second marriage was not turning out well. Events were battering me down, but I was never encouraged to see where my responsibility really lay. I felt it was my fault and if I said something or so-and-so is my fault, even if I wasn't sure about it, they'd say, Let's pray about it. It wasn't a case of them ever saying, It's not your fault. They never challenged my tendency to accuse myself. By and large the sin was that of my parents. Everything at the centre was either 100 per cent true or 100 per cent lies and I am still not 100 per cent sure where I stand with it all.

It would be good to record a happy ending for Kathleen's story. However, there is no happy ending, only some glimmers of hope. After breaking her links with the centre, Kathleen's relationships with her family remained tense and fragmented. Part of her recognized that she had absorbed considerable areas of fantasy about her family relationships, but another part of her could not let go of the alienation from them that she had imbibed through her counselling. Until I found Kathleen and her story, she had not been able to share any of her experiences or revisit them in order to obtain a new perspective on them. She was thus left with the raw, undigested emotions of blame, guilt and rejection. At various points in negotiating with Kathleen to tape her story, I was put off, as though the effort would be too much. The outcome, however, has proved positive. Even though I could not spend the necessary time to help her in the task of rebuilding her sense of reality and perspective, the telling of the story does seem to have given her a new relationship with it, and for the first time in many years the relationship with her family has moved in a positive direction. She was allowing herself the thought that she was a victim, not of witchcraft exercised by manipulative parents, but of a fantasy world created by the imaginations of zealous, but misguided, counsellors. She is beginning to consider the possibility that the counsellors might after all have been wrong.

Comment

Of all the stories that I have recorded in this study, Kathleen's is the most fragmented. Timescales and dates may well have become muddled over the years, though external corroboration suggests that the main events recorded did take place in 1992. One of the striking things about listening to her story was her description of what seemed to be a number of different charismatic counselling styles, all of which I was aware were being practised at the time, but in this case they were being practised on one person. Some of the diagnoses offered to her were at that time current in secular practice, notably Satanic Ritual Abuse and sexual abuse, while others, such as bondage to ancestors and witchcraft, were confined to Christian ministry. Whether or not the counsellors found all these things in a single session of ninety minutes or over several sessions is not important. The way that Kathleen had described so well the language and terms of all these different styles of ministry gave her story a credibility and coherence. In choosing to offer an interpretation of Kathleen's story I am aware that, once again, I am not able to check out her version of events with those who ministered to her. In my attempted reconstruction of what happened I am once again having to make a judgement based on the plausibility of her account, and the way that I cannot imagine any reason for the bulk of her testimony being fabricated. Such a reconstruction can, of course, be challenged, but there is no doubt from my own studies of other cases that all the styles of ministry were in operation at the time among Christian counsellors working within this particular culture.

According to the reconstruction, a pair of Christian counsellors had made up their minds that an apparent breakdown between elderly parents and an adult daughter was caused by the most heinous forms of abuse. Although much of the detail from 1992 has been lost to us, it appears that the 'technique' employed by the counsellors was a reliance on pictures 'given' to the patient or to them in the context of prayer. There was also a strong fashion at the time for 'recovered memories', however these were obtained. I have recorded one particular picture given to Kathleen of her being under the stairs and the way that this was interpreted as being indicative of an experience of attempted abortion. From the outside the picture might well be seen to be significant, but the particular interpretation given seems highly fanciful. It was as though parental abuse was read into the situation even before the picture was recounted. To add to this alarming interpretation of being unwanted, even before birth, the idea that you have been sexually and satanically abused meant that the counselling made no contribution at all to any kind of healing process. The speed with which these 'insights' were apparently revealed meant that the victim was re-victimized, and left battered and bewildered. As far I can tell, Kathleen added nothing to these revelations; she simply accepted them as coming from someone wiser and more spiritually experienced. The 'truth' in this case, even if it bore a genuine relation to facts, should have been disclosed far more gradually. If the saying that 'mankind cannot bear much reality' is true, it is still more true of someone who is emotionally vulnerable and suggestible.

The first consequence of Kathleen's counselling was that she learned to be suspicious of and alienated from her parents as well as the rest of her family. This was more than simply being unable to communicate with them on a regular basis; the internalized relationship with them which she had carried from childhood into adulthood was attacked and undermined. All of us will carry in our minds the memories of being cherished as small children. If the memories of being mothered are 'good enough' then our ability to trust and make new relationships throughout our lives is enhanced. Those whose memories are bad, or for whom there have been significant gaps in care and who thus have felt betrayed as small children, will carry scars into adulthood and all subsequent relationships will be affected to some extent. Therapeutic practice will sometimes help a patient go back in their memory to a time when they did feel safe and affirmed, and then help them from that position of safety to revisit episodes of abuse, to understand and relate to them in a new way. The opposite seems to have happened in the case of Kathleen. She was encouraged to believe that at no point in her upbringing had her parents wanted her or cherished her. Even if this were true, for which there was no external evidence, she was given apparently nothing in the way of love or therapeutic support to help her face this destructive and totally demoralizing affirmation.

Kathleen's parents were being accused of the most horrendous crimes that it is possible for parents to be accused of. According to the counsellors, the only thing they did not do was actually kill her. Wickedness on this scale is not normally affirmed without the suggestion of occult involvement, and here is seen the world of fundamentalist paranoia that existed strongly at the beginning of the 1990s, which will be looked at further later in the chapter. Here it can be remarked that the diagnosis of wickedness on this scale is likely to be highly destructive to a patient, and the 'revelation' of so much so quickly is likely to be damaging in the extreme.

In a moment the particular 'fashions' of belief and counselling that are apparent in Kathleen's tale will be examined. But it is necessary now to consider briefly what possible inner motivation there could have been on the part of the counsellors for engaging in such seemingly abusive and cruel practice as Kathleen has reported in her account. Details of the timescale involved in the counselling may well have been truncated, but even allowing for exaggeration of the speed with which 'truths' about her situation were shared, there are still a heartlessness and an inhumanity shown by this story which need some explanation. One theory that offers itself is that the counsellors were motivated by an age-old human need, the need to be proved right. A strong system of beliefs about the root causes of human distress had rooted itself in their minds, and Kathleen was a suitable subject through which to prove their theories correct. Within the particular charismatic culture the counsellors occupied, fashions of explanation reigned. Just as a Freudian psychoanalyst has a tendency, at least in popular imagination, to interpret everyone's problems in terms of unresolved Oedipal conflicts, so here Kathleen was understood to embody all the latest theoretical blockages to wholeness. The need to be proved right, if this was indeed the motivation, resulted in damage to an individual who was brought very close to breakdown and disintegration. Kathleen's fragility throughout my interviews with her suggests that had the damage been even slightly worse, the resulting trauma would have made it impossible for her to have ever revisited these painful events with me or anyone else.

In the 1950s a psychologist, Leon Festinger, studied a group in the United States who believed they were in touch with beings on flying saucers who were coming to rescue them just before the end of the world. The day for this rescue was precisely fixed and so the group faced the possibility of being proved to be totally wrong in their predictions. Festinger postulated that the believers, in the event of a non-occurrence of their prediction, would not simply fade away, but would find some way of continuing to maintain their belief system in spite of its non-fulfilment. In psychological terms there is a system in the ego for defending the belief, and this need to be right will seek to overcome the threat of dissonant information coming from elsewhere. The flying-saucer group drowned out their own disappointment and the need to admit that they were wrong by a renewed effort to spread their views, convincing themselves that God had spared the world at the last minute so that they could call everyone to repentance before the end finally came. Festinger's work illustrates the enormous energy that is given to the process of retaining beliefs rather than admitting doubt, uncertainty or ambiguity. The owner of a new car will seek confirmation from friends and colleagues that he has made the right choice of vehicle, and in the more serious business of religious faith there is going to be enormous resistance to admitting that there are in a belief or theory elements of doubt or ambiguity.

Within the strange closed world apparently occupied by Kathleen's counsellors there was a tendency to ascribe an infallibility not only to scriptures, but also to systems of ideas. If something was believed to be true then it had to be proclaimed as true without any doubts being entertained. For reasons known to themselves, the counsellors 'needed' to believe in their ideas, and that need was maintained by finding it 'proven' everywhere they looked. Kathleen seems thus to have been the victim of a 'need to be right', a system of thinking that put the infallibility of an idea or theory before the flexibility and need of an individual suffering human being.

Prayer counselling and words of knowledge

What are the ideas that were current in the early 1990s and seem to be at the heart of the counselling methods of the group who sought to help Kathleen? The technique at work was that of 'prayer counselling'. In my research for this book, I asked one respected charismatic leader what this expression really meant and where I could find some written explanation of what it involved. He replied that as far as he knew the technique was taught in workshops, but that no one had ever written down a clear guide to what was involved. He did not disagree with my reaction that such a situation in which no definitions were being offered was highly unsatisfactory. Anyone could claim to be using prayer counselling without anyone else being able to challenge what they were doing, either from the point of view of theology or technique. One major organization involved in teaching counselling and healing in a charismatic setting, Wholeness Through Christ, has now moved away from the expression to the name 'prayer ministry', possibly to avoid being associated with an unhelpful term.

In summary, whatever its name, this technique affirms that through prayer the Holy Spirit will reveal to the counsellors the true situation of the counsellee. It does not take much imagination to realize that what the Holy Spirit is apparently revealing may say as much about the inner beliefs of the counsellors as it does about the true situation of the patient. Nevertheless the possibility of supernatural knowledge is set out by Paul in 1 Corinthians 12 where the 'word of knowledge' is one of the gifts or 'charismata' given by the Spirit. A famous example of this gift at work is in a story told by John Wimber who, while travelling on an aeroplane, saw the word 'adultery' written across a man's face. Wimber tells how the name of the woman involved was also revealed to him so that he was able to challenge the man concerned and subsequently lead him to Christ. In commenting on the story Mark Stibbe agrees with another writer that the word of knowledge is an insight into God's thoughts and not some spiritual enhancement of a natural gift which all possess to some degree.

The immediate problem about this kind of teaching is that, however much it reflects Paul's own thinking on the subject, it fails to do justice to the enormous problem of distinguishing between a true inspired word and mere human hunches. In a healthy Christian community there may well be a sharing among Christians of insights given within the context of prayer, but these will always need to be tested. Also such 'words' should always be used for the building up and encouragement of others, and never in the context of some complicated game of control. Once a word of knowledge is detached from the context of the healthy functioning of a Christian community then it may well become a potentially abusive thing, because it is not subject to the checks and balances that operate within that community.

Paul's own words about the superiority of love over prophecies, tongues and words of knowledge in 1 Corinthians 13 are a healthy reminder that love experienced as both a human and a divine reality will always be supreme. In practice, this should mean that a person is never humiliated, browbeaten or shamed by the 'word' given to another Christian. Even if that 'word' is indeed an insight into the thoughts of God, it should not be shared if the individual concerned is not able or ready to receive it. When it is given it should be offered with sensitivity and humility, and without a trace of any kind of power manipulation. Humility is a word much used in the popular literature of Christian counselling. But in the face of a rigid belief in the sort of 'certainties' prevalent in the fundamentalist/charismatic culture that has so far been encountered, humility is not always experienced as humility, but is sometimes used as a cloak for coercion.

Christians against psychology

A further strand evident in Kathleen's story is the disregarding of normal counselling procedures in favour of Christian 'biblical' models. This reflects a strong tradition of writing and counselling that goes back to the 1960s in the United States. In this tradition, represented by writers such as Jay Adams, Dave Hunt and Tim LaHaye, psychology and psychiatry are aspects of secular humanism, which is seen as the chief enemy of Christianity. The danger of this view is that in identifying shortcomings in modern psychological approaches to the study of human beings, it overlooks their positive values, including proper accountability and the need for supervision of the counsellors.

Of these writers, perhaps the most influential is the American Jay Adams whose books have been read by hundreds of thousands of people since first appearing in the late 1960s. It is not difficult for him to do a devastating critique of psychiatry on the grounds of its ineffectiveness, expense and questionable scientific basis. Even in 1970 there were plenty of allies from within the profession to be found criticizing it, including Thomas Szasz and H.J. Eysenck. Szasz had suggested that the labels used by the mental-health profession to describe the mentally ill were merely fictions used to protect society from behaviour deemed by the majority to be deviant. Having, in his mind, successfully demolished psychology and psychiatry as rivals in the task of healing the human soul, Adams sets out his own biblical alternatives in his book, *Competent to Counsel*. All counselling, Adams claims, is the work of the Holy Spirit. Thus all personality changes to be sought involve the Spirit's work of sanctification, resulting in moving from the innate depravity of humankind to the state of regeneration and fruitfulness that belongs to the one who lives by the Spirit.

For Adams, buttressed by the arguments of such secular writers as Szasz, the fundamental problem for the individual is not mental illness, but the existence of sin. Counselling is, therefore, the task of enabling another to face up to sin in their life. Adams introduces an approach which he calls 'nouthetic confrontation'. The Greek word *nouthesis* is found in the New Testament and means 'instruction of another where change is required of the person being addressed'. From this word, Adams moves to a position where counselling is understood to be an activity which combines authoritative directive techniques and the uncovering of past sins.

Any process that consists of one party encouraging another to acknowledge and confess sin will set up a power dynamic which is unhealthy and potentially dis-empowering. The Catholic tradition of sacramental confession to some extent avoids this dynamic as the confessing is normally initiated by the penitent and not by the priest. In Adams' pattern the client is confronted by a need to confess his sin, and in this the power of the counsellor, backed up by his ability to quote scripture at every turn, will be impossible to resist. The client will all too easily take the role of the guilt-ridden child, whose only hope of escape is to adopt a passive role which will please the demanding parent. In such a situation the client will always find it difficult to move forward out of dependency on the counsellor to achieve a level of personal autonomy before God and his fellows. One could go further and suggest that such autonomy will never be found in the type of counselling that Adams is putting forward. As has already been suggested in the last chapter, inerrancy or infallibility within any system of thought will have the effect of producing one of two reactions in those who are subjected to it. Either there is total submission or there is rejection. If rejection is to be possible, then it has to be affirmed quickly before all personal decision-making and independence of thought have been destroyed through membership of the system. In many fundamentalist Christian communities that level of freedom and independence of thought is difficult to find.

In reading Jay Adams' best-selling book, *Competent to Counsel*, two things become apparent. The first is a complete lack of indebtedness to all approaches to counselling and healing techniques except those put forward by the writer. Other writers are only quoted in order to criticize them. The second thing is the attempt to look at human problems solely in terms of biblical models and images. Thus by implication it is denied that any Christian has been given new insight into human problems over 2,000 years. The result is a technique of care where love seems almost entirely absent and is certainly subordinate to the task of applying 'biblical responses' to complex human problems. There is never any facing up to uncertainty or ambiguity in the pastoral task. Love for another human being surely sometimes involves sitting with them in their place of pain or uncertainty. Failure to do that in favour of applying biblical answers is surely a failure of love and thus a failure of the spirit of Christianity. Nouthetic counselling may well constitute a contribution to a debate about the nature of Christian counselling as a whole, but as a pattern for pastoral care uncritically adopted without any compromise, it surely is a disaster area. When vulnerable people in search of healing, love and understanding are only presented with the 'certainties' found in the Bible, these same certainties are all too easily experienced as heavy, harsh burdens designed to crush them further.

Healing the family tree

A major part of the counsellors' practice focussed on the relationship of Kathleen to her parents and other relatives, some long dead. Although Kathleen did not know it, the ideas that were being presented combined those of orthodox psychotherapy with the beliefs of a Christian physician, Kenneth McAll. Dr McAll had worked in China and observed how a simple Chinese woman, who was a Christian, had dealt with an apparent case of possession through prayer. He came to the conclusion that many intractable problems in the area of mental ill health are caused by a bondage of the patient to others in the family, both alive and recently departed, through a kind of occult control. His book *Healing the Family Tree*, published in 1982, is a plausible account of many cases that he has dealt with who have been healed through some kind of 'cutting the bond' with ancestors. Kathleen's counsellors became convinced that she needed to break free of both living relatives, including her parents, and those who had died, especially on her mother's side on the grounds that witchcraft had entered into the family that way.

I would not wish to give the impression that there is nothing of value in this book since some of it does make sense. But there is an all too easy temptation to see the ideas in the book as a kind of panacea for all mental disturbance. One would have wished Dr McAll to have recorded examples where the theory did not work, together with a health warning that an obsession with dead relatives might be harmful. A positive feature of the book that does not seem to have reached Kathleen is Dr McAll's insistence on the importance of forgiveness of relatives, alive or dead, in order for the unhelpful bonds that link individuals to them to be broken. Kathleen seems never to have been made a fully active participant in the process of counselling. Even allowing for incomplete memory of the events of the time, she seems never to have been encouraged to develop a tolerant forgiving attitude to her parents and other ancestors whose actions had supposedly harmed her. Dr McAll's ideas are still current, but I have the impression that, like many ideas popularized in the 1980s, their impact is far less prevalent today.

Satanic Ritual Abuse

The final area of thinking that seems to have occupied the minds of those counselling Kathleen is that of Satanic Ritual

Abuse. Although the term was unknown to Kathleen when I tried it out on her, it is obvious that the speed with which they interpreted Kathleen's picture of walls and a skull meant that a belief in the power of the occult to cause ill health was close to the surface. In short, the counsellors were suggesting that one aspect of the abuse of Kathleen by her parents was linked to their own belief in and practice of witchcraft, a practice going back several generations.

Satanic Ritual Abuse (SRA) only emerged to claim public attention within the last twenty years. In 1980 a book by Michelle Smith and Dr Lawrence Pazder was published, called *Michelle Remembers*. The book was apparently an account of the sufferings by the author at the hands of a satanic cult, but it was soon discovered that much of the content derived from Dr Pazder's studies of African native ritual. Other books in a similar vein quickly followed, all of which were soon discredited as frauds. These had titles like *Satan's Underground*, *The Satan Seller* and *He Came to Set the Captives Free*. All these books made little distinction between witchcraft and Satanism as both were seen to be part of a widespread satanic conspiracy designed to undermine and destroy families and society as a whole.

As the paranoia gathered pace in the early 1980s, dozens of court cases were heard in the United States based on allegations which were almost duplicates of those in Pazder's book. A number of therapists began diagnosing SRA victims, though a survey in the United States revealed that while 70 per cent of therapists had never seen a victim, 1.4 per cent had over 100 each. This suggested at the very least that a belief in SRA was a prerequisite for diagnosing a victim of such abuse. Recovered memories of such abuse have proved remarkably difficult to substantiate. Claims of torture, mutilation and ritual sacrifice have never been confirmed by supportive evidence. When one group of SRA 'survivors' in the States claimed that bodies of victims had been totally destroyed by a bonfire, it was pointed out that the heat would not remove the evidence as bones would remain behind. The story was changed to involve a secret rendezvous at a local crematorium and this in turn was investigated and discredited. Finally it was claimed that the Satanists had mobile crematoria in which to dispose of their victims.

The beginning of the 1990s, when Kathleen was receiving her counselling, was a time when SRA fears were at their height in Britain. A number of 'experts' appeared, lecturing on the charismatic circuit as well as among concerned social workers who had the job of caring for abused children. Several television programmes were made between 1989 and 1992 putting the case for 'believers' in Satanic Ritual Abuse. Finally the belief system became entrenched among a section of the therapeutic profession and in 1994 an important book, *Treating Survivors of Satanist Abuse*, edited by a respected professional from the Tavistock Clinic in London, Valerie Sinason, was published.

In the same year, a measured scholarly report commissioned by the Government dampened the fires of enthusiasm for belief in SRA. The author, Jean La Fontaine, a former professor of social anthropology at the London School of Economics, wrote her report against the background of some serious cases which had attracted much public concern, including the Orkney Islands' allegations against a number of families. Her book, *Speak of the Devil: Tales of Satanic Abuse in Contemporary England*, published in 1998, brings the story right up to date. It is a story of paranoia, fear and panic and reflects the fact that large numbers of people of all ages have suffered, like Kathleen, because of this infectious irrational belief system. La Fontaine showed that while child abuse had occasionally taken place in the context of ritual activities, the ritual used was 'a ragbag of elements invented to further the abuse' with no connection to real occultism. Most of the cases of child abuse occurred in excessively disadvantaged families, while those involved in occultism tended to be drawn from articulate educated social groups. Her training as an anthropologist enabled her to rise above a tendency to view the material from an individual cultural or religious perspective, and view the phenomenon from a cross-cultural perspective. In short, she is able to be free of emotive bias as well as observe how the events of the SRA scare are paralleled in other periods of history and in other places.

The situation now (1999) is that what one writer has called a 'moral panic' has subsided in religious, therapeutic and social-work networks. Nevertheless in other chapters I shall have cause to note how the belief in the existence of Satan and demonic entities appears to be alive and well in other settings. Here it can be said that his existence seems to be necessary as an invisible but powerful enemy against which Christians can unite. To misquote an old saying, if Satan and his minions did not exist it would be necessary to invent them.

Thus Kathleen is a victim, but thankfully also a survivor (just!) of counselling fads and fashions which have disappeared, hopefully for ever. They have been replaced by more responsible and humane practices which reflect professional standards and accountability. If Christians are to retain their credibility in this area of counselling, they need to be able to show that they are prepared to be humble about past mistakes and able to learn for the future.

If they looked at me, I would put a curse on them.

Chapter Three

Devils in the Parish

Teresa's story of the life of her church sounded at first extremely ordinary, and for her part she was committed to it and useful to its overall life. To meet Teresa was to encounter a gentle, intelligent Christian who seemed a model of moderation and compassion. Her church, a daughter church of a large parish church, was in a fair-sized town in the British Midlands. The situation changed when a new priest-in-charge arrived. She explained,

> Before Mr Johns arrived I had been involved with the music and I was on the PCC. I was also involved in study or Bible-study groups, sometimes leading, sometimes taking part. It was the sort of environment where lots of people were doing many things. All the responsibility was quite evenly shared out. The year he arrived was 1994 and I had been involved with things in the parish since 1980. Whoever had been there as priest-in-charge had delegated really well. Somebody new would come every three or four years and they would pick up where the other chap had left off and move us a bit further forward. So the congregation was

taking more responsibility and involved in the decision-making. That's how it was.

The new priest-in-charge arrived a couple of weeks before Easter 1994. He appeared at an evening eucharist. When he saw me he actually vaulted over the pews from the front to the back of the church. He had been at the front of the church putting his arms around people that as far as I knew he didn't know – he was hugging them and kissing them. They had never met before. He jumped over all these pews and chairs to the back of the church, where I was with someone else, and came up to me as though we were long-lost friends. We had met once before in 1977 when I was doing a reader's course. I hadn't seen him during the years in between. He hugged me which I wasn't expecting and neither did the person I was with.

The new priest started work at Easter and Teresa found very quickly that hugging parishioners was not the only novel part of the style of the new regime. She had been part of a group that would meet with the priest to look at music and choose it for the weeks ahead. Her particular responsibility was making sure that the music was set out. The group was immediately disbanded. 'He said immediately there was no need to do this whatsoever because the Lord told him what we were to be having for music.' This in itself was not desperately serious, but Teresa found that the old balance of old and new was lost. During the offertory, a time when a hymn of some length was required, Mr Johns would choose a chorus with two lines of music which had to be sung again and again to fill up the space. He would then announce the end with a flourish. The liturgy itself became an area of unpredictability:

> Things would be shortened, things would be missed out and he would put things in. The Lord would be speaking to him at any one moment and then he would have to tell everybody what the Lord was telling him. There was one point when we were in the middle of the eucharistic prayer, and he stopped and said there were x number of people there that hadn't meant it when they had made the confession. They would have to make it right before they received communion. He knew exactly who they were because the Lord had told him. If they didn't do anything about it he would call them to the altar rail now and they would know about it. He would also tell the congregation that someone had said something or done something, usually behind his back. He knew and he would be able to sort it out, but we never actually heard any more after that.

The congregation began to dwindle and after a couple of months it was down to 50 per cent. The priest never seemed to mind when people left. The message, spoken or unspoken, was, 'Unless you are 100 per cent behind me, you know where you can go.'

Democracy also failed to flourish in the meetings of the Church Council. Teresa described what happened at the very first meeting. 'The secretary got out the minutes' book. The priest said, "There will be no need for that. The Lord tells me exactly what we have got to do and I'll tell you. We'll do it.

So that's fine.'" The advantage of this approach for Teresa meant that at least you knew where you were even if you didn't like it. The meetings used to last about ten minutes, during which Mr Johns would simply tell the meeting what was going to happen, the changes to the services, the changes in the way that people would do their jobs, and so on.

A major shift in the atmosphere of the church, however, took place when it was announced from the pulpit that the church was under attack. This kind of language, namely that the building and congregation were the arena of satanic conflict, was not unfamiliar to the congregation as they were used to this kind of rhetoric from the mother church in the town, though hitherto it had not made much impact in their church. Mr Johns indicated that the attack that was now under way was more serious than in the past because he himself was more in touch with God than the previous priests, and because he was more authoritative in his teaching and style of leadership.

It was generally known before he had arrived that the rector of the mother church had known Mr Johns as a member of his congregation, and at this church, which was in another diocese, the language of demonic possession and exorcism was regularly used. For Teresa herself the new atmosphere introduced into the church touched her directly. She started to feel a chill in the relationships within the church. People spoke less to each other generally, but after a period she noticed that there was an animosity directed at her personally. People avoided her and the regular stream of visitors to her home to see her sick father dried up. At a midweek service at the parish church she had a word with the rector about what was going on. He promised to look into it. But before anything transpired she had a phone call from someone who had been a friend to say, 'Don't you know what is going on?' She was puzzled by this message, but then further light was shed by a message from one of the recently lapsed members of the church. They had heard from someone still going to the church that everyone had been told to avoid her, because she was possessed by the devil. 'If they looked at me, I would put a curse on them.' At this Teresa paused for a moment, choking back tears. She again sought help from the rector at one of the midweek eucharists and he responded without surprise with a somewhat enigmatic, 'I thought it might be something like this.' Once again he promised to look into it, but nothing happened. The shunning continued and Teresa threw herself into the task of looking after her father of fifty-eight, who was suffering from multiple sclerosis and had only another six months to live.

Mr Johns' control of a central clique of twenty or so remaining parishioners was complete. All those upset by his harsh teaching and vitriolic temper had left, and the remaining clique were firmly convinced that the Lord was really speaking through him. The sense that the church body had completely turned their back on her was finally made abundantly clear when a lay person licensed to bring communion to her father failed to appear.

> She never arrived. I phoned up to see if she was all
> right – it wasn't like her just not to turn up – she
> answered and she decided to put the phone down
> when I asked if she was all right. I phoned several times

and she just put the phone down. From then it was a question of having to make a change and move on.

I suggested to Teresa at this point that something was missing from her account. There had to be something that would explain why Mr Johns had so easily and quickly persuaded a group of people who had been her friends to shun her and believe that she was demonically possessed. She thought for a moment and then recalled an attempt to contact a childhood friend still in the church who had written her a strange letter.

> She had sent a letter to say I wasn't to go near her, I wasn't to phone her and I wasn't to do this and I wasn't to do that. After a few months she would reconsider the friendship and see if we could get together again. When I got the letter, I phoned her and she put the phone down on me as soon as she knew it was me. I went down to see her and she let me into the house, which I was surprised about, considering, but, without looking at me – she stood looking out of the window – she said something about an attack and, 'You never told me. If you had told me about it, it would have all made sense.'

She also remembered hearing that Mr Johns had said 'that I was part of an attack against the church. I couldn't stay around because I was there for the downfall of him and his ministry and the downfall of the church. I never heard anything involving the other people who had left.'

Teresa then went on to tell me about a serious rape that she had suffered at the beginning of 1993. The man concerned had been sent to prison. Her sick father had been shielded from being told and few people knew. Thinking about this incident Teresa remembered something said about the man who committed the rape. Mr Johns, who had somehow got to hear of it, had told someone that the rapist belonged to a satanic group. I put it to Teresa that this rape might have been considered to have caused the demonization. I certainly knew that this was a theory that was held by many people who believed in demonization of individuals because of sexual violence or sin. It would certainly make sense of the words of her friend. Teresa further reflected on who had known of the incident. The former priest-in-charge had known and it would have got back to the rector. He in all probability would have told Mr Johns. Suddenly things started to fall into place. The mystery of the hurtful episode of five years before began to make sense. However dreadful this was, at last Teresa began to understand.

Teresa had a spiritual director to whom she said nothing initially, because as she put it,

> I think I was worried that she wouldn't believe it. It was so obscure really. But when she did come to know about it, she said that she thought that one of the bishops would like to know what was going on. She went with me to see him. He said that this chap had got psychological problems. They had been keeping an eye on him since he was ordained, but they weren't sure what was going on. He sort of apologized and said that they would keep their eye on him. Nothing came of it. There was no move to get the priest-in-charge and me together to try and sort it out.

The final incident in this tale came after Teresa had moved away from the area and she started to receive letters from Mr Johns. The first letter expressed regret that they had not talked things out, or allowed him to try deliverance. She ignored the letter and a second came saying similar things. A third arrived and, unread this time, was burned like the previous two.

I met Teresa in January 1999 in a town a long way from her parental home. After her father died her mother had moved into a one-bedroom council flat, so she no longer had a base back there. She had half completed a course in nursing, but the previous March she had fallen victim to an ME-type illness. By January, she could only walk for ten minutes before her muscles ached prior to going into spasm. Her student grant had stopped and she was managing on £35 a week after her rent was paid. After a period of going to a different church every Sunday, 'the last in and the first out', so she didn't have to get involved with a congregation, she had settled on a weekday eucharist at a local Anglican church. Her illness meant that she could not stand a lot of the music or noise that would come with a Sunday service. Her contribution to the parish was to receive an intercession list, but the church had still not got this properly organized. Before I left her we prayed together and I prayed that she would find her way through the illness and all the suffering that she had endured.

Comment

Teresa's story raises a number of issues about power and abuse within an Anglican parish. Even if the bishop's opinion that Mr Johns was 'psychologically disturbed' can be accepted, there remains a host of problems about the failure of an institution to stop a serious case of spiritual abuse. Teresa was not the only one to suffer under Mr Johns. The two-thirds of the congregation who had to move elsewhere suffered, particularly if, like Teresa, they had given their whole lives to the church. Those who remained also suffered though they would not have admitted it. They suffered because by their behaviour they showed themselves to be caught up in the paranoia suffered by Mr Johns.

What was going on in the parish? Before making any spiritual assessment of the situation, it is clear that Mr Johns was unable to deal with any kind of opposition. He got his own way by forceful confrontation and a readiness to use verbal violence, reminiscent of the technique employed by a small child in a supermarket. It was also backed up by a frequent reference to what the 'Lord' had told him. Here he was appealing to a common motif in charismatic theology that the man of prayer is given guidance. Protestant thinking about the inerrancy of the Bible could naturally be extended to include the inerrancy of what is believed to be direct spiritual guidance. Just as the 'truth' in the Bible needs no dialogue, so actions based on such guidance do not need to be justified or explained.

The story suggested that Mr Johns needed to control everything that happened in the parish, but in this case the indications are that it was more a reflection of his psychological state than any apparent enjoyment of power. It seems that negotiation and compromise were simply not part of his way of dealing with the world. It had the effect of isolating him from everyone except those that agreed with him. This would have further isolated him from the realism of a constructively questioning voice. The apparent collusion of the rector who had appointed him and who shared his paranoid fears of demonic attack would have isolated him still more. For a 'psychologically disturbed' person to be beyond challenge and also propped up by a theology that knows no compromise is a destructive and dangerous phenomenon. When a paranoid belief system is in place in an individual, he or she will constantly seek evidence around them to prove to themselves and their followers that they are right. Teresa seems to have been part of that 'proof' and no doubt there were other 'evidences' of attack produced by Mr Johns to bolster the belief system.

The group of twenty who gathered around Mr Johns to reinforce his perception of God and the world would have found themselves under enormous pressure to think exactly as he did. A group which feels itself under any kind of threat will knit tightly together and individual doubts will be banished by the pressure to conform. Initially the challenge to their loyalty would have been the sight of fellow parishioners drifting away from the church among which there were, as Teresa told me, husbands and wives of members of the group. There would have been an initial fierce test of loyalty, but once the choice had been made, the peer pressure of the inner group would have taken over. Any attack on Mr Johns would have been experienced as an attack on them personally because they had made the act of identification with him. Their inner need for consistency would have made them cling to his side because changing the mind is a painful step, particularly when it involves losing face with other people. Many studies exist to show the force of a public commitment and the consequent need to be consistent in one's actions, and this would be particularly true when backed by the power of a group.

The 'demonization' of Teresa can be seen as part of a group process. Her attempt to remain part of the church while not being in agreement with all its thinking was perceived as a threat to its existence. There is no room in a group of this kind for someone who does not go along with the group's understanding of itself. Teresa's rape and her consequent demonization were something that would have been seized on readily as explaining the failure of her non-compliance and non-cooperation with the rest.

In the next section I will be looking further at ways that certain charismatic theologies successfully make large areas of behaviour they do not approve of into entry points for demons. Some of these supposed entry points are acts committed by an individual, while others arise through suffering at the hands of other people. Sometimes the opportunities for entry of demons are believed to have come down from a previous generation, or arise out of some sexual molestation. The list of entry points is so long that someone who holds this type of theology will never need to listen to, or have dialogue with, another point of view, because the person offering another position can be said to be automatically demonized. Suffice to say at this point that sexual violence against an individual can be said to demonize them. Peter Horrobin in his book, *Healing Through Deliverance,* speaks of his belief in the way that sexual abuse in early childhood opens a girl up to the entry of a demon which will do all it can to interfere with subsequent relationships. Horrobin also believes in the idea of transference and generational demonization, the idea that demons can pass down the family line and affect those whose only fault is to have been born to a particular set of parents.

It does not take much imagination to see how this kind of thinking may have been transferred to fit the situation of Teresa's rape. If the act of parenting a child can result in the handing on of demons to an innocent party, how much more can a man reputed to be involved in a satanic cult pass on his demons to a victim of his sexual violence? The whole concept of demonization is fairly alarming, but still worse is the idea that an innocent person can simply pick up demons in this way and thus be doubly victimized.

The notion of the scapegoat is an old one in religious history. Leviticus 16 describes the day of Atonement when the high priest prayed over two goats. The first was sacrificed and the high priest then confessed the sins of the people over the second before it was driven off into the wilderness to perish of thirst and starvation. In modern psychological thinking this process is called projection. The things individuals most dislike about themselves are most fiercely resisted and loathed when they appear in other people. Hating another person or group on whom an individual has projected, or whom they have made to carry all their weaknesses and faults, helps them to relieve their bad feeling about themselves. Teresa became the scapegoat of the group around Mr Johns. Subconsciously they would have recognized that she continued the normality of the parish before Mr Johns arrived. In opting for the new pattern of the parish, they had to reject the past and Teresa who symbolized it. In hating and demonizing her they could drown their inner doubts about the situation, as well convince themselves that they were doing the will of God. Scapegoating is a common activity both in our society and in those of the past. The classic scapegoats were, of course, those accused of being witches, and one has only to read the play by Arthur Miller, *The Crucible*, to see the psychological processes at work in the accusers. Today, as will be seen in chapter four, some homosexuals have come to be the demonized figures that carry the shadow of many people. How convenient that Teresa had a history 'explaining' how she had become demonized!

As long as Teresa remained in the area, she served a function in binding the group together in their work of resisting her 'attack' against the church and the ministry of Mr Johns. By moving away she no longer served that function. One expects that in a paradoxical way the group would have missed her 'threat', particularly as the dynamic of the paranoid group 'needs' an external threat to function at its most efficient. The Nazi party came to power on the back of a paranoid fear and suspicion of the Jews. In the United States, Joe McCarthy achieved influence and power for a time by tapping into a deep fear of the 'Red menace' of communism in the 1950s.

The act of writing letters to Teresa in her new home can be interpreted in a number of ways. Perhaps Mr Johns missed having Teresa around, playing a part in the maintenance of his group solidarity. No one else, according to Teresa, functioned in this way. Perhaps now that the 'threat' had been removed, it could be seen that Teresa had never been a threat and Mr Johns was trying to make amends to her. The letters expressed regret, but no pastoral approach had ever been made to her while she was around and the only conversations with Mr Johns had elicited brief monosyllabic responses. The burning of those three letters was not an act of hatred, but a realization that any response would somehow drag her back to a stage of her life which was finished and needed to be let go.

Some final comments need to be made here about the way that the system failed Teresa. Taking such a case personally to the bishop is not an option available to the majority of Christians in the pew as most would lack the social confidence to approach a person in high authority. But having reached the bishop and explained the situation, the powerlessness of the bishop became apparent to Teresa. Technically Mr Johns was the responsibility of the rector, but the collusion of the two men in the paranoid world of demons meant that it was unlikely that the rector would ever fully face the 'psychological difficulties' of Mr Johns.

The Church of England does have guidelines given to all clergy over the issues of the occult and paranormal. Every bishop will have an adviser available to the clergy to help them with cases of 'possession' or demonization. In practice, the vast bulk of cases referred to bishops' advisers refer to poltergeist phenomena. Sometimes they encounter a so-called 'place-memory', a situation in which strong emotions from the past have somehow lingered and become fixed in a particular location. The language of possession and demonization is seldom heard outside parishes whose theology makes such phenomena possible. One adviser I know says that part of his job is to help people recognize that the demons they think possess them have been put there by zealous Christians operating a particular belief system, and normally have no existence except in the imagination. The consensus of the

Church of England is that possession is an extremely rare event and that lesser cases of 'oppression' are also seldom met with. Even with such guidelines, however, the Church of England has no power to curb the excesses of clergy who operate within a belief system such as that of Mr Johns.

To summarize, Teresa seems to have been a victim of a belief system, a parish power dynamic and a disturbed clergyman. More disturbingly the institution has no power at its disposal to rectify the situation, no means of disciplining anyone or holding anyone accountable. In the next section I will be suggesting that the theological roots which make the abusive system possible need challenging with considerable energy, rather than being ignored and written off as quirky and of no real interest. A theology that abuses is a theology that needs to be challenged and refuted. The power of the institution, in this case the Church of England, needs to be used with authority to outlaw anything that causes another to stumble or be harmed in any way.

The use of power in the parish

The issue of power and its abuse within the parish has not been one that has hitherto been openly discussed too much in Christian literature. Apart from a number of books from the United States which describe a somewhat different church situation, one of the first books to break this silence in Britain is one by Paul Beasley-Murray, *Power for God's Sake: Power and Abuse in the Local Church*. Power struggles within the institutional churches have sometimes come into public attention, as with the saga of conflict at Lincoln Cathedral between the dean and canons in the mid-1990s. In churches there is sometimes a power struggle by the clergy over the people, as in this story; in other situations it is the people who hold the upper hand over the clergy, who find themselves victimized and sometimes overwhelmed by the power of the group, who seek control within the congregational life. Beasley-Murray seeks to have this issue addressed openly so that the consequential dissipation of energy from the important tasks of church life can be halted.

In his analysis of power abuse, Beasley-Murray collected data through means of questionnaires sent to members of the Richard Baxter Institute for Ministry. This is an organization which holds conferences to 'promote excellence in the practice of ministry' and issues a magazine, *Ministry Today*. The questionnaire produced a 50 per cent response with a total of 116 replies. Baptist and evangelical churches were somewhat over-represented, reflecting the nonconformist roots of the organization, but nevertheless the results were striking and instructive. Some of the questions touched on quite sensitive areas of ministerial life, such as inappropriate touch with members of the opposite sex, but for the purposes of this chapter I need to focus on the findings about the use of power. Even allowing for a questionnaire that shows the respondent in the best possible light, it is disturbing to discover that 42 per cent of the answers were admissions that at times ministers had played on the guilt of their members to get their own way, and 32 per cent of ministers had 'hidden behind God' for the same purpose. As Beasley-Murray points out, the true figures may be much higher as some ministers will be lacking in self-awareness. 67 per cent of the ministers also saw themselves as having the most power within the congregation and over this percentage believed that their 'call', their special role as a messenger or agent of God, was their focus of authority. This was considered to be more important than their expertise and personal charisma. It is not hard to see how such an understanding of their role could be easily twisted to mean that the minister is above contradiction and permitted to control and manipulate the congregation. Another striking finding showed that only 7 per cent of those answering never preached 'aggressively'. Whether that referred to expressions of anger in the pulpit or manipulative 'hell-fire and damnation' sermons is not clear, but aggressive preaching is unlikely to be pleasant, either for those who preach or those who listen.

Beasley-Murray's survey indicates that issues of power in the church at large are alive and well, whether from the point of view of the clergy or the people. He concludes that there is a great deal of confusion about what power is appropriate and what is inappropriate, and not a little unhappiness in many of the churches because of this. His book ends with an analysis of what power consists of and the models from scripture that can be followed. To these I will return. In summary, then, the issues raised in Teresa's church are neither unusual nor unparalleled.

Healing through deliverance – a case study of the literature

I propose now to examine a recent and influential account of the ideas of demonization and theories about 'demonic entry points' that are in a book already referred to, *Healing Through*

Deliverance, by Peter Horrobin. The book is in two volumes, with the first given over to an examination of the New Testament evidence. The second, which will be examined here, is subtitled *The Practical Ministry*. The problem for any book which deals with matters connected with the demonic is that it will always attract the curious, the inexperienced and the naïve. Anecdotes about healings and cases of deliverance can all too easily be taken as models for actual practice. The art of diagnosis of demonic infestation is not something that can be readily taught from a book, so there is considerable scope for using a book like Horrobin's inappropriately.

Some of the theology in Horrobin's work is based on an appeal to the obscurer parts of the book of Revelation with its account of the end-time. From this book Horrobin obtains his belief in the unleashing of Satan to 'seduce the nations' (Revelation 20:8), and the continuing vulnerability of humankind to attack by Satan and his demons or fallen angels. The incarnation of Jesus is part of a divine plan to rescue humankind and deliver them from the power of demons. Thus to proclaim the gospel is to heal the sick and cast out demons. Horrobin makes it clear that Christians cannot be possessed by demons as they belong to God. But they can be and are oppressed and demonized in various ways and thus will need deliverance.

It is clear that in Horrobin's universe the Christian life is one of constant cosmic struggle between good and evil. This perspective is normally called dualism. The practical outworking of this belief for Horrobin and those who follow his ideas is that almost any disorder experienced by an individual may require some kind of act of spiritual deliverance. As I commented elsewhere in this book, the acceptance of needing to be delivered from some kind of malignant entity requires an enormous act of trust in the one ministering. This is something that can so easily be abused.

Horrobin's book shows that with many other Christians he is facing the whole range of sicknesses as well as all the issues from the past which contribute to various types of dis-ease. He writes well, for example, about the need for forgiveness in people's lives. 'To know that they are forgiven, sometimes for the very first time in their lives, can be the most significant healing experience that they will ever have.' But then he goes on to say, 'We have witnessed enormous battles with the resident demonic powers as they have employed every weapon in their armoury to try to prevent a person speaking out forgiveness of an individual who has abused them sexually.' The question of whether this really is a battle against a demon, or possibly an act of power against an individual who needs time and space to come to terms with a particularly vicious crime against the integrity of their being, needs to be asked. I will be considering the experience of sexual abuse in another chapter and the particular issues that are raised when violence of a sexual kind is involved. One cannot imagine Jesus wrestling on the floor with a sick person who was finding it hard to forgive! He goes on to say, 'The consequences of sin can leave us sick, or demonized, or both, as well as in need of forgiveness by God.' According to this thinking one of the overall effects of being demonized is to be under Satan's control, and thus unable ever to disagree with the spirit-filled counsellor who is offering ministry. Thus the power relationship is totally unequal. Submission to God in this case has to be combined with submission to another human being who may merely be using this teaching as an exercise in power.

Reading through Horrobin's list of 'observable symptoms of possible demonization', it is hard to imagine anyone anywhere who is not possibly demonized. One feels that anyone who goes to someone practising this kind of ministry will have some demon or other found. There are twenty-seven possible symptoms, including depression, hereditary illness and nightmares. Still more notable are the demonic entry points. I have already mentioned the way that Teresa may have become 'demonized' (though as far as I know she never showed any of the symptoms!), and it is necessary to pause to note another one of Horrobin's ideas, that of transference down the generational line. Generational demonization can take place at the moment of conception or death of a parent. Thus an adopted child needs to be 'delivered' from the sexual sin of his or her natural parents. Horrobin avoids facing up to the passage in John 9:2, in which the disciples ask Jesus whether the blind man sinned or his parents. 'Neither,' says Jesus. Horrobin rather lamely says that there would be no point in the question if suffering down the generations could not take place!

Among the many symptoms that may lead to demonization, 'denominationalism', alternative medicine and trial marriages are found alongside false religions, universalism and wrong attitude to the scriptures. In short, one could summarize the demonic entry points as living life in any way other than the particular approach to Christianity which the leader using such a list might approve of!

One of the things that would make the book far more

engaging would be some indication that in the twelve years of ministry at Ellel Grange mistakes had been made, people had been damaged and forgiveness for those mistakes sought. Once again in the inerrant universe that many fundamentalist Christians appear to belong to, everything seems apparently perfect and beyond criticism. To admit failure is not permitted. So there is a book which, through its failure to allow ambiguity, disagreement or possibility of error, is probably going to be less than helpful in the task of hands-on ministry. As I noted with my discussion of the Bible, people will always be in danger of abuse when they are brought to a place or person that 'knows' the truth and knows it without any possibility of error.

The charismatic movement and spiritual deliverance

In a previous chapter, I looked at the literature which emerged in the 1980s giving rise to the notion of Satanic Ritual Abuse, and making some sense of the fashions of diagnosis surrounding the counselling of Kathleen. It is necessary here to pause to look at the wider historical picture and ask whether the ideas in Peter Horrobin's book have a context in the broader international scene. The detailed research has not yet been done, but Andrew Walker, in an essay in the book *Charismatic Renewal*, helpfully points out the direction that should be looked in to understand the historical context of such beliefs . In his words, 'demons began to break loose from the subterranean moorings of the unconscious and surface in open rebellion'.

Through looking back to the start of the twentieth century and the beginnings of the Pentecostal churches, Walker claims that these churches, though believing in demons, kept them 'under the bed and firmly under control'. He traces the origins of the 'paranoid universe', a fear that devils are everywhere, to a 1950s' movement in the United States called Latter Day Rain. This movement of Pentecostal revival lay behind the shepherding or discipling movement, which will be further examined in chapter seven. One of the inspirers of this movement, William Branham (1909–65), was, during the 1940s and 1950s, given to somewhat bizarre teaching and prophecies. For example, in the style of David Koresh (see chapter six), he proclaimed himself to be the angel of Revelation 3:14 and 10:7, prophesying that by 1977 all denominations would be consumed by the World Council of Churches under the control of the Roman Catholics. This would usher in the rapture and the world would be destroyed! In spite of his bizarre theology, Branham had considerable influence, particularly in the area of healing. This somewhat maverick ministry was handed on to, among others, two young men, Paul Cain (later to be associated with John Wimber) and Ern Baxter, who will be mentioned later as one of those associated with the shepherding movement based at Fort Lauderdale in Florida.

Two other members of this group, Dom Basham and Derek Prince, promulgated strong views on demonology alongside their views on shepherding and male leadership. Their 'ministry of deliverance' came to be practised within charismatic circles and seems to have originated with these men as recently as the early 1970s. They seem single-handedly to have made fashionable the notions that our societies are strongly dominated by witchcraft, that charms and amulets can be infused with demonic power and that demonic strongmen can dominate churches, cities and even nations.

One particular book that captures the Prince/Basham style is one that appeared in 1973 called *Pigs in the Parlour*, by Frank and Ida Hammond. Frank Hammond famously declares that he has never met anyone who does not need deliverance! This style of ministry is continued to this day by Bill Subritzky, whose influence over the independent charismatic churches is extensive.

Andrew Walker, normally an irenic commentator on the charismatic scene, is fairly critical of the effects on many churches and their members by this creation of a 'paranoid universe'. He notes, as I have done, how difficult it is to escape possible 'demonization'. Anyone or anything that is detested or disliked, such as homosexuals or critics of your theology, can be seen to be under a demonic thrall. To be demonized, Walker points out, is to be dehumanized and when there is the threat of such demonization there is fear. A world where demons are seen everywhere is a world subject to fear. Where fear is dominant, it is hard to see how Christian love can be practised or known. Walker ends with the thought that paranoid beliefs create a need for strongmen of power who can show people how to protect themselves from spiritual danger. Perhaps here is the motive and the tragedy of the paranoid universe: devils are created in order for individuals to obtain power. In short, the whole demonic 'revival' of the past twenty-five years may be a complicated and bizarre power game played out on vulnerable and susceptible individuals. It may be that the 'demons' in fact reside in the power abuse that is taking place, rather than in the individuals named and 'demonized' by the exorcists!

Conclusion

Of all the belief systems that can potentially harm an individual, the idea that demonic causes lie at the root of many ordinary human problems is perhaps the most alarming. This writer is sufficiently flexible in his thinking to allow the possibility of demonic activity as being a factor in the diagnosis of human suffering. However, the regular discovery of 'demons' inside people is likely to be at best an evasion of responsibility and at worst an opening for serious power abuse against an individual. In an earlier chapter it was noticed how Rachel visited Ellel Grange for ministry and apparently benefited from the extensive attention that was offered to her in the course of her exorcism. For her, the deliverance facilitated the continuation of the belief that her problems were caused by something outside her, a demon, a father or her upbringing.

In other settings that I know about exorcism has not been experienced so benignly. It has been experienced as a profound invasion of the psyche, leading to nightmares and other forms of psychological disturbance. This is not to say that such rituals should never occur, but only that they should happen in carefully supervised ways so that accountability is retained. The theology that finds demons in people, caused by a multiple of situations and circumstances, also needs to be carefully examined. Is the devil being searched for in the wrong place? Perhaps he should be looked for in any situation of power abuse, including the use of inappropriate exorcism. Certainly, as shall be seen in chapter nine, Jesus himself seemed very clear about the evil that is present when power is inappropriately exercised in a religious setting. People could do worse than follow Jesus when he looks into the heart of man to find the cause of evil in him (Matthew 15:18), not in anything outside. If Jesus was reluctant to look outside an individual to locate evil, so should people be reticent in blaming outside 'demons' as an explanation for human sin and sickness.

And their feeling was that I had to physically say it myself. I had to be willing to say that I did not want these demons.

Chapter Four

The Church and its Response to the Homosexual

Of all the moral issues exercising the church today, the question of homosexuality is the one that perhaps engenders the most passion. The Lambeth conference of 1998, a gathering of Anglican bishops from every part of the world, deliberated on many important issues, but the one thing that attracted the media was the issue of homosexuality. Nothing else seemed worth reporting.

One Lambeth image that seemed to sum up the divisions of culture, morality and theology in the conference was the scene involving a Nigerian bishop seeking to exorcize a young gay activist Anglican priest. Clearly there were strongly held opinions on both sides, ones that would not go away simply as a result of a vote following a heated impassioned debate. To this topic I will return as it enables us to see, at least in the part of the Christian church represented by Anglicanism, that there is a real debate to be had and more than one way of interpreting the material from the Bible on this topic. At Lambeth 1998, in addition to the formal statements it was declared that compassion and understanding at the very least should be offered to the homosexual, and that a fuller acceptance of this lifestyle may eventually be possible.

Peter is a young Christian man for whom the debate about homosexuality reflects something more than an interesting moral discussion. He was at the receiving end of the indignation of a Christian community who had decided that standards of sexual morality were more important than the normal requirements of compassion and care. At a stroke Peter lost job, home, family and friends and almost his life. None of his accusers wanted to debate the issue or leave any measure of uncertainty about the rightness of their action. Peter was to be sacrificed to the principle that morality is fixed and beyond negotiation. It will be seen that what is mainly at issue in his story is how Christians should apply strongly held moral beliefs when dealing with fragile human beings.

I met Peter in London where he was working in a church-sponsored social project. He told me that he had grown up in a fairly 'liberal' environment. His family did not conform to a middle-class norm since none of the men who had been a father to him, nor his half-brother or half-sister, had stayed around. He had thus grown up with a somewhat insecure sense of identity. The pervading morality was that you can do what you like as long as you do not harm anybody. He started to have homosexual feelings from his early teens and this, combined with his existing confused sense of identity, meant that he was very much in search of answers. This led him to a Strict Baptist church to which a group of his friends belonged. As Peter put it,

And I guess from the very first meeting there was a sense of these young people having something that

I didn't have. They seemed to have their life sorted
and one of the attractions was that here was a group
of people that seemed to know definite answers about
things. Things were black and white, there were definite
rights and wrongs, they weren't allowed to have shades
of grey. They didn't go to the cinema, they didn't drink
alcohol and they didn't go to discos and things. But
somehow that seemed to make sense. Here was a set
of values that people knew were right or wrong. And
I found that attractive.

And so for the first few months that I was attending,
one of the things that I became aware of was that I
was a sinner, that I was going to hell, unless I accepted
Jesus as my saviour. In amongst all that I also heard
various comments made about homosexuality, which
confirmed my belief that it must be the worst possible
sin that there was and I was definitely going to burn
in hell for it. And so there was this terrible dilemma
early on between wanting to be saved and yet also
being made to feel that I was beyond the pale. That I
couldn't be saved. Until eventually I had this experience
of believing that Jesus really could save me as I was. And
so at fourteen I gave my heart to Jesus. And that was a
very affirming experience for me.

The feelings of homosexuality did not go away, and Peter tried
desperately for six months to subjugate them with various
spiritual exercises, Bible reading, prayer and fasting.
Eventually he was desperate enough to want to talk to
someone about it, so he tried to talk to the pastor's wife. He

reflected, 'It took some weeks to build up the strength to do it. And eventually I told her in her sitting room that I was gay. Her reaction was just to say, "Don't be silly, you're much too hairy."' After this less-than-helpful encounter he decided that the only way forward was to remain celibate.

Some years later Peter recalled a meeting at which a 'converted witch' was speaking. During it he had a kind of panic attack which left him breathless, and immediately those around him interpreted it as of spiritual significance and urged him to come out with whatever problem was being indicated by this attack. He wasn't at that point going to admit to his homosexuality, but in the prayer offered over him, someone came up with the insight that homosexuality was indeed the problem. Since Peter could not deny this piece of discernment, the prayers became prayers for deliverance and exorcism of the demons responsible for the homosexuality. Peter, however, was not allowed to be a passive participant in these prayers. He told me,

> They eventually convinced me that in fact the demons had left me and that they had seen the demons leave my body. But they had got stuck in my throat. They had risen up through my body getting stuck in my throat. And their feeling was that I had to physically say it myself. I had to be willing to say that I did not want these demons. And there was this tremendous struggle because I really could not say that. I wanted to, I desperately, desperately wanted to be what I considered normal. And eventually I did manage to say those words, and they all went away rejoicing.

The next day Peter was exactly the same, but his situation was by then worse than it had been because those involved in the prayer of exorcism had told everyone that a miracle of deliverance had taken place. Peter was now expected to live up to this miracle even though nothing had, in fact, changed.

At the age of twenty-one Peter went to theological college and spent three years studying theology. There was a problem with his choice of college as it contrasted with the church he came from, which was Calvinist and anti-charismatic, but Peter wanted to be exposed to the broader evangelical tradition that was represented by this college. There, he confided in a couple of people, but they encouraged him to think that there was a way forward through embracing celibacy. It was during this time that he met Charlotte, his future wife. He told me,

> We were actually introduced by my best friend, one
> of the people who knew that I had these feelings.
> Charlotte had expressed an interest in me and I knew
> she had this romantic interest. Very, very early on
> I took her to one side and told her that I was gay.
> Because I wanted her to realize that it was no good
> pursuing it. However, I kind of feel after that that we
> were pushed together by various people who may have
> thought that this was a kind of redemptive thing for
> me. Charlotte, having prayed about it, was convinced
> that this was the way she was going to be used. And
> there was a sense that I wanted to be normal, I wanted
> to be seen to be like everyone else. And marriage was
> part of that. And I think I felt kind of vindicated in it

because I had been honest with Charlotte from the start. I had told her that I had these feelings. Even up to the day we married I hadn't given any indication that those feelings had actually changed. We had always talked quite openly and honestly.

Peter's marriage and ministry were to last for seven years. His first job took him to a small church plant in Dorset, which was a charismatic breakaway from a Strict Baptist church. The congregation prospered under his leadership and he then left to go to the North of England to work with another church plant. Finally, he left to work in a mission. All through that time, when he was in smallish communities, he met no other gay people and he and his wife acted as a normal heterosexual couple, though he confessed that the pretence brought its own stresses. The situation changed once he received an invitation to go to work in London as an associate pastor to a congregation of around 1,000 people. Here he was expected to counsel young men like himself who were gay. He asked the other pastors what their opinions were about homosexuality. He told me, 'One of them thought it was a disease that should be healed. The second was very much of the opinion that it was demonic. And people needed to have demons cast out of them.' So Peter found himself putting off these interviews, feeling profoundly unhappy that he didn't know how to deal with the situation. He told Charlotte that he thought he would have to leave the church within a year as the situation he found himself in was impossible. As far as the rest of the work was concerned things were thriving. In one year he had baptized thirty teenagers and the youth fellowship was 150 strong. Peter, however, was conscious the whole time of living a double life, the inner life of a tormented homosexual man and the outer life of a successful and charismatic pastor.

In the middle of Peter's stress-filled existence, he allowed himself to be party to a homosexual encounter. He was immediately filled with a sense that he would be struck down by God and he vowed that it would never happen again. Nevertheless, in his words, 'it had opened up the floodgates'. He managed to keep it from Charlotte for a time, but unfortunately she found during the course of a medical examination that she had contracted a minor sexually transmitted disease. Peter was confronted and asked outright if he had been seeing another man. He confessed it and within a short time they had both gone to one of the other pastors. In his words,

Within half an hour I'd been sent away. His comments were, 'Well we'll just tell the church that you've had a breakdown. And you will be sent away.' And I was sent to the North of England. I was sent away but with no one to support me. Charlotte went to visit her parents. For two weeks I was left in isolation. There was no one there to give me support, no one to talk to. And it was during that time that I realized that life was going to change dramatically for me. I was never going to be allowed to return without certain restrictions. And so at that stage I sought out other gay people and was put in touch with gay Christians. But when I did return two weeks later, my resignation had been written for me. And so in a church that is supposedly congregationally

based, and where 97 per cent of the congregation had
felt it was God's will to invite me to join the church, on
the basis of a few old men, at the end of the day, I was
asked to leave. I was basically given three options. I had
to resign… I could publicly repent of my sin and my
sexuality; they would send me away for healing to one
of these groups like True Freedom Trust or Courage.
They would see to it that I was never a minister in that
or any other church again. The second option was that
I could go into a gay lifestyle and be oppressed by the
Holy Spirit for the rest of my life. The third option was
that I was never truly born again and that I was going
to hell anyway. And I left that day. I was told that the
elders would be coming to pray over me and so on.

Peter felt completely unable to handle the thought of the
entire eldership coming to pray over him that night. He had
spent two weeks in isolation and was now physically,
emotionally and spiritually drained. While driving back from
the North of England, he contemplated killing himself by
driving off the road to solve everyone's problems, his own,
Charlotte's and the church's. He left his flat the same day
with just one suitcase before the eldership could get near. He
didn't want to pretend that he really believed that prayer was
going to solve the fact of his sexual orientation.

Peter survived, though he was by then completely outside
the network of friends and support that had sustained him
throughout his entire adult life. He was simultaneously
homeless and penniless. Through a contact in the Methodist
Church he knew to be sympathetic to someone in his

position, he managed to cope with the early weeks, gradually putting his life back together both on a practical level and spiritually. He told me that at the end of three months he went back to visit the pastor of his old church and was asked, 'How are you?' In his words he responded,

> 'I said to him, "What you actually mean is how am I spiritually?" I said, 'Quite honestly I feel much better spiritually. I feel more in touch with God than ever I was in the last ten years. I feel I am being honest with God and I am saying, "God, this is who I am. This is how you made me, this is who I am." I feel that my integrity is much more in touch and so on.' His only comment was, 'No, you are living in a place of deception.' He couldn't accept the fact that I could be out and yet feel spiritually in touch.

By being forced to leave the church, Peter had been able to move to a new place, but not his wife Charlotte.

> During the interim three months that I was actually gone, the church had had large prayer meetings. Everyone had been told why I had left the church. Which was fine for me in a way because I was out of it, but I felt sorry for Charlotte. She had to go back into that church knowing that everyone knew all our business. Two-and-half months after I had left, they asked her to leave the manse. She had not worked [during the marriage]; she had always been a pastor's wife. She supported me. It wasn't part of the deal. She had lost her husband, everyone knew her

business and now she was losing her home and all our
furniture. The only thing she could afford was a bedsit
which was furnished. Everything that was done after that,
although we had always talked about unconditional love
in that church, everything was conditional so that when
they agreed to put in a telephone for her, it was on the
condition that she never told me what the number was.
She was to have no contact with me. Because that would
somehow taint her.

Contact from the church continued, but it was never to offer
any love or support:

For the first three months after I had left, I was having
letters from people telling me I would burn in hell –
people sending me photocopies from books about how
I could be saved, how I could be released from demons
and so on. Most of which I never bothered to read; they
just went in the bin. No letters of support, nothing.
I subsequently joined a group called Integrity which is
for gay men and women from evangelical backgrounds.
And actually I met two members of my congregation
there. And they told me that following my leaving,
the church had brought in people from these anti-
gay movements to give talks to the congregation, and
there were several months of intensive propaganda and
indoctrination. During this a number of people left the
church who turned out to be gay. But they had been in
the church for many years and subjugated those
feelings and so on.

That Peter had been able to move on into employment so quickly after seven years in ministry was a cause of deep thankfulness.

> I was very fortunate because I finally got a job. But I was six months from leaving the church to finding this job when I couldn't find anything. People looked at my CV and said, 'You've been in the ministry for seven years, why have you left?' I was left with this dilemma. Do I say to them, 'I came out as a gay man and so I was forced to leave the church'? I thought, if they write to the church, more than likely the church would write to them and say, 'Well we had to get rid of him because he was demon-possessed.'

Another thing that upset Peter after he had left was that his whole work with young people was questioned, and everything seemed to be done to suggest that nothing good had ever come out of his ministry. According to Charlotte, with whom he had remained on good terms, young men were asked if Peter had touched them inappropriately and, worse still, other young people whom Peter had baptized were re-baptized as if somehow their baptism had been invalidated.

> It was those things that really hurt me the most. And no one had looked back and said, 'Oh look how much blessing there was, look how we grew, look how many young people were baptized,' and no one used that as a stepping stone to questioning, 'Well, what was God doing in all this?' And the way in which they took it

upon themselves to tell everybody. Every church I had ever belonged to was informed. My mother, who is not a Christian, was informed and she wrote back and told me I was dead. She suddenly felt that the son she had known didn't exist. And I had hid something very important from her. Now we get on better, but there was this period when she couldn't accept it herself.

Peter found that the total condemnation he was receiving from Christian people forced him to look outside the Christian networks for support, and what he found there was not what he had been taught he would find. He found,

People whom I would formerly have condemned because they were not Christians. All my friends were Christians because you were not encouraged to have friends except with the express purpose of converting them. But suddenly I was experiencing more unconditional love and acceptance from people who didn't have any faith. There was a tremendous release very early on, because once I had left the church and opened up my sexuality and so on, it also led me to question other things that I had formerly held to be sacrosanct. The black and white. The issues around alcohol and so on. I still don't drink myself, but I suddenly realized that actually drinking in itself is not actually sinful. Going to a pub is not actually sinful, though previously I would never have entered a pub. And also along some theological lines. I suddenly realized that I did feel comfortable saying to somebody, 'I'm sorry, but I don't know the answer

to that.' Whereas previously, admitting that you didn't
know the answer to something, or that you had doubts
about some aspect of the faith, was actually almost
sinful itself. There wasn't room for that. I still feel
myself very much to be evangelical, but it is much
broader than that.

Peter then told me of his current work with his partner among
gay evangelical Christians, organizing a group of twenty to
thirty people. He told me, 'All of them have at one time or
another desperately wanted to be heterosexual. Nobody
could have wanted it more. They have been willing to
undergo the most extreme forms of therapy or ministry. I
know one person who went for electric-shock treatment
because his church sent him for it. All of them desperately
wanted to be saved from their homosexuality.' Peter was
describing a group of suffering gay people who had done
everything the church required of them over considerable
periods of time. They had arrived at a point where they had
become broken and embittered towards God and the church.
He claimed that, as far as he knew, all the evangelical
organizations set up to make gay people straight were
completely ineffective. He personally knew counsellors who
had left these organizations on the grounds that the
treatments being offered helped nobody.

Peter had at the time of my interview found an Anglican
church which accepted him and his partner for what they were.

I still consider myself mainly to be evangelical in my
theology. I'm very happy because I have found a very

evangelical church – with a little 'e' – which is very accepting. I am able to be out and yet I preach, I teach in the Sunday school and I'm on the PCC. I am very accepted as I am, for who I am. But there are for me still issues. Throughout my life there have been people who haven't been prepared to listen to the experience of gay Christians and how much they are really hurting. They are not willing to accept the tremendous things that gay people are actually doing in the church.

Part of the hostility to homosexuals, Peter conjectured, seemed to come from individuals who were homosexuals themselves, but because they repressed this aspect of themselves, were far more unforgiving towards those who did not. He told me the experience of his partner:

My partner also has an evangelical background and was an evangelical missionary. He was brought up in an evangelical Church of England, went to theological college and worked for a mission overseas. Later, he worked for a youth mission in this country [Britain] where he came out. In fact, he was outed by someone who was also gay. But they subjugated their feelings, and one of the problems we have to contend with is that sometimes the people who are the worst offenders against us are themselves gay. And their way of dealing with it is to out others. He was working with a ministry with the homeless and then overnight was made homeless.

It was interesting to hear of the impact that the Lambeth

debate on homosexuality had made on Peter when it was publicized in July 1998.

> My partner brought home the daily paper with the
> summary of what had been said at Lambeth. I was
> really, really angry. My first reaction was, What am
> I doing worshipping in the Church of England now?
> I should just leave it. It seems that there isn't a home
> for the gay Christian. If it hadn't been for the fact that
> my vicar rang me that same night and affirmed that
> within my local church they affirmed and valued the
> ministry that Andrew and I had within the church,
> I would have left. But what it brought home to me
> was that at grass-roots level, in the local church, it
> makes no difference. Andrew and I are both out and
> worship in the church together where we are known
> to be a gay couple. But we are valued.

Peter was grateful for the place that he found himself in. His experience of ministry had enabled him to counsel himself, and he was secure with an accepting church, a good job and a loving partner. For most gay Christians, that was not the experience they found. For most, it was an ongoing struggle to remain Christian in the face of such opposition and condemnation.

Comment

It would be wrong to portray Peter merely as a victim of Christian prejudice and moral harshness. Clearly, allowing himself to enter into a casual sexual relationship while married was inappropriate behaviour for a Christian, let alone a minister. It is, in fact, not easy to see how the leaders of his church should have responded to this revelation. They could, in another context, have claimed that the issue was more to do with infidelity to his wife than with homosexual inclination, and that discipline was necessary to uphold the integrity and reputation of the ordained ministry. That, of course, was not the position of the leadership in this case, who were apparently motivated by a strong hostility and paranoia towards same-sex relationships. It was this incredibly powerful antipathy towards homosexuals from part of the evangelical world that punished Peter so harshly and, many would say, excessively. It was in the context of a climate of hostility towards homosexuals that Peter had been pushed towards marriage, hence the involvement of Charlotte in the sad, tragic affair.

Any understanding of what might have been an appropriate response to Peter's action must be linked to an appreciation for what had brought him into this particular situation. Taken alone it was a serious moral lapse, but when seen against the background of his whole life up to that point, it can be seen as far less worthy of blame and condemnation. Peter's marriage to Charlotte could well be seen to have had an impediment to its validity from the beginning. Had Peter not been in his particular religious environment at the time of meeting Charlotte, then he might well not have experienced any pressure to conform to the expectations of 'normality' around him by marrying her. I do not know the extent to which Charlotte had bought into the idea that heterosexual experience and prayer would somehow change Peter once they were married. It is likely that some such idea may have been in her mind. For them to marry was by any reckoning a tragedy in the making. Peter did not claim to be bisexual, and told me that from the beginning the whole sexual part of the marriage was difficult for him.

Peter's expulsion from the ministry was the culmination of a sequence of events that one would describe as tragic rather than wicked. Clearly the tragedy of the whole episode was not in any way recognized by those who sought to deal with Peter after the facts of his casual affair became known. He was made the target of an enormous amount of vitriol and anger, and I suspect that the harshness of this response had a great deal to do with the need to preserve boundaries between the congregation and the 'fallen' world outside, which is an aspect of the type of congregation described here. An emphasis on being 'saved' will always heighten awareness of those outside who are unsaved and, as will be seen in chapter eight, there is sometimes a tendency to glory in that contrast. Behind the condemnation there is also a mechanism of scapegoating, which in turn, as has been seen, contains a refusal to face the 'shadow' part of the personality. To condemn the 'wicked' person among the group or outside it provides a relief from having to face up to the shadow or unacceptable part of one's own personality. According to Thomas Szasz the homosexual has become, for many people, the outsider on whom can be heaped all the hatred and loathing that individuals possess for the unacknowledged and unacceptable parts of the personality.

Even though the leadership may have had to take some action to deal with a case of infidelity among them, it could be suggested that there should have been some degree of compassion for the tragic aspects of the case. When everything is taken into account there is a certain inevitability about the way things turned out. From the whole story, what is most in evidence is the particular loathing for homosexuality among many conservative Christians. It is this loathing that led to the leadership being particularly ferocious in the way the punishment was handed out. There could have been an agreement to part company with Peter in a private way, but instead there was a massive vindictive campaign to humiliate, discredit and devalue Peter and all he had ever done. Particularly cruel was the letter writing to all his previous churches. This appeared to be saying, Just as our church has condemned you to eternal damnation, so we want to make sure that everyone else is going to do the same. It is also hard to imagine how a church would find it necessary to insist on re-baptism of an individual on the grounds of the 'unworthiness' of the minister. If blame-free behaviour on the part of the minister is the criterion for a valid baptism, then very few baptisms are going to be valid.

It seems that the real dynamic at work in this exaggerated response to Peter was a paranoid fear of homosexuality, and a recognition that in a tightly controlled Christian community, such behaviour was subversive. Were homosexuality to be considered an allowable option within the Christian community, that would be a challenge to the idea that only Christian heterosexual marriage can be read out of the Bible. If any alternative lifestyle were to be tolerated, that would be a challenge to the role of the Bible as interpreted by the church to guide behaviour. Homosexuality within the church can, in the last resort, be seen as an attack on a particular understanding of biblical authority, rather than simply an act of immoral behaviour. It is the claim of the homosexual lobby to read the Bible in a different way from the orthodox evangelical that is so feared and in need of vigorous rebuttal.

Michael Vasey's book, published in 1995, *Strangers and Friends: A New Exploration of Homosexuality and the Bible*, caused a major upheaval in evangelical circles, particularly as Vasey himself claimed to be an evangelical theologian. It was experienced as a subversive attack on the right of the evangelical establishment to decide the 'correct' biblical point of view on the subject.

Whatever one thinks of such claims by Christian homosexuals to read the Bible in a different way, one can see that the particular cruelty with which Peter – and Charlotte – were treated arose out of 'political' considerations. In the last resort, the church was not dealing with Peter's lapse of behaviour, but with an apparent total attack on its right to guide the lives of its members in a preordained 'biblical' way. Peter then can be seen to have been more a 'victim' of a system of ideology than an individual being disciplined by a church anxious to preserve standards of goodness and truth. My final criticism of Peter's church, then, would be that they totally failed to see the pastoral dimension of homosexual tendency and practice. Homosexuals are people, often, within the church, suffering people, and a failure to enter that suffering is a failure of love. The imaginative and loving pastoral support of homosexuals will, I believe, in due time lead the church as a whole to a far greater acceptance of homosexual liaisons as an expression of human love and commitment. The church is still a long way from that point, but when it arrives it will bring tolerance and healing to this significant minority of Christian men and women.

Homosexuality and the church

It is not the purpose of this section to deal fully with all possible aspects of the fundamentalist response to the issue of homosexuality, but to take as a case study some of the background events that have led up to the current polarized situation in the Anglican Church with regard to this particular area of applied ethics. While the Anglican Church is by no means the whole church, the traumatic time that it has been through has, in a short space of time, opened up all the arguments on behalf of the wider Christian body. Also, the debate about homosexuality has drawn more attention than anything before to the wide and barely containable variety of views within the Anglican Church.

To comprehend the debate among the Anglican bishops at the Lambeth conference at Canterbury in 1998, it is necessary to go back to an earlier Anglican conference in Kuala Lumpur in February 1997 which made a lengthy statement on homosexuality. It was this conference and the responses to it that made the Anglican preoccupation with the same issue almost inevitable at Canterbury in July 1998. The Kuala Lumpur conference gathered Anglican delegates mainly from the 'two-thirds' world and was chaired by Joseph Adetiloye, archbishop of Nigeria. The resulting statement on human sexuality appealed to scripture in a fairly uncritical way and speaks of it teaching both a literal fall, as well as defining clear boundaries in the matter of human sexuality. The condoning of same-sex relationships is seen to be not only condoning sin, but also undermining the authority of holy scripture. The statement also challenges those parts of the Anglican Communion that are pursuing 'radical changes to Church discipline and moral teaching' to be mindful of the need for 'mutual accountability and interdependence within our Anglican Communion'.

The Kuala Lumpur statement was the basis for the challenge by David Holloway, the prominent vicar of Jesmond in the diocese of Newcastle, against his incoming bishop, Martin Wharton. The Jesmond PCC took exception to the bishop's views on homosexual sex which, in keeping with a statement by the bishops of the Church of England, *Issues in Human Sexuality*, published in 1991, was tolerant of permanent loving homosexual unions. In response to their bishop's views, the PCC declared itself to be in communion with only that 'part of the Anglican Communion which accepts and endorses the principles of the Kuala Lumpur statement and not otherwise'. Thus, by implication, even before his arrival, the parish declared itself to be out of communion with its new bishop and asked for alternative episcopal oversight.

The Jesmond affair developed further when the conflict between the parish and the bishop resulted in an innocent curate being unable to proceed to ordination. The parish wanted to invite an 'orthodox' bishop to ordain him, but the bishop of Newcastle took out a legal injunction to prevent this ordination. Eventually, after the archbishop of York had been involved, a face-saving formula was found to allow the ordination to proceed, but not before a lot of damage had been done to the credibility of the Church of England and its ability to discuss, in a creative and constructive way, a moral issue that affects a large number of people in our society.

The debates at Lambeth must be seen against the background of not only the Kuala Lumpur statement, but also several other conferences in the United States which debated the same issue. The General Convention of ECUSA (the Episcopal Church of the United States of America), which is the sister Anglican body in the United States, passed in July 1997 a fairly liberal and irenic statement about homosexual liaisons. This led to a conservative reaction from both Catholic and evangelical bishops and clergy, and their disquiet was articulated in an open letter 'to all faithful people in the Anglican tradition'. It was a call for faithful Anglicans not to 'leave', but to be 'out of structured fellowship with those who defy the clear teaching of the Bible and the consistent witness of the historic Church over fundamental doctrine and ethics'. The *Open Letter* drew on Catholic as well as evangelical Anglican support, while further statements, the *First Promise Statement* and the *Dallas Statement*, both published in September 1997, were evangelical documents produced by sections of ECUSA firmly opposed to any weakening of the line taken at Kuala Lumpur. The Lambeth conference thus had to face up to these profound disagreements within Anglicanism and try to find a way to move forward in this area of moral debate.

Lambeth 1998 may well be seen as a watershed in the history of worldwide Anglicanism. The debates on homosexuality were important in themselves, but more important was the deeper issue of the nature of authority, the place of the Bible and, in short, the nature of truth. Was Anglicanism going to become a largely conservative body or was it to continue to reflect a diversity of opinions and a mutual tolerance towards those holding differing positions in theology? The answer to this question was, in a typically Anglican way, ambiguous. On one level a large majority was obtained in an important debate which sought to restate traditional values with regard to homosexual behaviour, while the issuing of a pastoral letter to lesbian and gay Anglicans by 182 bishops seemed to blunt the impact of the main debate.

The conference took place over three weeks during July and August 1998. During the first two weeks, a lot of activity went on behind the scenes in committee work preparing for the main sexuality debates that took place in the final week. The final resolution on sexuality reflected the conservative bias of the conference, but when the proposals are studied carefully they reflect a patchwork of attitudes on the topic. The third resolution stated a commitment to 'listen to the experience of homosexual people'. There was also an assurance that they are 'loved by God' and 'are full members of the Body of Christ'. The next resolution, however, included the words 'while rejecting homosexual practice as incompatible with Scripture'. These words were proposed by the archbishop of Tanzania, a more conservative alternative having been rejected. A further resolution stated that the conference 'cannot advise the legitimizing or blessing of same-sex unions, nor the ordination of those involved in such unions'. The word 'advise' is perhaps a weaker one than 'approve', which some bishops wished to use for this proposition. It could be said that although the conference voted for a fairly conservative set of resolutions about homosexuality, it did so in a way that showed Anglican reticence for outright condemnation and scapegoating of the gay/lesbian community.

The way that the conference dealt with the Kuala Lumpur statement is instructive for some insight into the minds of the bishops. In the main resolutions on sexuality the Kuala Lumpur statement received a mention: 'This Conference notes the significance of the Kuala Lumpur statement... and asks the Primates and the ACC [Anglican Consultative Council] to include them in their monitoring process.' When the issue of the statement came up again two days after the main debate on sexuality, the conference decided not to debate the issue any further as, to quote the bishop of Guildford, 'we've gnawed at this bird long enough'. The conference appeared to feel that a closer identification with the statement was not required, though clearly, as has been seen, much of the conservative stand against any acceptance of homosexual behaviour within the church had been based on some identification with it in the first place. For the conference to pass over the Kuala Lumpur statement, in the way it did, expressed some distaste for its style and theology. Clearly there were many bishops at Lambeth who may have felt that simple appeals to scripture do not resolve complex moral issues on their own.

Before leaving Lambeth and the way that it tried to grapple with one of the most complex ethical issues of the day, I should note once again the pastoral letter which was written during the conference by Ronald Haines, bishop of

Washington. It was circulated around the conference for supporting signatures and, by the end of October, it had received 182 episcopal signatures, including those of eight archbishops. The letter acknowledged that the voices of lesbian and gay Anglicans had not been heard adequately and sought to assure such people of their continued 'respect and support'. It went on to express a need to continue 'prayerful, respectful conversation' since 'there is much that we do not understand'. The letter concluded with a promise to give the whole issue 'a more thorough hearing than you received over the past three weeks'. While the pastoral letter should not be seen as a final word, it does articulate a way of doing ethical debate which is always conscious of ambiguities and uncertainties. In short, the pastoral letter was an affirmation of a way of receiving the gospel for which this book has consistently pleaded – a way of humble seeking after truth as opposed to one of grasping it and codifying it that may damage people. A codified, certain 'truth' with an emphasis on non-negotiability will always have a harsh edge to it, and for some that harshness will be a stumbling block to any possibility of hearing the words of Christ.

Conclusion

I recall listening to a Christian speaker reflecting on her attitude to the issue of homosexuality. She said that before she actually met anyone who was homosexual she had all the conventional evangelical answers on the topic, that it was wrong, that it was a state which could be altered through prayer, that it contravened what was written in the Bible. And then, she said, she heard a gay person speak about his relationship. What he said about his relationship of love with his friend was a moving account which taught her some things about the nature of commitment she had never heard before. Her eyes were opened to the depths of love and commitment that were being expressed, and she declared that she could not regard the issue as being open-and-shut any more. There was nothing that linked this relationship with some stereotypical notion of a crude casual pick-up in a gay bar.

I remember this talk because it seemed to sum up the conundrum of almost every moral dilemma that you care to name. It is possible to go off and study moral theory, read the Bible and have a clear grasp of the principles of ethical debate. It is possible, then, to declare that one particular course of action is right, while another is wrong. The problem with this position is that, as the speaker above found out, the moment you enter the real world of people with their longings, aspirations and ideals the theories break down. Rules and regulations are fine in the abstract, but the task of applying them to real situations and real people is immensely complex. Moral principles, of course, have their place, but they should be applied only when the person holding them has internalized the greatest Christian principle of all – the principle of love.

They prayed with me… then told me that I had to forgive and forget. They laid hands on me… They re-abused me, they silenced me.

Chapter Five

Responding to the Problem of Sexual Violence

My meeting with Rita took place in some rooms belonging to a church in a large city in the North of England. She had contacted me by phone some months before because she had heard through a mutual contact that I was interested in the problems of Christian abuse. She was in the process of coming to terms with a horrendous episode that had blighted her life some ten years previously, a rape by a Christian minister after she had sought help from him. The story that unfolded was not just about a single episode of sexual violence, but contained a series of quite alarming incidents of incompetent and inept help from Christian churches and individuals. That Rita has remained a Christian is something of a miracle, though it has not happened without some considerable testing of her faith.

Rita explained that she had been converted at a Baptist church in 1986 and was baptized at that time. A minister who was on the circuit was brought into the congregation by one the deacons, and she confessed to seeing him very much as a father figure. One Sunday morning he had laid hands on her and asked for her to be filled with the Holy Spirit. At that moment she had experienced something quite powerful, and so she asked a friend of hers to come with her that evening, when he was to preach again, and 'check it out'. She wanted to know, 'Is this off the trolley or on the trolley?' As the service ended and they were leaving the building, the minister 'put his hand on my shoulder, and said, "The Lord has given me a personal prophecy for you. It is not right to give it to you now. I am in the telephone book. When you feel the Lord's prompting to have this personal prophecy, make an appointment to come and see me."'

Nine months later, when Rita was going through a crisis with her work, she felt it was time to receive her personal prophecy. She was feeling fragile and vulnerable because in her work as a health visitor she was dealing with child-abuse cases which put her in touch with the abuse she had suffered as a child. On arriving at the minister's house, she was not, as she put it, well protected or alert to various inappropriate gestures. Hugging her, he succeeded in dislocating her shoulder. She managed to excuse him in her mind by thinking he didn't know his own strength. As she began to pour out the issues of her own abuse, he responded by inviting her to go out in the car to a park so they could walk. In fact she was whisked away far out into the country where the rape took place. As a defence mechanism she blacked out during the actual assault and only realized what had happened when she came round. The physical evidence of bruising all over her upper body was apparent as well as abdominal pain and vaginal bleeding. She recalled how the minister, as if to complete her humiliation, had forced her to swear on the Bible that she would never tell anyone what had happened. In her state of total trauma she consented, recognizing that she was in a totally unknown place and was still dependent on him to get her home.

Finally she received the prophecy she had travelled to him to obtain. The prophecy was, 'God has made me beautiful so that I can sexually appease Christian men.' The minister then went on to describe how he was going to arrange for others to do the same things to her, in short setting her up as a kind of 'holy prostitute'. Rita was convinced that at their first meeting he had spotted her extreme vulnerability and low self-esteem, caused by her father's violence to her as a child. By singling her out and complimenting her he had been 'grooming' her for abuse, like a paedophile attempts to come alongside a child and build up a relationship which can then be used for sexual abuse. The whole episode ended up bizarrely, with the minister pouring out his own problems – the recent suicide of a brother and how he had had to take the funeral. Rita, the abused, then found herself in the role of counsellor to her abuser.

The oath on the Bible prevented Rita from saying anything to anyone for six days. Eventually she provoked her friend into forcing her to tell what had happened, but the help she got was counterproductive, and she received the first of many attempts by Christians to 'heal' her.

She took me down to what I thought at the time was a retired Anglican vicar and his wife who were evangelical/ charismatic. I took two days off work, went down and they talked and talked to me till midnight. I was saying,

'I am bound by an oath to God not to say anything about this. But I need to say what has happened to me.' About a quarter past midnight I exploded, started sobbing, named him and said, 'Something has got to be done.' They prayed with me... then told me that I had to forgive and forget. They laid hands on me, all this sort of thing. They re-abused me, they silenced me. The message was that if you forgive you are instantly healed, you are called by God to forgive. But in fact you are unchanged and at the same time you can never talk about it again. You certainly don't have anything done about the minister who abused you. Because it's dealt with, under the carpet.

Rita recalled many times how at the hands of Christians she had heard this message. Forgiveness was demanded instantly and then, when the outrage was 'forgiven', the past was expected to be left behind. If she found this hard to do, then the focus of the counselling shifted to her, the victim, and how the failure to forget was a sign of deficient faith. Suddenly the abused became the one who was being blamed for the situation. Rita realized that what had really been going on was that the counsellors could not deal with the enormity of it all, and so retreated into well-tried clichés and other methods to avoid facing up to both her pain and the unpalatable truth that a spiritual man of God could be a sex abuser. She also realized that in the particular charismatic culture to which they belonged there was little understanding for an individual who was not capable of having their problems resolved instantly and thus be filled with the joy of victory.

The situation was still desperate and Rita found herself contemplating suicide as she walked across Waterloo Bridge on her way to work. Her Baptist church, to which she returned every weekend, three hours by car from London, had advertised a twenty-four-hour counselling service. She rang them and found them unwilling to see her, suggesting she sought help nearer home. Rejected, she started to attend an Anglican church near her home which was evangelical/charismatic. Here she had a further spiritual experience, a 'slaying in the spirit', when she found herself falling to the ground. This suggested that she make it her spiritual home. But once again she was hearing the same message from the pulpit about the need to forgive, and she found herself arguing with both the rector and the curate that this was not always realistic if the perpetrator was not forced to accept responsibility for his actions. She also became angry at one particular sermon in which was stressed the biblical requirement for two witnesses to an offence to be found before an accusation could be made. After that sermon she tackled the rector and pointed out that rape was usually a crime without any witnesses except the victim. Rita spoke about the incident as having happened to a friend, but the rector still looked at her strangely.

Her situation in the church further deteriorated when the congregation had a weekend visit from a charismatic luminary. In the course of the proceedings the visitor encouraged the people of the congregation to minister to one another, and Rita found herself with a younger woman, a pupil nurse at a college where she taught. They both went to the visiting curate, a former medical doctor, and Rita found herself asking the curate for help with her situation and telling him, in the hearing of the pupil nurse, about the rape, at the same time requesting confidentiality. On the following Sunday, she heard the rector talking to a group of people with a voice she knew she was meant to hear. 'He said, "Priests do not abuse; if a person says that a priest abuses they are either liars, or they are witches who have set out to seduce ministers to break their ministries down." I was being told, It didn't happen, you're a liar, you're making it up.' She then discovered that the student nurse had betrayed her secret.

> I wasn't invited to people's homes; women started protecting their husbands from me like I was going to seduce them. I was asked to stop doing various things in church which they had been happy for me to do before, like I was not nice to know. They made me unclean, but not demonized. I had been giving prophecies at that point and I was stopped when they got the knowledge about the rape because I was deemed not to be sound. Something was not quite right.

Rita's position in the church was further undermined when the rector refused to accept her application to be on the electoral roll on the grounds that she was a Baptist and, after losing her job, was no longer resident in the parish. She was further kept in her place by having the student nurse who had betrayed her secret put over her as a discipler. Alone of all the people in the church Rita believed in the ordination of women, and this was somewhat awkward as the parish was deeply into the ecclesiastical politics of the time, trying to get candidates up for election to synods to vote down the proposals. She avoided two meetings when the topic was 'discussed', and when a woman challenged her for her absence, she admitted her support for the proposal. As Rita put it,

> She practically fainted. She rushed off to the rector
> and he came over and said, 'I understand you stupidly
> believe in the ordination of women – justify yourself.'
> And then he said, 'Sit down.' And I said, 'I am not
> going to argue with you, Peter. I am perfectly aware
> of all the bits in the Bible that we disagree on. There
> is no point in me saying what I believe about and you
> saying what you believe. We believe different things.
> My personal opinion is that if there is not complete
> equality between men and women so that where it
> says "disciple" in the Bible, it means me, I would not
> be a Christian.' And he got really annoyed and didn't
> say anything and stormed off. And then he went round
> telling everybody in the church that I was too intelligent
> for my own good, especially as I was a woman.

Once again Rita had to move on; once again she had been identified as a problem. Her instinct when in a difficult situation was to stay and fight, but the very act of fighting made it more difficult to leave. And yet she knew she did not want to become a butterfly Christian hopping from church to church. She knew deeply that she wanted to belong, but her intellect did not allow her just to submit and conform to everything said by the leadership. But to question the teaching of the leadership meant people questioning her faith. The message in both these churches was, If you conform, you can have membership of the family, you can have acceptance in the family and be loved. Rita further reflected,

> In charismatic/evangelical churches they emphasize the family, which is what I was looking for. I was looking for parental figures, grandparental figures; I was looking for a partner. Also, I wanted to take up the offer of friendship, acceptance and love, but the cost was complete and utter obedience to the leaders and their view of the Bible.

At the next church she attended, a community church, Rita saw the process clearly at work. 'The pastor stood up in church and said, "This is not a democracy, this is a theocracy. I have been appointed your leader by God and therefore all decisions are funnelled from God through me to you."' Even prayers in the church had little to do with seeking God's will for a situation; God was instructed to act in a way that the leadership had decreed. Coupled with a stern authoritarianism was a strong anti-intellectualism. Training for ministry was given within the ranks so that the party line was preserved without contamination from outside. The same control was exercised over the thinking of the membership. Rita told me,

> When I went into the church, I was told it doesn't matter who you are, where you have been in the past, if you've been a vicar in another church or a bishop even, you've all got to go into a foundation group. So that you know what our aims and objectives are. The first lesson is about Genesis and you are told that it is a completely inerrant historical document. And there are no inconsistencies.

Rita allowed herself to question where the wives of Cain and Abel came from to find out the boundaries of church thinking. The response was that 'holy incest' had been allowed because it was just after the Fall. She was given photocopies of an American book which 'explained' the line taken.

Socialization into the group required complete conformity to what was being taught. Other strands of teaching concerned with the demonic also had to be accepted . This affected her directly as it was taught that it was dangerous to work as a nurse or a health visitor in case you became 'demonized from the people who are sick and dying'. The situation became simultaneously farcical and threatening when Rita had five leaders of the church call on her to say that she had been seen going into a health-food shop. She showed them the Barley Cup she had bought and explained that she was on a vegetarian diet for health reasons. The discussion then led on to an exchange of texts about vegetarianism. Rita was convinced that their line about vegetarianism was connected to a passage in a book favoured by the leadership in which it was reported that a man was not be delivered of a 'New Age spirit' until he had renounced his vegetarianism.

In time the fact of Rita's sexual assault became known to the leadership. It led to an apparent moment of acceptance by the pastor of the church, in contrast with what up to then had been constant demands for control over her thinking and actions. She was called to his office one day and asked if she would be willing to speak about her experiences of sexual abuse to the five local leaders of the church network. She agreed, but as the time drew near for the meeting, Rita found that she couldn't do it, particularly as she was being plagued by nightmares which somehow merged her abuser with her own father. She offered instead the services of a friend who was an expert in sexual abuse and was a lecturer on this theme to various theological colleges. The leader became irrationally angry at this and Rita became convinced that the motive for inviting her to speak was pure voyeurism. Throughout the church a somewhat unhealthy attitude towards sex seemed to prevail and this was articulated forcibly when the leader told her that all but one of the leaders had had affairs with women in their pastoral care. He, the leader, thought that such affairs were therapeutic for all concerned. This conversation had created a rather curious inverted dependency as the leader made subsequent attempts to get Rita to collude with his perception that sex between pastor and people was good for those involved.

Rita's gradual recovery from the rape was badly shaken by finding a brochure advertising holidays which were to be led by her abuser. It was aimed at those who had been abused or were in difficulties. It seemed that complaints she had made to church authorities were bearing no fruit. She decided then to go to the police. It was in the end to be an unproductive process as a lot of time had elapsed since the event. This attempt also led to further difficulties with her church: when it was discovered, she immediately had quoted to her the text about not going to law against a brother. She immediately challenged the leader by referring to the text about going to an erring brother with witnesses. Was he as a Christian leader prepared to come with her to do the biblical thing? Her main concern was to stop anyone else being damaged, by ensuring that her abuser never counselled women alone. He declined. The following day he had Rita into the church office and he told her,

> I've prayed about it overnight with my wife and we have decided that you are bitter, you are looking for revenge; this is not a Christian thing to do. If you persist in doing this, we will excommunicate you from the church. We will treat you like a non-believer, we will not pray for you; when we meet you in the street we will not speak to you.

So Rita left.

Rita had now run out of charismatic churches to attend locally, but she called in at an Anglican church where she knew the vicar socially. The vicar and his wife were clearing up after a midday service and she asked if she could just be there to pray as she was in a bit of a state. 'He left me alone and he then said, "Do you want some prayer?" And we knelt at the altar and I completely and utterly sobbed my heart out all over the altar. And he put his arms around me and I was aware his wife was there and I felt safe. If I'd gone in and there had not been a woman I would not have stayed. I wouldn't have felt able to. And he hugged me. And eventually he became chaplain to a healing trust. The centre became my church.'

Looking back on all her experiences of church life since her rape, Rita realized that no one in any of the churches had known how to handle her situation. Eventually she found a Baptist church which started to listen to her for the first time. She was, by the time I met her, having psychotherapy as it was recognized during the unsuccessful police procedures that she was suffering from post-traumatic stress disorder. The Baptist church cooperated with this process and encouraged her to write a healing service which would express liturgically and symbolically the path to wholeness that she was seeking. The service involved an anointing, the wearing of a white robe to symbolize the virginity that had been lost through the rape, and the proclamation that she was not unclean before God. For her it was like a re-baptism and a new beginning, as well as a statement that the sin involved in the event was not hers.

Rita is still sadly not free from the effects of the rape. Various medical conditions emerged as the result of the stress, and the psychological effect on her has meant that she has been unable to work in her old profession as a health visitor. Nevertheless she emphasized to me that she was not a victim, but a survivor. She meant to go on and, if possible, move into a new career, one that combined her knowledge of the health profession with her faith in God. Her faith remains undiminished, and any naïvety that belonged to her earlier years has been burned away in the crucible of experience.

Comment

Rape is something that few people who have not experienced it can imagine. It is the ultimate degradation of one human being by another, the profoundest misuse of power that can be conceived of, short of actual murder. The power that Rita's abuser used was not just physical power, it was also spiritual power. The same power that had apparently been used to release individuals into a spiritual experience was being used to make them subservient to his will for base and ignoble ends. As such there was a kind of blasphemy at work, the mixing of the holy with the base, and the lack of realization by the perpetrator that in this there was something profoundly demeaning to him as well as to the victim. There is also something shocking in the way that the rapist combined a terrible act with spiritual activities such as prayer and an enforced oath on the Bible.

While words fail to describe the horror of the original deed, Rita's actions after it were dogged by a combination of misfortune and an unhappy dependence on the same culture from which the perpetrator came. The circumstances that took her to the retired clergyman and his wife damaged her chances of finding real help for a long time, as she allowed herself to collude with the idea that a simple act of forgiveness accompanied by prayer would solve her problem. Just as in the last chapter I noted how the homosexual tendency could not be 'cured' by a simple prayer, neither could Rita simply turn her back on the rape and pretend it had never happened.

The formula of the Faith churches that says that one only has to name in faith what one needs for it to be given was the main source of help that was on offer that night. Rita presented the couple with a disturbing story. A man rooted in scriptural learning had committed a terrible offence. They were powerless to confront the perpetrator so they looked to scripture to assist the victim. The only relevant passages that they could find to meet this situation were those which spoke of forgiveness. By exhorting Rita to forgive they put her in the position of obeying scripture or not obeying it. They were asking her to do something that at a human/psychological level was unrealistic, and at that point contrary to all accepted secular practice. They also, by implication, threatened to make her into a 'sinner' if she went against the scriptural command to forgive. In short, their 'help' was to force her to act in a particular way which denied her pain, her integrity and her inner voice. Common sense, as well as the accumulated wisdom of those who work with trauma victims, recognizes that the path to wholeness lies in a realistic facing up to the past event and slowly, in the context of supportive relationships, rebuilding the shattered trust in themselves and in other people. To offer Rita such an instant cure seems to have been an attempt to avoid having to cope with their own pain, rather than providing her with the best possible help. The instant solution of the Faith system was far more preferable to them than facing uncertainty or doubt as to what to do in the situation.

Rape victims as well as victims of all sorts of trauma such as kidnap and torture are often plagued with guilt, in addition to all their disturbing memories. They go endlessly over the ways in which they might have done something or said something that might have changed the event. They blame themselves and that blame is often reinforced by the attitudes of others around them who collude with their beliefs in their 'stupidity' or 'naïvety' at best, and at worst their 'asking for it'. The first task of any helper is to assist the victim to name clearly and unambiguously what has happened, to move from guilt to realistic judgement. There needs to be a rebuilding of a moral awareness of what happened, not a tacit acceptance of the victim's confused indulgence in grief and self-blame.

Beyond such help, rape victims need time in a safe place to mourn their loss. Rape is similar to a bereavement and the traumatized person needs time to heal after the experience.

To deny that process is to perpetuate the trauma. In Christian practice there has always been a recognition of the importance of ritual in the process of grief and the funeral service has always fulfilled a key role in moving a bereaved person on towards the eventual new self-integration beyond the loss. All this is done much more effectively in the company of supporting and caring people. There is need in both cases for repetition of the story, the full exploration of feelings aroused and the rebuilding of a secure self-identity based on a rediscovery of the trust which had been so brutally maimed. The literature on the treatment of victims of trauma gives no encouragement to believe that there are any short-cuts in the process.

In identifying with caring professional therapists with wide experience of dealing with victims of trauma, it can be seen that naïve exhortations to forgive instantly will not help individuals like Rita, merely compound the pain. Just as it has been seen that the act of quoting the Bible is sometimes an attempt to avoid responsibility, so here, I suggest, biblical teaching was being paraded to distance the counsellors from looking at the full extent of Rita's pain. The belief on the part of the various churches from which Rita sought help that their 'biblically based' methods of help were totally adequate and complete meant that Rita was effectively re-victimized. Professional help, based on secular assumptions and methods, was not made available to her. There seemed to be in this culture no recognition that the ideology followed was totally out of its depth to meet this situation. The ghetto of Christian belief and practice in effect became her prison because it refused to go outside its boundaries to seek help.

A dogmatic belief in the 'sufficiency' of scripture became once again a cause of continuing suffering.

When looking at the urging on of Rita by certain Christians to forgive, it can be seen that theologically it was inadequate. The act of forgiveness is bound to involve, if possible, more than the victim, and there seemed to be no attempt either by the local church or by the institutional church to bring the perpetrator of the rape to account. In South Africa, the body assigned to attempt to heal the wounds of the country's past was called the Truth and Reconciliation Commission. No one in the story seemed to be interested in establishing truth and accountability as a prerequisite to reconciliation and forgiveness.

The comments by the Anglican rector, intended for Rita to hear, that priests never abuse women and that if an incident takes place it is because the woman has seduced the priest are shocking for their callousness. They suggest that he had internalized the literal story of Adam and Eve and remembered the words of Adam: 'The woman you gave me for a companion, she gave me fruit.' He seems to be perpetuating a quasi-medieval view of women, which sees them as seductive temptresses not to be trusted. It is small wonder that he demanded so shrilly the non-ordination of women. He might have found that he would have had to change his ideas, once it was asked of him to work alongside them and treat them as equal partners. If, for any reason, a parish comes to a common mind on a subject, it is good to have the opposing point of view expressed so as to check out the validity of the common opinion. Rita's articulation of the opposing point of view about women's ordination was impressive, and considering her opinion had been dismissed as 'stupid' even before it had been uttered, it was courageously given.

The dynamic of a parish where everyone is expected to have an identical opinion is profoundly unhealthy. The only way that such a dynamic can be maintained is by some sort of coercion from the top. It is very rare that a large group of reasonably intelligent adults will all agree on a subject like the ordination of women unless they deem it expedient to do so. Here it was expedient to agree with the rector to avoid the social ostracism that Rita was to suffer. I pick up here the influence of fundamentalist ideas where it is assumed that what is perceived as truth is fixed and non-negotiable; obedience and submission are required and demanded. When the mere holding of a point of view attracts such hostility, this is evidence of a culture where 'truth' is not simply a guide and inspiration to the faithful, but a means of coercion and control. The rector's opinions in this case seemed to have acquired inerrancy, no doubt bolstered up by his privileged position as the mediator and expounder of the word of God. In this case, judging by the comments about 'intelligent women' and 'stupid' views on the part of Rita, the 'inerrant' opinions of the rector appeared to be based on his own psychology rather than a profound grasp of spiritual or biblical truth.

Many readers will wonder why Rita kept going back to situations which made her into a victim. The answer lies in the perception she had, not without cause, that charismatic/ evangelical churches were those where she would find a sense of love, warmth and family. The same search inspired John and Rachel. Evangelical churches do put these values high on the agenda and in this way set an example to churches where formality and ritual are seen to be more important. Although this book is fairly critical of the direction taken by some churches within the evangelical/charismatic fold, there are many places where the lack of pretension and acknowledgment of common humanity under God in prayer and fellowship do release genuine gifts of love into a congregation.

The price for this warmth, however, was, in Rita's case, too high. In the particular churches she joined, she had to swallow without complaint the highly controlling dimensions sometimes encountered in that culture and begin to deny aspects of herself, her dignity, her freedom and her integrity, in order to survive. The community church that she joined also operated a harsh model of parenting which forcibly demanded her submission when she chose to step out of line. Such controlling coercive behaviour is not, of course, necessarily typical of charismatic/evangelical churches, but the issue of power and control is one that needs to be observed closely. Perhaps the simplest test to see what kind of church one has arrived in is to observe the pastor deal with disagreement. Does he allow genuine dialogue with a differing point of view, or does he use weapons of divine authority to short-circuit the discussion and insist on obedience? Does the leadership bear with the failures and fallibility of the 'children' with patience, or are there unwritten 'family' rules of instant compliance to the requirements of the head of the family?

The story of the visit of the five elders after her visit to the health-food shop is laughable and tragic at the same time.

The belief that one could be contaminated by demons had percolated into the minds of the leaders and they had adopted a position of protecting themselves from such influences at all costs. The story of the man who had renounced vegetarianism had become a rule of behaviour for the leaders of the church. Such slavish following of an idea contained in an anecdote is the sort of thing that could have been avoided in a leadership who had taken on board the sort of education and learning that teaches appropriate discrimination.

In conclusion to this section it might be said that Rita was a problem to all the churches she attended for two reasons. First, she had a problem that neither their theology, nor their notions of healing through prayer, could deal with. In this way she threatened their self-understanding as being able to meet all the needs of its members in the spiritual, social and emotional realm. To have sent her outside the system for help would have been to acknowledge that there was a wisdom, in other words psychotherapy, which knew more about the world of human distress than they did. Secondly, being an articulate questioning person, Rita threatened to show up the pretensions to a monopoly of 'truth' based on scripture, through her questions and answers, and that was unforgivable. No doubt the Anglican rector was a well-educated man, but, in his determination to run a parish which maintained the illusion of perfect agreement, he had apparently forgotten how to handle the dissident voice. In the wider culture, the dissident is welcomed, even honoured, as being able to sharpen up the grasp of truth by the majority. Here, in this particular fundamentalist mindset, the dissident is only able to be seen as a nuisance and a distraction. Debate and dialogue as means to the discovery of truth are strangers in this kind of world.

Biblical and social control of women

In recent years there has grown to be an increasing recognition among professional groups that perpetrators of domestic violence and sexual abuse against women often claim to be Christians, and even justify their behaviour by quoting biblical texts. Although Rita's rape was not in any way part of recognizably Christian behaviour, it did take place in the setting of a church where, it could be imagined, women were often put in a position of subordination and powerlessness. Her subsequent failure to find an effective voice in later dealings with clergy and others suggests an implicit acceptance of the subservience of women among Christians, which has already been met in consideration of the treatment of children. There are four particular beliefs based on extracts from the Bible which, when read in a certain way, appear to put women at a distinct disadvantage in the matter of finding their power within the church.

In the first place there is a belief, claimed to be found in Genesis, that God intends that men should dominate and that women should submit. The first account of the creation of humankind in Genesis 1:27 represents God as creating men and women together, while in the second man is created from the dust of the ground (Genesis 2:7), and only subsequently is woman made out of one of his ribs. This text from Genesis 2 can be read to imply that man has a role of dominance over women as well as children. Some of the humiliating treatment that Rita experienced can perhaps ultimately be traced back to this chapter. Needless to say, a strong belief in the dominance of the male sex as being divinely sanctioned will also reinforce tendencies to wife battering if they already exist. Equally, there will be many women who will accept being physically or verbally dominated in their families and churches because they believe this to be part of the divinely ordered pattern. If a proper consideration of the biblical material about male–female relationships were to take place, this interpretation of Genesis 2 would need to be balanced out by an appeal to the parts of Paul's writings which speak of mutuality between the sexes, not to mention the revolutionary approach of Jesus to women and their needs.

A second belief common in fundamentalist circles, which is an outworking of the first, states that women are morally inferior to men because of Eve's role in the Fall. A book by Elizabeth Handford, published as recently as 1972, states, 'Women are more often led into spiritual error than men. This is the reason God commanded her not to usurp authority over man, so she can be protected by him from false doctrine.' Once again such beliefs may have lain behind the expectations of compliance and passivity that Rita found in all the churches of which she was a member. It goes without saying that this kind of passivity will make women in violent relationships far less able to defend themselves and their children from their husbands.

Christian beliefs have also indirectly countenanced abuse of women by teaching the importance and virtue of suffering. Various passages in the writings of Paul can be read to suggest that an individual is in some way a better disciple for having endured suffering, and that the suffering itself in some way adds to the effectiveness of Christ's suffering for the church. The various passages about suffering in the New Testament are far more complex than this summary implies, but a sophisticated reading of the text is not often an option to a battered or demoralized woman who chances on them when trying desperately to find meaning for her unhappy state. A clear distinction needs, for example, to be made between voluntary suffering endured for a greater good and involuntary suffering that is the result of arbitrary violence. One Christian writer describes this latter enduring of pain in a spirit of passive submission as Christian masochism. The cross needs to be seen not as a symbol of defeated endurance of pain, but the consequence of Jesus' constant challenge to and struggle against the powers of evil.

A fourth doctrine, which has been met in this chapter, that has the effect of putting down women declares that forgiveness is to be given to an abuser, and that if it is not forthcoming quickly, then the victim is to be shamed. Such a practice is carried out perhaps because it is easier to deal with a wounded and traumatized victim than with the perpetrator, who may be in a position of power and thus more difficult to challenge. Forgiveness and reconciliation are, of course, important ends to be aimed at in the case of an act of violence against a woman. Such forgiveness, however, must not be sought at the expense of dealing with the issues of responsibility and truth that are involved in the offence.

In the face of such doctrines it is unsurprising that there is a certain genre of evangelical writing about women which stands in stark contrast to the tenets of equality between the sexes. Diane Liftin asserts that 'Feminists find the biblical vision of a divinely ordained male/female hierarchy galling... They have embraced a profoundly unbiblical – indeed anti-biblical – ideology and are pressing it on the church.' A further exponent of this doctrine of submission, Beverly LaHaye, writes, 'Submission is God's design for woman... God's design is that the husband be in charge... Oh that we could just grasp the attitude in the heart of Jesus – the willingness to be humbled, to be obedient unto death, and to be submissive.' These kinds of submission and dependency on the part of women, surely a one-sided reading of the biblical witness, are thus believed to be part of the natural order of things, reinforced not only by the traditions of the institution, but also apparently by the ultimate authority, the word of God himself.

Towards an understanding of power and sexual violence

Sexual violence against women by figures of authority in the church is slowly emerging into the consciousness of Christians alongside the parallel, but distinct, issue of child abuse. Perhaps it should not be surprising that when half of all women in the United States have experienced a rape or attempted rape, the church should also have a problem with this distressing area of life. Perhaps the problem has always existed, but it has been silenced by attitudes similar to those encountered by Rita in her story. In recent years evidence has been uncovered as to the way some Roman Catholic authorities in Ireland and the United States have allowed their institutional power to be used to suppress information about the activities of paedophile priests. Comparable attitudes among some conservative Protestant believers, who *need* to believe that their leaders are incapable of such action, have contributed to an atmosphere of denial and thus occasional tacit collusion with such behaviour.

An important book on this issue of power abuse was published in 1991 in the United States by James Poling, *The Abuse of Power: A Theological Problem*. He focuses on the nature of power and the way that sexual abuse, whether of women or children, is a distortion and corruption of the ideal forms of power that should exist between human beings. Poling has some interesting things to say about the way that power functions within the context of a relationship, rather than being a one-way act of coercion against another person. The power of the individual is enhanced in an environment which encourages individual creativity and maximum relatedness to others. One writer quoted by Poling, Rita Brock, describes the energy involved in relating to others as 'erotic power'. While erotic power has as its aim the enhancement of the relational power in oneself and in those around, sexual power, which is closely aligned to it, can be easily perverted into the destructive and life-denying behaviour of sexual abuse. Why should power be so readily abused? The answer suggested by another quoted writer, Daniel Day Williams, is that power is abused because of human fear and arrogance. The path to communion with God and fellow human beings lies in openness to and movement towards a future that cannot be seen. Immediate gratification of that hoped-for communion cannot be expected. Sexual gratification appears to offer something in the present without any waiting. So some compromise and weaken their humanity in order to satisfy one part of their longing. Anyone who is the victim of sexual or any other kind of abuse is damaged. To the extent that an individual's misuse of power damages other people, they are damaged because their relationship with them can never have the elements of creativity and freedom that true love makes possible.

Poling notes the particular abuse of power that takes place in families. Parents can trample on the spirits and souls of their children to fulfil needs in themselves, and also because they lack in themselves the strength and discipline for the creative task of nurture. Also, in a society that gives value to power and aggression so that worth in a person is measured by his or her capacity to influence others, there will always be individuals who express aggressiveness in the one place available to them, their own families. Abuse of power in the family, as elsewhere, is also fed by ideologies in society as a whole. Poling notes in particular the ideology of patriarchy, a system of male–female domination that, as has been seen above, is apparently sanctioned by scripture itself. Society has institutionalized a situation of inequality between men and women, so that women, for example, do not easily receive adequate protection for themselves and their children against abusive husbands.

A further example of abusive power is found in racism. Society often appears to collude with racist attitudes by defining a norm for itself which shuts out people of different races. Privilege for the powerful is maintained by making their assumptions, values and needs the ones that everyone else's are measured against. The same thing operates in the relationships between the nations. Just as the glory of the ancient world was made possible by a huge, suffering underclass of slaves, so the comfort of the 'rich' nations today is made possible by the continuing economic and social structures that hold the 'developing' countries in a permanent state of dependence and relative poverty.

Poling paints some broad brush strokes in his description of power and the way that it operates in human relationships and society. His analysis, because it touches on political issues, is likely to be controversial and in need of further debate, but I have quoted him because I feel his initial observations about power profoundly reflect the spirit of the Christian gospel. According to him human beings are created to use their power 'to enter into communion', and all true uses of power serve to further mutuality and encourage and enable others to move further into their true humanity. Power abuse of whatever kind is a grasping after the immediate, the thing that gratifies needs and appetites. Because another's humanity is, in the process, damaged, our own humanity suffers because we put ourselves outside the network of relationships on which our humanity ultimately depends. Abuse of power is quite simply a denial of love.

The pursuit of immediate gratification by sexually abusing or controlling another person provides a simple way of understanding what is happening when one person abuses another. Another model which I have found valuable in thinking about what is happening in these situations is the idea of spiritual vampirism explored in a book by Marty Raphael,

Spiritual Vampires. Raphael claims that each of us is given a certain life-force or quasi-physical energy which is part of our being alive and human. This life-force interacts with that of others, in the case of love and mutual respect by building them up in this energy simultaneously with ourselves. When, however, for any reason our inner power becomes depleted, we may seek domination over others in a way that uses them to replenish our sense of power. Such abuse can happen whenever a weak or vulnerable person hands over their power to someone stronger who, in some sense, feeds on it and leaves his or her victim still weaker. The experience of being abused in this way may happen in perfectly acceptable social contexts, between priest and parishioner, therapist and client, but it will be very much like being sucked dry by the so-called helper. There are also more obviously extreme examples of spiritual vampirism such as domination, sexual abuse or terrorization. All these will, in different ways, deplete victims of their inner spiritual power, while giving the perpetrator some artificial 'high' through what is, in effect, a transfer of energy from the victim to the power abuser. The problem with 'spiritual vampirism' is that it sometimes takes place subtly, not only in professional-care relationships, but also in socially approved institutions such as particular styles of parenting, firms, schools and other organizations. It also, of course, happens within the context of socially reprehensible events such as torture and rape. Perhaps the reader of this book is better sensitized to the possibility that actions, even those sanctioned by religious tradition and authority, can on occasion be examples of a cruel abuse of power.

The naming and confronting of abusive power wherever it

occurs in societies and churches should be an important part of the role of the church. Something of the way that Jesus responded to the abuse of power in his time will be seen in chapter nine, and it could be claimed that it was more of an issue for him than for any other. Meanwhile, there are the words of the prophet Amos who, looking on the corrupt Israelite nation, declared the words of the Lord,

> For crime after crime of Israel
>   I will grant them no reprieve,
>   because they sell the innocent for silver
>   and the destitute for a pair of shoes.
> They grind the heads of the poor into the earth,
>   and thrust the humble out of their way.

(Amos 2:6–7)

There was for any reader of the Bible a sign that… he believed his followers were in danger of being slain as martyrs by the enemies of God.

Chapter Six

Millennial Madness

Beyond rape and gross physical injury, there is only one worse crime that can be committed against someone, and that is causing their death. Death can befall an individual not only as the result of actual murder, but also as the consequence of being encouraged to go to a place where there are severe dangers to life and well-being.

The saga of Waco

The victims of the Waco fire in 1993 were not technically victims of murder by their leader, David Koresh, but it could be argued that the paranoid and bizarre belief system put forward by him put all his followers into great danger the moment they chose to identify with him. David Koresh was an example of a particular tradition at the edge of fundamentalist Christianity, characterized by an obsession with issues concerning the fulfilment of scriptural prophecies about the end of the world. When a group of Christians spends a lot of time looking for signs of the imminent collapse of the world as a prelude to the second coming of Christ, the fate of individuals becomes of little importance. In summary, much of the belief system concerned with the end of the world is obsessed with death and destruction, whether of the believers themselves or of the world in general. The wide popularity of so-called prophecy writings, particularly in the United States, shows an unhealthy interest in the way that certain people, particularly scoffers and unbelievers, are going to receive their come-uppance at the time of the second coming of Christ, and in the catastrophes that are to come both before and after the event.

On 28 February 1993, FBI agents were called to the Mount Carmel centre outside Waco, Texas. Seventy-six armed agents of the Federal Bureau of Alcohol, Tobacco and Firearms had earlier attempted to storm the centre and had been repulsed with the death of four and the injuring of twenty of their members. There followed a siege lasting fifty-one days, ending in a tragic fire in which seventy-four Branch Davidians died, including twenty-one children under the age of fourteen. Throughout the siege the negotiators and the media were subjected to what were perceived to be the paranoiac ramblings on the subject of end-time prophecies by David Koresh. The tragedy of the whole episode is that none of those in authority was able to penetrate the convoluted thought processes that were involved in these apparent rantings. And yet, as I shall attempt to show, there was in Koresh's thinking a logic at work, albeit a tortured logic, that gave his ideas a coherence and pattern. Extreme and fanatical as he was, David Koresh was no madman. In his eyes and in the eyes of his followers Koresh was following the teaching of holy scripture, and the part that he believed he was to play in bringing about the final events of history before the second coming of Christ.

Throughout the fifty-one-day siege Koresh talked incessantly about the seven seals mentioned in the book of Revelation. At the beginning of Revelation 5 there is a scene in which a mysterious book or scroll is introduced, which has been sealed with seven wax seals. The question is raised, 'Who is worthy to open the scroll?' According to Koresh the scroll or sealed book was the entire Bible, particularly the prophetic writings. To open the scroll is not only to explain it, but also to set in motion the events it sets forth, leading to the climax of history, the end of the world. Koresh had arguments to show that the figure called 'the Lamb', who is said to be worthy to open the book, could not be Jesus Christ as commonly supposed. The events belong to the future and thus he believed there must be another Christ or Messiah at this time to accomplish this task. Through a complicated piece of biblical exegesis, and following a logic that few outside his group could follow, Koresh succeeded in convincing himself and his group of followers that this Messianic figure to accomplish God's purpose was to be none other than himself. It was he who would reveal to the world the full mysteries of the entire Bible.

The communications of David Koresh to the world media and to the FBI negotiators were thus wrapped up in an almost impenetrably dense discourse which very few could understand. When Koresh announced to the waiting FBI agents at an early point in the siege that they were in the fifth seal (Revelation 6:9–11), there was for any reader of the Bible a sign that the siege had in his eyes entered a dangerous stage, as he believed his followers were in danger of being slain as martyrs by the enemies of God. The situation of siege and barricade perfectly fitted Koresh's, and thus his followers', perception of what was happening – that they were in the end-days and that their enemies were seeking to make them martyrs. Allowing those inside Carmel to believe that their deaths were inevitable, as suggested by the fifth seal, and that that would then lead to the cosmic judgement which followed the sixth seal created a scenario in which tragedy was highly probable.

Nevertheless, through the long days of the siege, Koresh did show signs that he was not absolutely certain of his own interpretations of events. The negotiators on the outside were told that Koresh was waiting for a sign from God, and that he also believed a waiting period was required by the fifth seal. At the very least this implied that Koresh and his followers did not feel they had all the answers about what was going to happen next. Had the FBI negotiators been able to enter the mind of Koresh and allow themselves into the apocalyptic discourse that he so passionately believed in, then tragedy might well have been avoided. Instead Koresh's words were a monologue and the negotiators a group of mystified and exasperated men who had no comprehension of what was being said to them.

The final tragedy of 19 April 1993 came four days after Koresh received a long-awaited 'word from God'. In a letter he declared that he would come out as soon as he had finished writing his message on the seven seals, and which might have the effect of convincing the world of what they meant, and that they 'will bring New Light and hope for many'. Koresh believed that he was to reveal 'the mystery of God as declared to the prophets', which was contained in a small scroll held by an angelic figure in Revelation 10. In fact he claimed to be that angelic figure so that he could 'prophesy again before many people, nations, and tongues and kings'. The significance of Koresh's claim to have finished the waiting period, as dictated by his apocalyptic belief system, was not picked up by the negotiators and a decision at a high level was made to attack the compound with CS gas. A psychiatrist who was shown Koresh's final letter concurred with the general consensus that he was a conman interested in power and manipulation, and was simply trying to buy more time. Thus the fatal decision to attack was given. During the night before the attack Koresh worked hard at composing his exposition of the first seal, a work which, for all its strangeness, is a unique insight into the man's beliefs and mind as well as having its own internal if bizarre logic.

The background to Waco

It would be convenient to categorize the Branch Davidians led by David Koresh as a uniquely strange and offbeat expression of Christianity led by a mad power-crazed individual. The reality, however, appears to be somewhat different. In the first place Koresh was representing, at least as far as he was concerned, a distinctly American tradition of biblical interpretation which found its origins in the writings and speculations of William Miller, a Baptist farmer living in early nineteenth-century America. After a verse-by-verse study of the Bible, Miller had concluded that the second coming of Christ would occur 'about the year 1843'. He based this teaching on his own close study of the Old Testament prophetic writings and the book of Revelation. Between 1831 and 1844 he addressed vast crowds throughout the United States and it is estimated that he reached some half a million souls with his message. That such a relatively ill-educated man should have had such a powerful influence on the religious thinking of the age is worthy of comment. A teaching which was in essence an explanation of the text of scripture by reference to other passages in scripture can be accounted for in part by a principle proclaimed in early nineteenth-century America, that the Bible was accessible to the common man. That belief was based a popular philosophical idea of the time which stated that the plain meaning of any statement is the correct one. One does not need sophisticated understanding to arrive at the truth of a text. As the Bible appeared to talk about future events which had not yet come to pass, it was 'obvious' that a close study of the text might reveal the occurrence to which they referred. If these prophecies were not fulfilled then the Bible would be seen to be a 'lie'.

Miller's speculations on and interpretations of the prophecies of the Bible were finally shown to be wrong on 21 March 1844 when a final date for the fulfilment of the prophecy passed without incident. But the enthusiasm of the Millerites, as his followers came to be known, hardly abated as they found ingenious ways of resetting the time for the prophecy to come to pass. The opposition of the mainstream Christian bodies was, however, intense and the Millerites found themselves forced to become a separate body, meeting in halls and homes outside the churches. They believed that they were the faithful 'remnant' of God's people, likening the religious and political establishment that persecuted and despised them to the Babylon of Revelation 18:2–3. This Millerite movement eventually became the Seventh Day Adventist Church with its distinctive tradition of keeping Saturday rather than Sunday as a holy day. A further distinctive feature of their teaching concerned the interpretation of Adventist history in the light of the text in the book of Revelation. Miller identified himself with the angel mentioned in Revelation 14:6–7, sent to proclaim that the 'hour of his judgement has come', while Koresh, 150 years later, in addition to identifying with the angel in Revelation 10, claimed to be the seventh and final messenger mentioned in verses 17–18 of the same chapter.

The actual details of both Miller's and Koresh's teachings are complex and indeed tedious to the non-Adventist reader. It is, however, clear that though Koresh lived and died outside the mainstream Adventist community, he lived and breathed Adventist thought forms which had been the norm for debate among Protestant American theologians in the early nineteenth century. One of the pictures of life inside the beleaguered Mount Carmel that has been described is that of David Koresh surrounded by his admiring followers, who were totally mesmerized by his exposition of scripture in sessions that lasted up to nineteen hours at a time. Finding passages from the Psalms, the prophets as well as his beloved Revelation, Koresh had a rich mine to quarry to support his ideas about the end of the world and its imminent arrival. From the tradition he had inherited there were no restraints in his method of interpretation. The obscurities of the book of Revelation could be and were interpreted in ways that gave him personally enormous power and responsibility in the events leading to the end of the world.

If it is claimed that Koresh was suffering from delusions of grandeur, as indeed he almost certainly was, then it should be recognized that the tradition of biblical interpretation in which he moved seems to have helped create these delusions. Although he could be accused of many things – power abuse, sexual exploitation of the female members of his community and so on – his actions do not seem to have been those of a cynical calculating person who consciously uses the Bible and the weakness of others for his own ends. Nineteen-hour Bible studies were the hallmark of a person who was passionate about the Bible and its meaning and wanted to communicate that meaning to others. Koresh could be described as obsessive, paranoiac and deluded in the way that he interpreted scripture for his own ends; I would, however, not also want to write him off as mad or even insincere. Within his own belief system, and the belief system that he inherited from his own Seventh Day Adventist tradition, there was an inexorable logic at work, a biblically based logic which led him and his followers to confront the might of the American state. They had the firm belief that they were somehow instrumental in setting in motion the cataclysmic events that were biblically ordained to take place before the second coming of Christ. Their trust in the words of scripture as interpreted by their prophet David Koresh led them to pay for this belief with their lives.

Before leaving Mount Carmel, David Koresh and his small band of devoted followers, it is necessary to reflect on the fact that the ultimate key to the power of David Koresh, and indeed many of the leaders in this book, was the ability to say, This is what the Bible says and if you do not believe what it says you have no knowledge of God or access to his salvation.

For David Koresh's followers, belief in the exact words of scripture became a litmus test as to whether they were to be saved or not. In this system of Christian belief the Bible takes on the role of being the controlling reality of an individual's life, even a quasi-deity. I have, however, already noted that in such systems the Bible is never presented directly to a group of Christians. It always comes ready packaged and digested to suit the purposes of the leadership. The purposes of mere human beings will always contain aspects of greed, power abuse and other forms of exploitative behaviour. These are at their most dangerous when, as in the case of David Koresh, they are apparently unrecognized and unacknowledged.

Millennarianism and dispensationalism

David Koresh belonged to a particular American tradition of thinking about the way that the obscure prophecies of scripture were going to be fulfilled in contemporary history. Another strand which today has far more adherents is that known as dispensationalism, a set of ideas about the end of the world first put forward by an Englishman, John Nelson Darby (1800–82). Beginning life as an ordained member of the Church of Ireland, Darby soon withdrew in order to present his ideas of radical rejection of hierarchy and links with the State. He emerged as the leader of a faction within a sect called the Brethren, who became known as the Darbyites or Plymouth Brethren. Darby's importance went far beyond his own group as he preached widely in Britain and, after 1859, in the United States. His teaching proposed an ingenious way of understanding prophecy in the Bible which avoided the problems of date setting faced by Charles Miller and his followers. His theological system also benefited from a degree of theological sophistication not evident in Miller's speculations.

The essence of the teaching was the claim for there to be apparent in scripture a series of epochs or dispensations where God deals with humanity in distinct ways. In each of these dispensations the means of salvation offered is different. The present dispensation, that of the church, lies between one that ended with the crucifixion of Christ and another that begins with the rapture of the faithful and the events that follow that moment, including the tribulation and the final millennium, Christ's 1,000-year rule on Earth. The prophetic writings of the Bible, while having much to say about the coming of Christ and the events following the rapture are silent about this church epoch. Miller thus avoided any need to link particular biblical prophecies to events happening in the present. His teaching was thus better able to avoid the pitfalls of having particular prophecies unfulfilled through the unfolding of history since all events predicted lie in the future beyond the rapture.

Darby's ideas found widespread acceptance in the United States where they satisfied a need to take seriously the parts of the Bible that appear to talk about the future. The latter half of the nineteenth century was a time when literalist readings of scripture were under attack, and the concept of dispensationalism allowed conservative Christians to have a system of exegesis which gave proper attention to the prophetic passages without having them liable to ridicule by their non-fulfilment within contemporary history.

The prophecy conferences, which took place from 1875

onwards in the United States, were an important part of the building up of conservative Protestant morale by showing the truth of the Bible in the way that prophecies had been fulfilled. It was out of the milieu of these conferences that the most important instrument for its propagation arose, the Scofield Bible. Cyrus Scofield (1843–1921), after a somewhat murky beginning, became pastor of Dallas' First Congregational church in 1882, and later gave himself to full-time lecturing and writing on Darby's dispensational ideas. The most enduring monument to Scofield was his edition of the Bible, first published in 1909 and brought out in a further edition in 1967. In essence the Bible was the King James Version with Scofield's notes on the text in the margins. The notes were a confident exposition of Darby's main ideas about the way that prophecies had been fulfilled and were to be fulfilled. The dispensational ideas within the commentary allowed Scofield, as Darby had before him, to state confidently the 'true' explanation of the most obscure parts of scripture. Thus readers felt they possessed a Bible which had its secrets and obscurities laid open, and that with it they could understand and explain all that might otherwise be thought to be difficult.

Hal Lindsey and the prophecy writers

The Scofield Bible, of which 12.5 million copies had been sold by 1990, has had a massive influence on conservative Christianity all over the world, but particularly in the United States. It has made possible a literalist reading of scripture, particularly in relation to the way prophecies are believed to be fulfilled. A reader of the Scofield Bible who sees 'proof' of the fulfilment of Old Testament prophecies in the New Testament will have no problem believing that the obscure parts of Revelation refer to a cataclysm that is to take place in the near future. It is on a Christian public which has for a long time been sensitized to the idea that the Bible contains a great deal about the fulfilment of human history that the present generation of prophecy writings has been unleashed. The most famous of these, Hal Lindsey's *The Late Great Planet Earth*, contains (in my edition) 177 pages of extremely tortuous prose, relating the Bible to events in the near future connected with the forthcoming end of history. The main contemporary event that has Lindsey and many other prophecy writers excited is the foundation of the State of Israel. This event has set the 'end-time clock ticking' for the final events including an invasion of the Middle East by Russia, the rule of the Antichrist based in Jerusalem and the rapture, when faithful Christians will be snatched to meet Christ in the air. Different prophecy writers disagree as to the order in which these events will take place. Lindsey's book alone has sold over 20 million copies worldwide and has to be taken seriously for that reason alone. He appears very enthusiastic about the violence that appears to be foretold for the future and he turns the Bible, to quote one commentator, 'into a manual of atomic-age combat'. Thus he interprets 'fire and brimstone' to mean nuclear weapons, and the falling stars and stinging locusts of Revelation to mean warheads from space platforms and Cobra helicopters spraying nerve gas. Every phrase and image of the apocalyptic scriptures is translated into the 'vocabulary of the Pentagon strategists'.

It is not here my purpose to offer more information on this

genre of prophetic writing which has flooded the bookshops over the past thirty years, or to offer reasons for rejecting it. · Others have done this and their works will be referred to in the bibliography. My purpose in introducing Lindsey and this genre of writing is to focus on one theme particularly relevant to the overall topic of this book. It will be my claim that prophecy writing is responsible for reviving, albeit indirectly, one of the most sinister forms of Christian abuse, anti-Semitism.

Attitudes towards the Jews in prophecy writing

Anyone who reads the prophecies of the Old Testament in a literal way will be struck by the number of promises to and threats against the Jewish people. In the Middle Ages it was taught by such figures as Joachim of Fiore (c. 1132–1202) that while all Jews are destined to be converted at 'the day of the Lord', in the meantime they are destined to follow the figure of the Antichrist and bring terrible suffering on themselves and the whole world as a result. Darby, following the teaching of older traditions, taught that after the rapture, the Jews would establish a nation in Palestine where they would, after terrible persecution, hail Christ as Messiah after Armageddon. Thus there was always a great deal of keenness in prophetic circles for the Jews to settle back in their land, as a way for the fulfilment of prophecy to be made transparent, and the ultimate restoration of God's kingdom on Earth to be set in motion.

Among prophecy believers the proclamation of the State of Israel was among the greatest announcements ever as it made the rapture an event that could happen at any moment. The same excitement occurred when the old city of Jerusalem was recaptured in 1967 after the Six-Day War. The existence and welfare of the State of Israel had been decreed in the prophets. Streams of premillennial tourists flocked to the Holy Land to witness the literal fulfilment of biblical prophecy which 'proved' that God had begun the final countdown to the end of history. In Britain, such speculation about the way that the founding of Israel is the final countdown to the end of the world has largely passed people by. Nevertheless, there is a tremendous passion on the subject in other parts of the English-speaking world. Needless to say, as with every other area of prophetic interpretation, the variations on the basic theme are endless and few writers are agreed on anything but the broad outlines. Events after 1948 and 1967 failed to live up to the biblical prophecies, especially in the description of the extent of territory controlled by Israel. A considerable swathe of Protestant opinion in the United States would have the Palestinians expelled from the West Bank on the grounds of such passages as Jeremiah 31:5, where it is stated, 'Again you shall plant vineyards on the hills of Samaria.'

One detailed part of the prophecies about the restoration of Israel that has exercised interest in the events of 1999 and the build-up to the millennium concerns the rebuilding of the Jewish Temple in its historical place on the Temple Mount. Prophecy believers see this as an essential part of the end-time scenario. As the tribulation prophesied for the end of the world comes to pass, the Antichrist ruling in Jerusalem will encourage the Jews to resume Temple worship. After three and a half years, the prophecies proclaim, the Antichrist will set up his image in the Temple, whereupon Christ will destroy this Temple and build a new one for his millennial reign. The fact that the site of the Temple is now occupied by the Arab holy site known as the Dome of the Rock has not passed unnoticed, and fervent Christians have been arrested for plotting attacks on this building. Most Israelis are, in fact, totally uninterested in the possibility of rebuilding the Temple and they see the intervention of Christians as misguided and dangerous. One attempt to lay a foundation stone for a new Temple in 1990 led to an ugly and tragic incident when twenty-one Arab protestors were killed and 125 injured by Israeli police. It is hard to see how this particular 'prophecy' will be fulfilled.

Beyond the rebuilding of the Temple and the rule of the Antichrist a time of slaughter is prophesied, when two-thirds of the Jews gathered in Palestine will be destroyed. This, according to Darby, is prophesied in Zechariah 13:8. Scofield adds an explanation for this period of suffering by saying that they would atone for the 'murder of Christ' through it. A certain acquiescence by some Christians in the events of the Holocaust is detectable in the prophecy writings of the pre-war period. The prophesied punishment of the Jews was being 'fulfilled with poignant reality in Germany today' declared one prophecy writer in 1937, while another in 1942 grimly declared that the Nazi attacks on Jews were 'foretold in God's Holy Word thousands of years ago', and that they were as nothing in comparison to the mass slaughter to take place during the Antichrist's reign.

An influential prophecy book by John Walvoord, *Israel in Prophecy*, embellishes the belief that Israel is to enter a terrible period of suffering. Taking passages from Deuteronomy,

Daniel, Matthew and Revelation, Walvoord foresees a time of dreadful adversity for the Jews at the hands of the Antichrist, but he sees this as 'the searching and refining fire of divine judgement' which is designed to 'produce... an attitude of true repentance and eager anticipation of the coming of their Messiah'. In other words the suffering is provided by God to force a small remnant of Jews to accept Jesus.

There is, then, in prophecy writing an ambivalent relationship towards the Jewish people. In the first place there is a recognition that they play a crucial part in the events of the end-time but also that they, in order to fulfil prophecy, will suffer in an unprecedented way. Writers such as Walvoord and Lindsey, in their sketching out of the events on which the whole history of the world depends, accept the extent of the appalling suffering to be meted out to the Jews. Their books allow the reader to believe that such suffering is inevitable and a reflection of God's will. If my beliefs tell me that the suffering of an individual or a group in some way furthers God's purposes, then I will have no obligation or indeed right to relieve that suffering. I will stand idly by and watch while it takes place. Colluding with evil in this way, particularly an evil which involves the death of one's fellow human beings is, whatever the belief system undergirding it, profoundly morally repugnant and unrecognizable as an attitude worthy of the name of Christian.

It is, indeed, not a large step from this to think as Hitler did when he said, in *Mein Kampf*, 'I believe that I am acting in the sense of the Almighty Creator. By warding off the Jews, I am fighting for the Lord's work.' I would thus claim that Christian prophecy beliefs in their passive acceptance of and collusion with the potential deaths of millions of their fellow human beings are morally reprehensible at best and abusively evil at worst. The whole genre of prophetic writing never once stops to consider the question of Jesus' own attitude to such horrors being perpetrated 'according to God's will'. The books march blindly on, laying horror upon horror, all in the name of the fulfilment of 'prophecy' so that a narrow interpretation of scripture can be upheld. Thus the price of being a Bible-believing Christian may involve in some cases a belief that God actually wills the death and destruction of innocent human individuals.

Conclusion

In this chapter it has been seen how two traditions of millennial belief involve an acceptance by Christians that violent death and destruction are in some sense willed by God. In the case of the Waco 'cult', David Koresh allowed his followers to believe that their death might be made inevitable because of the role they were to play in the scenario of the opening of the seals of Revelation which was to lead to the end of the world. In the second pattern of belief in the millennial traditions which go back to Darby and Scofield, the violent destruction of two-thirds of the Jewish people settled in Palestine is seen to be inevitable and foreordained. From the perspective of Jesus of Nazareth it is hard to see how either view deserves the name of Christian. There is a lot more that could have been written on other prophecy beliefs and the way that violent destruction is predicted not only for the Jews, but for all the participants in the end-time conflicts, particularly Russia, which is likened to Gog found in Ezekiel

38 and 39. This book only has the space to touch on a cross-section of this strange world of Christian beliefs about the fulfilment of biblical prophecy. If, however, it is being suggested here that the Christianity as expounded by these prophecy writers is condoning death and violence, it should at least be attempted to offer some kind of explanation in the realm of psychology as to why such beliefs not only exist, but also have a large degree of popularity.

In his book, *Apocalypse*, Charles Strozier tells of an interview with a white woman in her thirties called Mary, whose mind was full of the details of the way that the destruction of the world through nuclear devastation is foreordained by scripture. For her, all was made bearable by the thought that she was destined to reign with Christ in his millennial kingdom. In being asked about her background Mary revealed that her early life had been full of terrors of apocalyptic events, and she remembered, as a child of six, hiding under the table of her grandmother's house during the Cuban Missile Crisis of 1962 as she awaited the arrival of missiles which would bring in the end of the world. As a young woman with a good voice she made her way to the Juilliard School in New York, the best conservatory of music in the United States. She failed subsequently to find a professional singing job and was left adrift and alienated in the city, doing such menial jobs as came her way in order merely to survive. It was then that she went through a conversion experience, becoming a 'follower of Jesus' and attached herself to a church known as Abiding Light. Here she found ample scope for musical expression and dreamed of becoming a full-time minister. Strozier, in making a psychological comment on her story, noted that her reborn Christian self connected up with an innocent self that she had known as a child between the ages of three and five. The contrast between that time of innocence and what she had later become filled her with self-loathing. With her conversion she had become contemptuous of her physical body as a reminder of her state of alienation from her childhood innocence. Images of decay, both in herself and in the whole of society, filled her imagination. Thus she could contemplate the future with satisfaction, with her split-off idealized self finding its true home, leaving all that she had come to despise about herself behind to be destroyed.

I have already, when discussing Philip Greven's book in chapter one, suggested that there is a further explanation for the immense popularity of the images of violence and destruction that abound in prophecy belief. He claims quite simply that the fascination with the texts from Revelation, Ezekiel and Daniel that spell out destruction and doom arises out a life history of experience of pain and suffering, meted out in Protestant households as part of the understanding of biblical discipline. Both he and Alice Miller before him linked physical punishment of children to the creation of a culture which is filled with fantasized and actual examples of violence. Greven stressed the way that the anger felt by the individual who was physically punished might well spill out into images of death and destruction being meted out to other people.

Any condoning of the destruction of whole masses of people, innocent and guilty, even if that destruction apparently makes God's purposes possible, is a strange sentiment for a follower of Christ. When a grim acceptance of such events gives way to joyous satisfaction, it is possible, like Greven, to see some profoundly unhealthy psychological dynamics at work. Lindsey reassured his readers, 'Even though many of these signs are appalling in themselves, their tremendous significance should gladden the heart of every true believer in Christ.' Greven claims that the Apocalypse of the book of Revelation is 'one of the most enduring sadomasochistic fantasies [which] has provided and still provides endless pleasure and satisfaction to those who consider themselves safe from the punishments... The rest will be tortured in hell eternally.' In summary, Greven makes the bold claim that the hate and murderous aggression created by childhood abuse finds 'displaced expression in apocalyptic visions of End Time'. Nevertheless, as he points out, the Christian tradition does not demand that people have images of God as a wrathful punisher and destroyer of the world. There are other models available. In particular, and I will turn to this in chapter nine, such aggression, cruelty and violence find no place in the teaching and life of Jesus.

When such an infallible belief system is applied consistently and strictly, there will be little sense that there are many things we simply do not know, that humble silence in the face of mystery is sometimes a more appropriate response to difficult issues than dogmatic certainty.

Chapter Seven

Fundamentalist Christianity and the Bible – the Wider Context

In attempting to describe a disturbing aspect of church life, power abuse, I have had to use words in a way that, to some readers, will seem provocative or, worse still, dangerously misleading. In this chapter I will set out more information about the background to these stories by discussing further the meaning of the words and concepts that I have used, as well as providing some extra background historical material.

The attempt to write about an issue in church life where the words in use have imprecise meanings is fraught with problems. A word like 'fundamentalist', as shall be seen, can be understood to have a whole number of meanings, depending on who is writing and from what perspective. I, therefore, thought it important to give some additional space to describing the background to the word and something of the various movements that constitute Christian 'fundamentalism' in Britain and the United States. Also, some definitions are given of other words that are used in the stories, particularly 'evangelical' and 'charismatic'. Chapter eight follows with some psychological material that will also, hopefully, elucidate understanding from other perspectives. So let the voyage of exploration continue with a discussion of the key words and their meanings.

An attempt at definitions: fundamentalist

The word 'fundamentalist', though found in the title of this book, is one that I have used with a certain reluctance because it has gathered associations that are considered by many to be unhelpful. Nevertheless, even though I might want to avoid the word, it is still useful as a way of describing a particular way of thinking and acting that is commonly encountered in the styles of church life that have been met in this book. It needs to be noted at this point the way in which the word is used in current writing and an attempt made to pin it down to a consistent meaning. According to a recent definitive study by Harriet Harris, the words 'fundamentalist' or 'fundamentalism' are normally used in the literature in one of three senses. The first two are meanings which are precise and refer to particular identifiable Christian groups. The third sense refers to a tendency of thought, a distinctive mindset rather than as a member of a particular group.

The first use of the word 'fundamentalist' to describe a Christian body refers to a movement of separatist Protestant Christianity which emerged in the 1920s, in self-conscious opposition to what it perceived to be the onslaught of modernism in the American churches. This group of Christians was so-called because it was identified with the theological position taken in a series of twelve booklets published between 1909 and 1915, entitled *The Fundamentals*. These articulated the beliefs of many conservative Protestant Christians coming under increasing pressure from the liberal ascendancy in the main denominational structures. The booklets were an attempt to respond to that challenge by setting out what were considered to be essential beliefs, as well as meeting head-on the threatening ideas, including Darwinism and higher criticism of the Bible. The high point for this movement was in the 1920s, when attempts were made to take over various denominational structures in the name of orthodox opinions. But the movement suffered defeats, partly because of its own internal disunity, and by the 1930s it was far less visible in American life.

In popular perception the fundamentalist cause suffered a severe setback in the Scopes trial of 1925. In that year John Scopes, a teacher in Tennessee, was prosecuted for teaching evolution. He was defended by Clarence Darrow, an eminent New York lawyer, and prosecuted by William Jennings Bryan, a former presidential candidate, and an avowed opponent of the theory of evolution. Scopes was found guilty, but not before Darrow had put Bryan himself in the witness box and shown him as ignorant both of science and the Bible. The trial was followed by the whole nation and confirmed in most people's eyes that fundamentalism as a movement was clearly out of touch with the mainstream of modern thought. The subsequent history of the fundamentalist movement after the 1920s was one of withdrawal into the ecclesiastical undergrowth, with re-emergence into the light of day only in the last couple of decades, reinvigorated, and with powerful political and educational institutions, particularly in the United States.

The second sense in which it is accurate to use the word 'fundamentalist' is in reference to those Christians today who use the title as a self-description. There are relatively few in Britain, and in the United States the title would be owned by those Christians who are associated with institutions such as the militantly conservative Bob Jones University. The word implies strict separatism from other bodies of Christians who do not share their beliefs. For example, in the eyes of Bob Jones, Billy Graham does not merit the title of fundamentalist because he has chosen to associate with other Christians of a non-conservative position, not to mention Roman Catholics. The American manifestation of strict self-designated fundamentalism tends to have, in addition, a strong set of beliefs connected with the future end of the world as it is claimed to be found in scripture.

The third way that the word 'fundamentalist' is used is in describing a particular style of belief found in all religious traditions. For the sake of clarity it is helpful to distinguish between a fundamentalist mentality as displayed by the leadership within a church and the way that this same mindset is taken on board by those in the pew. The leadership or the institution of a church will normally adopt a far more consistent approach to the proclamation of the Christian faith than the ordinary Christian among the membership. For the latter, there may well be areas of inconsistency or even contradiction in their belief systems, as there tend to be among all religious believers. The main feature of a fundamentalist attitude among ordinary Christians seems to be deference to authority, whether that of an institution or that of a book. Such deference might reflect a genuine admiration or respect for authority or, alternatively, a sense that an air of submissiveness to authority is the price to be paid for the perceived advantages of belonging to the group. The displayed deference thus may hide considerable areas of independent thought, and it might be suspected that amid the apparent unanimity of thought in conservative churches there may be a certain amount of 'subversive' thinking. Alternatively there may be a reluctance to engage in thinking about the issues at all. A claim that large numbers of people all believe identical things is probably unrealistic and unattainable. From the perspective of this book such unanimity of thinking is probably an undesirable state to seek or to obtain anyway. So consistent and identical patterns of belief among large groups of Christians are probably a fairly rare phenomenon. Yet large groups of people may well seek to bind themselves securely to the institution for reasons that I will examine further in the next chapter.

Among the Christian leadership the adjective is most appropriately used to describe those who seek to present a particularly strict adherence to the written word of scripture as the defining aspect of their Christian identity. The Bible comes to represent a reliable foundation, a 'fundament', for everything about their lives and the lives of those they seek to minister to. While everything around them is changing and uncertain, the Bible is seen as a fixed point offering certainties and grounds for strong Christian proclamation amid the apparent confusion and subjectivity in the world.

How is it possible to distinguish such loyalty to scripture as may be displayed in a fundamentalist Christian from an attachment and devotion to the Bible that would be owned by all evangelicals, and indeed all Christians? The answer would seem to lie in the particular way that the fundamentalist Christian leadership has come to regard other Christians that do not share its particular rigorous approach. Those in the pew may also have an acute sense that their strong loyalty to scripture separates them both physically and psychologically from all who do not share their beliefs. So I would maintain that all those who operate within the orbit of fundamentalist Christianity, both the leaders and the led, have absorbed a deep sense of what they are not. Their sense of what makes them Christian has perhaps allowed them to feel somehow above other groups of Christians who do not share their perspectives on the essential content of the faith.

So fundamentalist Christians, particularly those in leadership, are often identifiable by a tendency towards a certain militancy. Other groups, whether Christian or non-Christian, may represent all the things they have been taught to despise as being in some way 'against' the Bible. They are liberals, they have sold out to secular-humanist ideas and they accept the fruits of higher criticism of the Bible. The true 'Bible-believing' Christian will always be encouraged to reject any ideas or people if they appear to contradict the 'truth' of the Bible. The image of the fundamentalist Christian, whether from the leadership or from the pew, as regarding his or her faith to be a belief in the Bible before a belief in Christ is often no caricature. Another Christian will be assessed, not on his or her acceptance of Christ, but on whether he or she has similar 'sound' views on the place of scripture. Such views will involve an acceptance of their total accuracy and inerrancy.

It needs, however, to be recognized that there are wide gradations in the level of commitment to this approach. When talking about those at the receiving end of a fundamentalist style of preaching I would not want to imply that he or she has necessarily bought into a whole system of belief, or a consistent position about the 'fundaments'. Human beings are normally riddled with inconsistencies, and while the 'correct' belief system is set out for them by their preachers and the books they read, it is quite likely, as has been suggested above, that an individual member of a congregation may have allowed a number of assumptions about God into their thinking that are officially not permitted by the overall system.

The adjective 'fundamentalist', when used to describe an individual or a church congregation, will outwardly signify a particular way of embracing the Christian faith that is strict, exclusive and uncompromising. The fact that a person who is completely consistent in his fundamentalist beliefs is relatively rarely encountered outside the leadership has to do with the fact that such an exclusive position is quite hard to sustain over a period of time, particularly when the 'enemies' of your position often seem less threatening than those in authority have taught you to believe. But most members of 'fundamentalist' churches will accept that membership of it requires an outward conformity to the system of belief that the church has defined for them. Some will genuinely come to a similar belief system as their leaders, but others will conform, as has been suggested above, for the rewards of belonging, and suppress doubts and disagreements. Others will conform and believe what they have been taught simply because they have invested a great deal of human trust in the leadership. In effect, they allow the institution or leader to do their thinking and believing for them. For these last two groups of Christians it would be more accurate to say that they have become fundamentalist in and through their membership of a fundamentalist institution, rather than because of an individual, thought-out position. When a situation arises in which an individual hands over his thinking for it to be done by others, it can be seen that what has been surrendered is considerable. What is wholly or partially lost is the self-determination and decision-making processes of the individual. The fundamentalist mindset might call this attitude 'obedience', but it could, particularly in the light of the stories that have been told, be called an abdication of responsibility.

Bruce Bawer in his book, *Stealing Jesus*, well describes the attitude of defensiveness combined with a loyalty to the truth of the Bible among some fundamentalist Christians and calls it 'legalistic'. Describing the phenomenon from the perspective of the leaders, he sees a division between Christianity understood as a system of control, finding its identity in tightly defined systems of belief and institutional authority, and a broader, more generous manifestation of Christ's teaching and spirit. The word 'legalistic' suggests an inflexibility of attitude believed to be necessary in order to protect the certainties contained in the 'fundaments', and this is a key aspect of the manifestation of Christianity that has so often been met in this work. It is a particularly good word to describe the way that fundamentalist church authorities sometimes enforce the principles of their faith system.

It is true that Catholic and liberal expressions of Christianity can be and are sometimes inflexible, so that they could at times incur the accusation of being legalistic. Indeed, other books could be written about the victims of almost any belief system that you care to name. But the fundamentalist Protestant leader operates in a distinctive way with a significantly powerful weapon. He claims that he possesses the inerrant truth of God in a written form, and that this truth must be obeyed without any compromise. As has been seen throughout this book, when such an infallible belief system is applied consistently and strictly, there will be little sense that there are many things we simply do not know, that humble silence in the face of mystery is sometimes a more appropriate response to difficult issues than dogmatic certainty. So the word 'legalistic' used in a Protestant context is a good one to capture the meaning of fundamentalist approach, because it describes well this minority tendency within Christianity to put law and non-negotiable principles before love. Law, by its own self-understanding, has to be applied consistently and inflexibly. Love, conversely, while not a stranger to issues of justice and truth, will always approach issues and people with mercy and understanding. It will seek to find a way forward which is devoid of harshness and is marked by generosity and hope as well as an appropriate flexibility.

Evangelicalism

The word 'evangelical' also appears throughout this book. This word describes a Christian movement which looks back both to the Reformation in the sixteenth century and to the revivals of the eighteenth. Evangelicals would be those who emphasize that Christianity is not just about a formal belonging to the church, but also involves an inner conviction of being 'saved' by an acknowledgment of the lordship of Christ in their lives. In the past as well as the present the evangelical tendency has also been to sit lightly on the authority of formal church institutions in favour of the authority of scripture. Scripture alone had been the rallying cry of the Reformers and modern evangelicals would generally agree that the Bible contains all that is necessary for a Christian to believe and know for their salvation. The exact relationship between evangelicalism and the tendency that I have referred to as 'fundamentalist' is complex and is the subject of a detailed study by Harriet Harris in her book, *Fundamentalism and Evangelicals*. Having chosen to define fundamentalism in terms of its militancy and separatism, I do not wish to follow her arguments, which link fairly closely the two movements. The connections that she makes between the two have, however, more to do with the formal work of biblical scholars and theologians than with the typical believer in the pew, or even the local church leader.

An assessment as to where the boundary between evangelical belief and behaviour and that of the fundamentalist might be placed will be a difficult task. It could be suggested that a boundary might be drawn, as indicated above, at the point where some Christians begin to stand apart and separate themselves from their fellow Christians on the grounds of scripture and belief. There is a world of difference between mainstream evangelical figures represented by Billy Graham and George Carey and the styles and behaviours described in this book. In summary, the two words 'evangelicalism' and 'fundamentalism' are descriptions of fairly different things. One is a fairly coherent system of thought and theology with a distinctive ethos and intellectual history; the other, fundamentalism, is, as has been seen, a mindset within evangelicalism with a tendency towards militancy and separation. Evangelicalism may indeed contain many people who might possess a fundamentalist or near-fundamentalist mindset, but it would be unjust simply to link the two as being the same.

In this brief survey of what is meant by evangelicalism it is right to note its intellectual achievements, recognized within the universities of both Britain and the United States. The universities have, by contrast, largely rejected the scholarship presented by fundamentalist writers. This has forced such scholars as work within the fundamentalist network to serve institutions outside the academic mainstream. These are built and paid for by church rather than state funds. Evangelicals in Britain especially have always retained a high profile in the academic world of the universities and theological colleges, and in such academic circles the stridency of fundamentalist rhetoric is seldom heard. It needs, however, to be suggested that, outside the world of academic evangelicalism, fundamentalist tendencies do creep into the thinking of large numbers of Christians, not just within the evangelical churches. It may be easier to hold a congregation together with the black-and-white certainties of fundamentalist ideas, rather than allow in a host of different opinions which might cause division. The convenience of unified thinking has also been apparent to dictators of every hue throughout the ages. Democracy is far more untidy and difficult to manage. So evangelical reverence for scripture all too easily becomes subordination to the party line of the leader's interpretation of scripture. As I commented in one of the incidents connected with Rita, it is unlikely that any large group of intelligent adults will have an identical view on anything. If that does occur it may be as the result of the working out of a church dynamic that forces people to suppress their real thinking. It is here that a link between the dynamics of an extreme right-wing political system and the workings of church life might be postulated.

In summary, the situation as regards this complex question of the relationship between evangelicals and fundamentalist Christians, could be presented as a continuum. At one end there are, in Britain, evangelical Christians who fulfil all the qualifications of strict fundamentalism, with an emphasis on separatism and beliefs in the imminent second coming of Christ, as well as a strong, uncompromising and militant belief in the inerrancy of scripture. At the other end of the continuum there are evangelical Christians who would reject ideas they consider to be extreme, but would want to describe both their faith and spirituality as being evangelical. For them, Christianity has been discovered in an experience of conversion and emotional warmth, and for this the evangelical tradition is acknowledged and valued. Their relationship with the Bible would be strong, but it would be defined in ways that avoided any suggestion of militancy. In the middle are many Christians who are capable of being pushed into a conformist mode of thinking by the 'politics' of their church life, which could be described as fundamentalist by those outside. When such an individual moves beyond that particular setting they may revert quickly to more mainstream independent thinking. In the last resort the labels that can be given are not really important as the concern is, after all, with the fruits of particular belief systems. Whether or not a particular Christian is evangelical or fundamentalist is not important. What is important is the fact that Christians are, on occasion, using their beliefs and doctrinal systems as a means to control, manipulate and sometimes damage other people. The concern of this book has been to show the nature of this abuse and examine how particular belief systems and emphases within traditional Christianity give rise to it. When something thought to be wholesome and good becomes a cause of stumbling, that is a concern for every Christian.

The charismatic movement

In the introduction I spoke briefly about a personal involvement with what is known as the charismatic movement. Throughout the text there have been accounts of congregations that have been described as 'charismatic'. In itself, the word describes a style of spirituality, one that gives much attention to lively open prayer within the context of exuberant worship and music and close interaction with other Christians. It was, in part, a reaction to what were perceived as dry formal styles of prayer which show little involvement of the emotions or the 'heart'. The 'charismatic movement' emerged in the early 1960s in Europe and the United States to become a powerful force in worldwide Christendom by the middle of the 1970s. Its main theological and spiritual roots owe much to the somewhat sectarian Pentecostal churches which have been on the world scene since the beginning of the twentieth century. In its early days the movement caught up into itself many Christians from the main denominations including Roman Catholics. By 1975 charismatics seemed to offer a new ecumenism, a joining together of Christians right across the denominations based on their common joy and celebration of the Christian faith. From the beginning the striking exuberance of charismatic worship, the emphasis on 'spiritual gifts' and the rediscovery of a spirituality which has the effect of binding people closely together have all led the movement to have a wider influence than just on those caught up in it directly.

Much good has been released into the church by the charismatic movement, but the problem has been, as the introduction pointed out, that charismatic churches have, in some places, become infected with authoritarian styles of leadership of a fundamentalist kind. In the sections that follow, two particular strands of authoritarian teaching that have come to be part of much charismatic thinking throughout the world will be looked at, both of which have the potential to harm individuals. In following one or other of these strands of teaching, leaders or pastors are able to claim substantial power over their communities. The power used may well claim to follow and reflect the models of the New Testament church, but too easily there may be a shift towards patterns of power that are experienced as abusive. The word 'charismatic' in this book has referred not only to the spontaneous spiritual style of prayer and worship, but also, regrettably, to the fundamentalist authoritarian style of church government not infrequently found within these churches.

Charismatic Christianity compromised?

In the introduction I described some personal involvement in, and appreciation for, the charismatic movement as it affected the denominational churches in Britain. I also recorded how I found myself less and less able to be part of it as fundamentalist modes of thinking seemed to take over within its structures. Finally I found myself an outsider, but in the situation of using my sympathy for the movement in seeking to help its casualties. These have become more numerous as the movement in many places has become less tolerant and, on occasion, abusive and harmful. It was at quite a late stage in reading the background material for this book that I began to formulate a theory as to how this new less sympathetic tone had developed. It was in analysing the stories that have been recorded in the previous chapters that I began to see a certain pattern emerging. The authoritarianism that is a feature of so many of the stories was not simply due to powerful leaders backing up that power with quotations from the Bible, but also echoed the ideas of particular individuals and movements in the American charismatic scene during the 1970s and 1980s. The history of the charismatic movement has not yet been written, but the final story will, I am sure, show that two particular strands of interpretation and understanding have come to have considerable influence in this worldwide movement. Both of them, in different ways, illustrate how an appeal to the authority of the Bible can have practical and, in this case, harmful consequences for individuals and churches. These strands, known as the Faith movement and the shepherding movement, have, I believe, made their influence felt in Britain as elsewhere, and from my perspective they can be seen to have helped to distort the charismatic movement and make it a potential cause of stumbling for a large number of its adherents.

The next three sections will attempt to tell this story in brief. It is a story worthy of far more research than I have been able to give it. In sketching the outline I make no claims of proving anything in detail. I merely suggest that the atmosphere these two movements have created within the charismatic world has, to some extent, compromised its theology and witness and muddled its thinking. Until these influences are thoroughly understood and their harmful effects exorcized, they will continue to have a less-than-wholesome influence on the movement as a whole. Almost as importantly, the Faith movement and the shepherding movement have meant that the charismatic movement has been increasingly less accessible to Christians like myself of a more mainstream temperament. In brief, what began as a movement for unity has become, in many places, a movement for division and exclusion, as well as creating, on occasion, harm and abuse.

The Faith movement

The origins of the so-called Faith movement can be traced back to the United States of the 1950s with the ministry of Kenneth Hagin, a pastor in a Pentecostal church. He himself was indebted to (though some would say plagiarized) the writings of E.W. Kenyon, another American writer and preacher linked to Pentecostalism, who was active until his death in 1948. Kenyon's ideas have been described as a 'Pentecostal Christian Science'. He had trained in Emerson College in the 1890s, a centre of the American metaphysical tradition known as New Thought. His writings betray an indebtedness to these traditions and in many ways they reflect an attempt to enable Christianity to compete with them. In essence Kenyon took over from the American metaphysical traditions the notion that there are two levels of knowledge, sense knowledge and revelation knowledge. With this latter, Christians are able to transcend the limitations of the physical dimension and have a higher sense of God's presence, so that he can act directly in their lives, especially in terms of providing healing and material prosperity. revelation knowledge will allow the individual to have accurate guidance and 'perfect knowledge' of God, and this not unnaturally has a tendency to create a grandiose personality cult led by powerful charismatic supermen.

The path to revelation knowledge is the path of faith. Faith is rising up to the higher dimension, where an individual can lay hold of the promises of God to provide everything they need. One particular verse that is key to this exposition of the Christian faith is Romans 10:10 with its idea of positive confession, 'the confession that leads to salvation is upon the lips'. From this principle, or 'law', Hagin taught that there were four steps to receiving anything from God: '(1) Say it, (2) Do it, (3) Receive it and (4) Tell it.' According to this, faith-filled words have a kind of impersonal power to effect anything that is required. For Hagin's critics this impersonal-formula approach to faith has far more to do with the metaphysical cults, or even magic, than with the Christian God. The New Age idea that everyone, through the content of their minds, creates their own reality is similar, and no doubt ultimately can be traced back to the same nineteenth-century New Thought ideas. The same principle applies to negative thinking. Kenyon wrote, 'It is what we confess with our lips that really dominates our inner being… They confess their fear of disease and the disease grows under the confession.'

The Faith teachers, Kenneth Hagin, Kenneth Copeland and Frederick Price, to name a few, were able to mine the scriptures for quotations to offer support for their ideas. Superficially their ideas appear to have biblical support and there are many references in the gospels to the need for 'faith'. But equally clearly the non-biblical roots of this whole system of thinking, which has been well explored by Dan McConnell in his book, *The Promise of Health and Wealth*, cause some disquiet. Without becoming deeply involved in the whole debate, it can be noted that for Jesus, faith was far more an attitude of trust and openness to a divine reality than a working out of some divine law to achieve one's ends, however worthy they may be. When the faith formula fails to work, the leader can always suggest to the disappointed follower that he or she has not reached the right quality or depth of faith required. For those who teach Faith ideas, it is a win-win situation. After failure of the formula, the disciple will need to depend more on the teacher to help find the right method of practising Faith confession.

It should be recognized that the formula does contain a modicum of truth, since clearly an individual's attitudes towards health and the future will affect the way things turn out for them. Nevertheless, the fact is that Faith teaching will often tend towards cruelly manipulating vulnerable people who seek health or riches in the name of biblical Christianity. Some writers within the charismatic movement, such as William DeArteaga in his book, *Quenching the Spirit*, have made good cases for supporting Kenyon and Hagin, pointing out that the metaphysical traditions from which the ideas came were not all bad. Even if this is conceded it is difficult to see how such ideas will avoid becoming more corrupted as they are reinterpreted over and over again to a vast range of audiences. Human nature being what it is, an idea, if it is capable of being corrupted, will on occasion be corrupted if money and power are there to be had through it. In the last resort, any idea should not be evaluated on its purest and highest manifestation, but on how it is actually used. DeArteaga may have many valid points in supporting the ideas of Kenyon and his followers, but the fact remains incontrovertible that these same ideas have often been used corruptly and abusively, not least by a number of the so-called 'televangelists' in the United States. A few of these broadcasters, through a series of financial and sexual scandals from the late 1980s until the present, have done more than anyone to cast a shadow over the Faith teachings, Christian broadcasting and, by association, the whole charismatic movement.

The history of the Faith movement, since its first origins in the early 1960s under the leadership of Kenneth Hagin, is a complicated one. Suffice to say that it has been enormously popular, not least within the multi-billion-dollar Christian broadcasting industry throughout the world. The owners of vast television empires, including the infamous Jimmy Swaggart and Jim Bakker, by giving prominence to the basic theology of 'name it and claim it', have, many would argue, generated vast sums of money for themselves. It is this extension of Faith ideas beyond the actual Faith movement that is important for the current theme. Faith ideas and assumptions have crept into the thinking of countless Christians who have never heard of the movement presided over by Kenneth Hagin. What is important from the perspective of this book is to identify it as one of the strands of charismatic Christianity that has sometimes been taken and used abusively against vulnerable people. My concern is not to argue for or against the biblical correctness or otherwise of Faith ideas, but simply to claim that they can be and have been used corruptly.

The shepherding movement

The so-called shepherding movement emerged in the United States and South America simultaneously in the late 1960s and early 1970s. In the late 1960s, an Episcopal charismatic congregation in Houston, Texas, began caring for people with special needs in members' homes, and soon this 'shepherding' form of care was extended to include all members of the congregation. The thinking in part came from a 1950s' Pentecostal movement known as the Latter Rain movement, which taught a system of church government according to the pattern of Ephesians 4:11–13. This passage sets out a divinely ordained five-fold ministry to govern the church. Latter Rain taught that the ultimate purpose of the five-fold ministries was to unite all believers, and 'to acquire a divine nature'. Another influence was a book by a former Communist, Douglas Hyde, who urged Christians to adopt the Communist cell system to recruit, inspire and train new members. Yet another source of inspiration were the writings of a Chinese Christian, Watchman Nee, particularly a book called *Spiritual Authority*, which was written against the background of Communist persecution. This book was published in the West in the early 1970s.

In the early 1970s, an organization called Christian Growth Ministries was formed in Fort Lauderdale in Florida. This was headed up by prominent shepherding leaders such as Derek Prince, Bob Mumford and Ern Baxter. This organization cross-fertilized with another charismatic community called Word of God in Ann Arbor, Michigan. These communities, with others, sponsored the National Men's Shepherding Conferences during the 1970s. Their leaders also formed a somewhat secretive General Council, which controlled, through magazines and books, much of the charismatic media of the time.

The ideas that were emerging were also encouraged and cross-fertilized by those of a South American, Juan Ortiz, who moved to the United States from Argentina in the early 1970s and spoke at numerous conferences. His books, *Call to Discipleship* and *Discipleship*, were widely studied and destined to be influential. The movement that Ortiz helped to get off the ground was widely popular because the charismatic style of church life was felt by many to be too indulgent and permissive. There was a need for a stronger sense of discipline, and the discipleship leaders promised their followers that theirs was the way to a more total commitment to Jesus. Reading the book, *Discipleship*, as well as having a discussion with someone who knew about Argentinian Christianity in the early 1970s, I was not entirely unsympathetic to Ortiz's case. For example, when he called for the local church to break up into 'cells', he was no doubt in part seeking to prepare it for possible persecution by a right-wing dictatorship. The pattern of authority within that cell, however, emphasized strict discipline, and words like 'submission' and 'submit' are freely used. Nevertheless, what might be justified in the context of possible persecution did not settle well in the new cultural setting of the United States. Instead a darker side to submission appeared. Not only did submission to a shepherd promote a form of bondage and lack of human freedom, but also the shepherds or disciplers, often new and immature Christians, were permitted to exercise power without any restraint. Horror stories emerged about the total control that shepherds exercised over their flock. Families were required to move at the whim of their shepherd, and the sheep were expected to seek permission before they made any decisions of any substance. By about 1990, the movement had begun to disintegrate and the shepherding leaders began to 'release' their disciples to find their own way.

In 1991, the Word of God community in Ann Arbor, Michigan, called in a specialist in cults, James LeBar, to assist the membership to understand the abuses that had been practised on them over the previous twenty years. The list of problems identified in that community was chilling. It included 'elitism, thought control, unnecessary shame, loss of personal identity, loss of freedom and soul, dependency, loss of personal initiative, extreme negative world-view, extreme sex role differentiation and extreme secrecy'. An in-depth study of the mainstream Church of Christ, which had been greatly affected by the shepherding movement, by Flavil Yeakley, called *The Discipling Dilemma*, examined the personalities of the members using the Myers Briggs Type Indicator. Yeakley found that instead of the wide variety of personality types he would have expected in a normal group, as measured by this particular method, all the members converged on a single type. In short, the discipling process had caused the personalities of the members to be changed to fit in with the group norm. Such personality changes, which were a denial of the core personality, would, he predicted, cause major psychological disturbance in later life. This, sadly, turned out to be true and the 1990s have seen a rejection of the formal shepherding ideas. Nevertheless the influence of the movement remains and it was seen most chillingly and abusively at work in the Nine O'Clock Service in Sheffield in the mid-1990s.

The Faith and shepherding movements – an unholy alliance?

Mention has already been made of an important study by Dan McConnell on the Faith movement. In it there is a fascinating section on the way that the two streams of charismatic thinking I have briefly discussed, having both independently entered into a situation of controversy in the 1980s, proceeded to cooperate and build up an alliance against their critics. Shepherding teaching had always attracted fierce criticism from its rivals, and a standard defence from the leaders was that they could do nothing if someone took a basic principle of their teaching and misapplied it. Bob Mumford, a shepherding leader, wrote, in defending the Faith movement, and Kenneth Copeland in particular, 'What they have gone through in teaching the faith message is so analogous to what we have experienced that it's brought a certain sense of camaraderie.' This coming together of Faith leaders with those from the shepherding movement became a reality at the meeting of the Network of Christian Ministries in 1985. Kenneth Copeland even called for a merger of the two revelations given to the Faith and shepherding movements. Charles Simpson, speaking for the shepherding movement, declared that if the respective leaders would express their need of each other's revelations, 'that same attitude would follow among the people'.

The Network code of ethics required that members refrain from criticizing one another, and that ethical violations should be confronted in private, according to the principles of Matthew 18:15–17. Since both movements were subject to criticism, not only from a doctrinal point of view, but also in terms of the ethics of their practices, such an appeal to scripture could be regarded with a certain amount of cynicism. In 1985, the two movements accounted for a considerable proportion of the Pentecostal/charismatic body of Christians, not only in the United States, but also in the world. Any 'gagging' of theological or ethical debate would be unhealthy for those movements and for the charismatic movement in general.

In recent years both movements have lost their high-profile organizations, especially the shepherding movement. The Faith movement has retreated somewhat under the fierce onslaught of mainstream evangelical critique. This book cannot chronicle the full story of the debates and there has been an enormous literature generated to 'expose' the heresies of both movements. The internet, too, is awash with material that attacks the 'unbiblical' nature of both these emphases within charismatic teaching.

Two things remain to be reiterated. The first is that shepherding and Faith ideas, in spite of their controversial nature, appear to remain deeply embedded in much that passes for charismatic Christianity today. Secondly, it is one or other of these ideas that lies behind much of the abusive practice discussed throughout this book. In short, some expressions of charismatic Christianity in Britain, in their absorption of Faith and shepherding ideas, have become, to a greater or lesser extent, tainted by this influence. The health of the movement in the future will depend on the extent to which it is able to identify and re-examine the influences of Kenneth Hagin, Derek Prince, and so on, and rediscover a new 'purer' theological voice as it moves into the twenty-first century. In that way it may be able to regain an important role among the churches of Britain.

Fundamentalist Christianity is, then, a shorthand for a particular kind of authoritarian and exclusive Christianity, whether or not it is combined with a form of charismatic Christianity which has been compromised by the influences I have sought to describe above. Charismatic Christianity itself, as mentioned earlier in the chapter, has no inevitable link with fundamentalist ideas. In principle it can be described quite separately as a form of spirituality which spills over into distinctive styles of worship. In practice, as will be seen, it has often and regrettably allowed itself to become deeply entwined in fundamentalist modes of thinking, using the Bible as its source of authority and power. In the last resort, both of the influences causing the aberration of charismatic Christianity have to do with power. Power in their country of origin, the United States, means money, incredible amounts of it. The truce between Faith teachers and shepherding teachers in 1985 could cynically be thought to be a means of protecting the money-making industries of two massive empires. The church was ill served by the perpetuation of these easily corruptible doctrines which have come, as I would claim, to compromise one of the great movements of the Spirit in our time.

The doctrine of the Bible in fundamentalist Christianity – an overview

At this point in the chapter a key idea that lies behind all the stories in this book needs to be considered further, namely that the Bible contains and reveals the true word of God. Thus the beliefs, teachings and practices found within the congregations represented in this book will be believed to be rooted in God's word, and thus reflections of his very will. It has already been suggested that the way this doctrine is understood and implemented in a particular church will vary considerably. Decisions will have to be made about the way that certain parts of scripture are chosen in preference to other parts of scripture in the way the church is guided. Even the most detached observer of the church knows that scope for disagreement among Christians about what the Bible actually says on any topic is infinite. It is hard to see how the choices that are in fact made will not in some way reflect the particular interests and concerns of those in leadership.

In his important, but highly controversial book, *Fundamentalism*, James Barr claims that a doctrine of the divine authorship of the Bible is rooted in a particular kind of religion rather than the other way round. In other words, the Bible is a shield or support to a particular religious tradition whose roots lie elsewhere. The main historical basis for what Barr describes as biblical fundamentalism is in the revivals of the early nineteenth century in the United States. During these revivals there was a strong recognition that individuals were being brought into touch with a warm, living and saving faith which had not been a feature of the formal denominational churches. There thus came to be a sense that people within those churches were at best nominal Christians who had never heard the true gospel of salvation which was proclaimed in the revivals. Once, however, the existing mainstream church and its life and teaching came to be looked down on and mistrusted, there had to be a different norm which would guarantee the purity of doctrine – that central point had to be the Bible.

In the Bible are grounded, or claimed to be grounded, all the distinctive doctrines of conservative revivalist Christianity, the substitutionary doctrine of the death of Christ, the virgin birth of Christ and a belief in his bodily resurrection. All this and much more is read from scripture, so that the first act of belief required of the fundamentalist Christian is in the reliability and inerrancy of scripture, because God is the author of the scriptural text. Once this is accepted all the other beliefs become less acts of faith than articles of certain knowledge. In short, a belief in the utter reliability of the text of the Bible is the defining quality of fundamentalist Christianity in its Protestant form. All forms of criticism are resisted because the traditions of revivalist Protestantism have no other foundation. Barr, however, points out that the relationship between the Bible and the tradition is not a simple one. Logically, one would expect the Bible to check and question the tradition, but in practice there is an unquestioned assumption that the tradition as it stands is based on a true interpretation of the Bible.

The outcome of this belief in the reliability of scripture means that the Bible is used in a distinctive way within fundamentalist discourse. A biblical quotation is held to clinch an argument one way or another and preaching will make frequent use of biblical texts. There will be little or no questioning on the part of the congregation as to the way scripture is used by the leadership. It is the preacher's use and application of the Bible within the context of worship that sets the tone as to how it is actually to be regarded by the congregation. So it could be claimed that alongside a belief in the infallibility or inerrancy of scripture there may well be little appetite on the part of an individual congregational member for examining the contradictions and complexities of the actual text. The task of interpretation is left, in practice, almost entirely to the leadership. So, as Kathleen Boone points out, inerrancy quickly passes from the text of scripture to the words of the preacher. There is thus within the doctrine of inerrancy of the Bible, a powerful institutional authority, which, though hidden, controls how the Bible is read by its adherents. The notion that a simple reader can extract guidance and right teaching outside the context of this hidden authority is a myth.

Within the fundamentalist world the Bible is read against a background of anxiety. So much hangs on its utter trustworthiness for the whole edifice of Christian belief, that any apparent deviation from this reliability is seen as an attack on faith. This sense of fear may also emerge from the experience of conversion, as will be described in chapter eight. But for whatever reason, the anxiety to maintain the words of scripture against doubt or questioning may explain why many Christians in this world remain largely ignorant of its contents. They prefer to hear scripture presented in a pre-packaged form by an authoritative interpreter who 'explains' and harmonizes the difficulties that may soon appear when the text is examined with any degree of objectivity. All believers within the fundamentalist culture have heard the 'thin end of the wedge' argument. This states, in brief, that if the Bible is found to be in error in any of its particulars then it is impossible to know that any of it is true. The whole basis for Christian belief is thus destroyed because there is no reliable basis for knowledge about what God has done. A further refinement of this argument, famously presented by James Packer, states that if Jesus quoted the Old Testament, believing it to be true, yet was wrong about this, how can we know he was not wrong about everything else he taught? Thus many fundamentalist Christians prefer to use the Bible more as a quarry for proof texts than as a narrative revealing a remarkable kaleidoscope of events, beliefs and insights which represent a human response to divine activity perceived through the events of history and the life of Jesus Christ.

The roots of the style of biblical interpretation practised by modern fundamentalist teachers lie less in the text of the Bible itself than in an unconscious assimilation of some quite modern philosophical ideas. In her recent book, Harriet Harris has set out clearly the way that modern conservative ideas about the Bible are greatly influenced by a set of eighteenth-century ideas known as Common Sense philosophy. This philosophy is associated with two names, Thomas Reid (1710–96) and James Beattie (1735–1802). Both these philosophers lived in Scotland, but their ideas had widespread influence in nineteenth-century America. They resonated well in this young republic with its robust defence of the rights of the individual. In essence, the philosophy stated that Common Sense perception was a reliable form of knowledge, and thus truth was accessible to all but those of an unsound mind. This principle was taken and applied to scripture in opposition to other methods of interpretation emerging from Germany, which assumed a level of philosophical sophistication.

Common Sense ideas allowed the ordinary reader to have access to scripture because 'the meaning that the plain man gets out of the Bible is the correct one'. The Bible was understood to be true with a scientific precision that earlier centuries would not have understood, not having encountered such ideas of historical and scientific accuracy.

The Common Sense view of scripture reigned supreme for the first half of the nineteenth century in the United States, but in the latter half of the century was seen to be at odds with a whole host of new scientific facts that followed on from the discoveries of Darwin. Conservative biblical scholars clung tightly to a notion of biblical truth about the origins of humankind, but in reality they were supporting a now obsolete philosophical vision of what truth consists of.

Conservative scholarship to this day finds itself defending 'Common Sense' ideas of biblical truth in the apparent belief that these are the only ideas about truth in existence. Meanwhile, the rest of the church has long since recognized that language in general, and the Bible in particular, offers a whole variety of insights into truths, transcending mere historical or scientific fact. The Bible itself contains poetry, drama and symbolism, all of which are flattened and destroyed by a single notion of 'Common Sense' truth. The situation at issue between conservative and other interpreters of the Bible is not in the last resort about whose interpretation of the Bible is correct. It is a profound philosophical disagreement about what 'truth' is. Is it the same as 'fact', as defined by Common Sense philosophers, or is it a far richer and broader insight into reality.

Conclusion

In this chapter I have sought to set out the broad outlines of what is meant by fundamentalist Christianity. In addition, I have sought to sketch out some of the recent history of what is known as the charismatic movement. It has been suggested that two particular strands of teaching, both strongly fundamentalist in tone, have come to have a fairly dominant role in the thinking of the movement, making it harsher and, in many places, less accessible to Christians who had hitherto valued it for its style of spirituality and vitality. In short, where charismatic theology comes into contact with fundamentalist styles of theology, particularly an insistence on the infallibility of scripture, it too easily slides into a style of authoritarian church life capable of harming individuals.

Any insistence on the inerrancy of scripture is often accompanied by increased and often inappropriate power on the part of the leaders in a church. When a particular course of action is forbidden on the grounds that a passage from the Bible says this, it is just as likely to be result of the human fallible notions of the leadership as a perfect expression of God's will. It is the use of the doctrine which equates God's will with a selective reading of scripture without allowing any appeal to dialogue that is strongly questioned in this work. In particular, when the enforcement of biblical 'truth' is made the means of obtaining inappropriate power over an individual and thus the cause of actual pain or suffering, it then becomes a doctrine to be resisted and in need of restatement. From the point of view of this writer, my relationship with the Bible will always be one of continuous questioning and dialogue, rather than involving its use as a final knock-down proof for a point of view that I already hold.

Literalism, by seeking to interpret scripture with completely the wrong set of tools, comes to destroy the reality of God.

Chapter Eight

Towards an Understanding of the Fundamentalist Mind

Understanding the fundamentalist mindset is not an easy task. It would be quite wrong to suggest that all those who belong to churches such as those described in the earlier chapters possess an identical personality or emerge from a similar social or psychological background. Among many observations, two things were noticed about the mindset. Firstly, individuals will sometimes pay lip-service to the fundamentalist ideology when it is expedient to do so, but drop out of it when the external situation compelling them to conform is no longer there. Secondly, a totally consistent fundamentalist position in one person is probably fairly rare. Nevertheless, it is important to consider some of the models that exist within psychology when thinking about the nature of the militant/authoritarian personality found in fundamentalist circles, as well as those who allow themselves to submit to such authority. What are the particular aspects of the fundamentalist mindset, which have been identified in the book so far, that need further elucidation?

The desire for absolute certainty within religious belief.

The apparent intolerance of, and sometimes violent hostility towards, those who question the belief system.

The demonizing of those who do not collude with the group.

The readiness to surrender to a powerful, wise personality who appears to have the answers and who will make decisions on their behalf.

The readiness of some church leaders to use power in a totally negative way.

The tendency to think in a polarized fashion – something is either right and good or wrong and totally evil.

The inability to handle ambiguity or doubt.

The defensiveness and fear of fundamentalist belief. Compromise can never be allowed in discussion.

These are just some of the issues that have emerged in my survey of a variety of church situations where fundamentalist modes of thinking have been in operation. All of the above patterns of behaviour are, I would suggest, at the very least unhelpful in the task of promoting Christianity and achieving any kind of personal integration and spiritual and emotional wholeness. During my reading over a number of years on this whole topic I have sought models of understanding which would help me towards some appreciation of why these distinctive patterns of behaviour and belief should arise. I realize that there is no overall explanation for fundamentalist patterns of behaviour, nor should one be sought as the variables within individual Christian stories and institutions are just too numerous. Nevertheless, I felt it right to share some of the fruits of my reading which offer models of understanding the reader may find enlightening as I have done. Such models, whether from philosophy or psychology, can be useful in helping us to look at the stories described in the book with a fresh language and set of concepts. Even if the models are themselves subject to controversy within their various disciplines, it does not make them without value for the current purpose. While the arguments from various authors are presented more or less uncritically, it is hoped that at least the ideas they are based on are reproduced accurately. The main thesis of the book does not depend on the correctness or falsity of these theories. If a single model contained in this chapter is found by the reader to be useful in helping them to think with greater clarity about the subject matter of the book, then this chapter has been worth writing.

The language of signs and symbols

In my discussion of the traditional interpretation of the Bible that I have identified as fundamentalist, I noted one particular word to describe this approach – inerrancy. This implies that a statement within scripture which has reference to an apparent fact about the world will be true in what it affirms. To quote the Chicago Statement on Biblical Inerrancy published in 1978, 'Scripture in its entirety is inerrant, being free from falsehood, fraud or deceit.' The word 'inerrant' is not one that is in common use, but can be and often is loosely translated into a word of similar meaning, 'literal'. The two words do not in fact have the same meaning, and indeed the latter word appears nowhere in the Chicago statement. To take a passage 'literally' is to, if possible, read it as a statement of truth or fact. The commentary on the Chicago statement does in fact pay lip-service to the notion that the Bible may contain poetry, hyperbole and metaphor, but in practice many conservative commentaries will find factual history or scientific descriptions of reality in the text where most other readers not tied to notions of divine authorship will see more easily poetry, story or mythological material. For example, most Christians, when reading the book of Revelation, will recognize that it is an immensely complex symbolic work, containing allusions to events and ideas that in places are at best obscure and at worst unrecoverable. Thus, apart from the first three chapters and certain other sections of great inspirational beauty, much of Revelation will, for practical purposes, be largely left to one side. Conversely, some schools of conservative fundamentalist interpretation, particularly that known as dispensationalism, will scrutinize the text with great enthusiasm, because their ideas of inerrancy lead them to believe that every detail has great significance and that a hidden meaning can be uncovered by diligent study. In particular, so-called 'prophecy' writers have discerned in the book references to happenings in recent history or events shortly to come to pass.

Kathleen Boone examines several conservative interpretations of Revelation. In one by Oliver Greene, there is space given to a consideration of how the 200 million horsemen mentioned in Revelation 9:16 can be literally feasible. Boone also notes how, in another book by Leon Bates, the desire to find a literal meaning in the passage leads the author to speculate that Revelation 9:17 is describing modern missile-launching tanks! Such extremes are, to be fair, not typical of conservative interpretations of scripture. Nevertheless, once one accepts a teaching which involves words like 'inerrancy' or suggests that God is in some way the 'author' of scripture, it is hard to see logically how such 'extreme' interpretations can be outlawed. A popular belief in the Bible being 'true' will always at a grass-roots level create potentially serious misunderstandings of the meaning of the text. Such misunderstandings are, of course, not confined to conservative Protestant churches but are widespread among Christians of all denominations.

In this section it is intended to show how a 'literal' reading of scripture can in many places destroy the meaning of what is being written, due to a profound misunderstanding of the nature of religious language. The fundamental point to have in mind as this theme is explored is the distinction between sign and symbol. A failure to distinguish between these words will lead to confusion. A 'sign' is a representation of an idea or object which points to the thing thus signified. A sign is a precise representation in the sense that the understanding of it is either correct or wrong. A no-entry sign, for example, has only one meaning and anyone claiming that its meaning is not clear is unlikely to impress a policeman! Within Christianity the sign of the fish has a single meaning, namely that the word for fish in Greek spells out the initial letters of 'Jesus Christ Son of God Saviour'. Signs are, then, a form of language which has to be learned. Their meaning has been defined by convention in much the same way as words come to describe particular objects within language. There is far less an element of subjectivity in the language of signs. Signs are only so described if their meaning is fixed and agreed by all who use them.

The way that symbols operate is similar to but distinct from that of signs. Instead of appealing merely to human understanding and capacity to recognize particular shapes and colours, symbols touch people at a much deeper level. They expose the observer to levels of meaning unfound in signs. Water, for example, when used as a symbol, crosses cultures; sometimes it symbolizes refreshment and fertility, but alternatively it can symbolize destruction. Light as a symbol can also be apprehended in a range of ways. Sometimes it will speak of the power to transform and give life, or it may be a symbol of the divine itself. The power of such symbols is that they touch an individual at a level of subjectivity far deeper than the trained intellect. All of us have a relationship with light and water which goes right back to the preconscious experience of our infancy and all of that experience will be fed into the way the symbol is apprehended. When symbols are used as part of language they can be seen to evoke and suggest meanings, rather than making that meaning precise. It is through symbolic language that we approach things that are not immediately knowable. The whole realm of what, in religious terms, is described as the transcendent, the spiritual dimension beyond the visible world, is approached through symbols, whether verbal or visual, and that enables the listener to use his entire subjectivity to 'know' what is in front of him. Religious knowing has always involved this subjective way of apprehending reality. There is simultaneously a recognition that the reality evoked by the symbol is beyond full human comprehension. Nevertheless, the symbol allows people to approach that reality and to some extent participate in it. Both the reality to which the symbol points and the symbol itself function in very different ways from a sign and the thing which is signified.

This discussion of a distinction between signs and symbols has been sufficient to indicate that if symbols are understood as signs, there is a case for much confusion. There are, of course, many biblical passages which can be read as statements of literal fact, in terms of things said and done in the past. Such a way of reading scripture, however, does not seem appropriate when used, for example, to interpret the book of Revelation. The book seems to be written almost entirely using symbolic language. If this symbolic material is understood in the way I have indicated, then it will be read in a way that is suggestive and evocative of God's glory and power, at the same time hinting at the reality of heaven and the cosmic struggle between good and evil. The 'literal' or fundamentalist approach that entails interpreting these same passages as being full of signs will also encourage discovery of exactly what they are signs of. Such an attempt to elucidate the exact significance of symbolic language as though it were the language of signs will only result in confusion.

This desire to read symbolic language as signs comes from the eighteenth/nineteenth-century belief in the superiority of physical reality over any other. This stimulates a further desire to purge language and thinking of any symbolic meaning on the grounds that symbols are an inferior form of discourse.

Symbols, however, in their power to speak to an individual at every level of being and orient him or her towards a particular way of living, feeling and believing, cannot be so easily dispensed with. They are part of our way of relating to the world and its mystery, a language of power which touches the heart. To suggest that all symbols can or should be reduced and flattened to correspond to the language of signs, which merely speaks of physical and historical realities, is to empty and destroy them. Thus an attempt to rid scripture of its symbols is to remove its power to move and inspire a believer. Literalism, by seeking to interpret scripture with completely the wrong set of tools, comes to destroy the reality of God. Literalism can only describe physical reality, never evoke the transcendent mystery of God's being.

The preconscious roots of personality

It has become a commonplace of psychological insight that many aspects of human personality find their origins in the period of life in a child that is pre-vocal and preconscious. Many of the psychological ills to which human beings are prone are traceable back to the environment of the first months and years of life. While the writing in this area is extensive and difficult to summarize, there are a few broad principles connected with the early experience of the child that may shed light on this chapter's subject – the emergence of the fundamentalist mindset.

The newborn baby emerging from the womb finds his or her new world far less comfortable than the one known before. The womb had been a haven of warmth, comfort and continuous nourishment, but now the baby has to face many new experiences. There is a new intensified experience of light and noise alongside the unwelcome sensation of hunger and being left alone. The mother's breast is a place of comfort and nourishment and when the baby is there it is able to fend off for the moment the deep fears that it has begun to experience. The breast as well as the physical protection of the mother are the source of the baby's attachment to her, for without them there is the threatened abyss of physical extinction.

According to Melanie Klein, an important writer in this field, the mother creates ambivalent feelings in the child. At one moment she is the loved object, the source of reassurance and sustenance. At another she is, however, also the one who sometimes withdraws, leaving the child to experience total helplessness. The child has no means of knowing whether she will return, and so each time the withdrawal occurs, he or she will experience fear and deep despair. Thus the mother who often withdraws becomes the object of intense negative feelings, and the child will experience violent, destructive rage towards her. It is this ambivalence or duality of experience within the small child, consisting of total devotion or total anger towards the mother, that is sometimes carried into adult life. In most people the process of growing up and being adequately parented allows the extremes of response and experience to be muted. The mother and father are seen for what they are, 'good enough' to allow the normal process of growing up to occur. Some individuals, however, have this process fractured by enforced separation from the mother, through war, abandonment or death. When such a break occurs there may well be within the personality a primal rage against the parent, combined with a desperate fear of being abandoned, and these may emerge at times of stress. Such internalized rage as well as the accompanying fear are, of course, capable of being projected outwards in the process that is known as transference. Relationships with other people in adult life can lead to re-enactment of these strong feelings which draw on the experiences of early infancy. Equally there are others who are idealized and adored with an irrational and uncritical zeal.

What I am claiming here is that certain individuals, as the result of experiences endured in early life, may have an inbuilt tendency to see the world in strongly polarized ways. The good is idealized and the bad feared, execrated and loathed. There is no room in their minds for anything other than the black and the white; all is seen in crystal-clear terms with no room for ambiguity or doubt. Such is a mindset that appears very similar to that already described in the previous chapter as a feature of fundamentalist religion. Perhaps fundamentalist Christianity, with its claim to possess clear unambiguous truth, will have a special appeal to those who have, for reasons of internal psychology, a need to deal with their history in a particular way. Some people will always have a need for total certainties, but this need may be rooted in long-forgotten experiences of trauma through separation and neglect. Such a person would find attractive the idea and promise of a God or a religious system which allows no uncertainties. Unlike the real parent who may have neglected or abandoned them, the divine reality or the scriptures given by that God are utterly reliable and certain.

Conversion and fundamentalist belief

The path to becoming a Christian convinced of the creed of the inerrancy of scripture does not, of course, arise out of being persuaded logically of such propositions. Individuals are converted to Christ in a variety of ways and contexts and it is in no way the intention of this book to doubt the sincerity of such experiences.

Of all the descriptions of becoming a Christian through sudden conversion, perhaps the most vivid is contained in a book by a Brazilian author, Reuben Alves, called *Protestantism and Repression*. Like many other commentators, Alves notes that conversion normally follows a crisis of some kind, a collapse of meaning and the consequent rise of anxiety. There is nothing around which to organize properly one's inner being. There is a void of identity which seeks to be filled. From the perspective of evangelical insight, this state of crisis and anxiety is a message from eternity. A diagnosis is offered in terms of the soul and its relation to God. The problem is not an awareness of a failure to be good, but a profound existential alienation from God, given the name 'sin'. The convert is called upon to surrender to Christ, who can rescue the individual from that anxiety, that sense of profound alienation and fear of eternal doom. These anxieties resonate with the earliest experience of the small child. In classic conversion sermons there is a twin pole of hope and reassurance opposite a 'matrix of terror'. The convert moves from fear and isolation to a deep sense that he has accepted Christ, a reality who is a focus of curative power, a being who gives access to eternal salvation in freedom from the former anxiety and fear. At the point of conversion, the details of the life of Christ, his teaching and death, are not important. He is welcomed into the heart as a source of peace, joy and certainty.

Once the convert has passed through the metamorphosis of surrender to Christ, Alves says, the community in which it has taken place quickly moves in to provide a framework of interpretation in which to express the new-found faith. The emotional language of freedom and joy becomes codified in the language of Protestant orthodoxy. In providing a brief description of the conversion experience, I have not attempted to suggest that there is anything other than a real dynamic life-changing event occurring in the life of individual Christians, and that warmth lives on in the way Christians continue to celebrate their faith within their Christian communities. There is, however, an uncomfortable fact that if the conversion has taken place against a background of induced guilt and terror, one reason for remaining in that state of conversion could be a deep fear of falling back into a state of despair once more. In other words Alves' model suggests that anyone who converts in such a context may possess a faith that cannot grow and change because it is functioning in the same way that a neurosis enables a patient to avoid facing up to an inner emotional problem. In the convert there will be a certainty about the reality of their experience, but that certainty will have qualities of absolutism and finality which leave no room for doubt or critical questioning. In short, the classical conversion experience required of evangelical believers may itself feed into the dogmatic cast of mind that is a feature of fundamentalist believers.

In another study of religious conversion by Chana Ullman, where the focus was wider than Christianity alone, it was noted that 80 per cent of those going through a religious conversion had experienced a problem in their relationship with their fathers. Twenty-three per cent of the non-convert group reported similar experiences. Only 18 per cent of the converts reported a positive relationship with their fathers. Ullman is reluctant to make too many conclusions from her findings, but she notes an old study from 1957, looking at the conversion of St Augustine from a psychoanalytic perspective, by C.A. Kliegerman. In it he had traced Augustine's conversion to a close relationship with his dominant mother in contrast to his failure to bond to his ineffectual and distant father. Kliegerman speculates that the moment of conversion was precipitated by a visit from his mother 'which rearoused and intensified the old conflicts of Augustine's youth'. The words of Augustine, 'It was her earnest care that Thou, my God, rather than he [natural father] shouldest be my father,' could be interpreted as the final victory of Augustine's mother, Monica, over her husband.

The mention of psychoanalysis brings us once again into contact with the writings of Melanie Klein and, behind her, Sigmund Freud. The theories of Freud made much of the way that belief in and understanding of God were supposedly linked to the patterns of relationships between children and their fathers. Religious faith, according to Freud, arises out of the disappointment in their parents that children experience and this gives rise to a need to transfer expectations for protection and safety to a new superior invincible power. For

Freud, God was a wish-fulfilment and an illusion which spared the child the recognition of his own helplessness. Religious conversion was thus a defensive process which had the effect of reducing anxiety. A real but unconscious anger against a natural father was replaced by a surrender to an illusory father.

Few interpreters today accept Freud's ideas without a great deal of qualification, but the work of Chana Ullman suggests that his insights into the meaning and interpretation of conversion are not entirely misplaced. Freud's interest in the role of the father, of course, belongs to a later stage in the child's development than the studies by Klein which were touched on earlier. His work has helped create the climate for an increased appreciation for the role of the father in the process of rearing a child. Consequently when there is an absent or ineffectual father there may sometimes be problems in a child's socialization and sex-role adaptation. The traditional role of the father is first of all as the mediator between the family and the outside world. Through his role of protector from its dangers, he helps the child to be assured that he or she will eventually be able to deal with that world as he has done. A father also traditionally takes a crucial role in the process of developing a social and moral awareness by setting limits on the child's behaviour. One interpretation of Ullman's observations is that when the father is for any reason absent, both these developmental processes may be compromised. In the first place there may arise a deep-seated anxiety about the outside world and its dangers. Secondly, the internal urges and impulses which have never been brought properly under control threaten to overwhelm the child or the adult who has grown up without the benefit of that role model of a father.

It does not take a great deal of imagination to suggest that the absence of a father figure early in life may produce in an individual unfinished business, both in relation to the outside world and to the inner world of impulse and instinct. There will have been a significant loss of control experienced both internally and externally. Conversion provides the individual with access to an omnipotent figure, under whose protection the world can be faced. This God will also 'save' the individual from the anxiety created by a failure to master the internal urges and instincts that have become so unbearable. It will not only be an internal God figure that can provide a father substitute for the one who has hitherto lacked such a role model. Within the orbit of the Christian community there can be a transference to any male individual in authority. It is not a coincidence that the title 'Father' has been given to significant male leader figures within some Christian communities, though not, of course, those within the fundamentalist orbit.

Conversion and faith

From this discussion about the dynamics of conversion and the earlier observations about Kleinian psychology it is possible to argue that the converted individual may, according to the first model, have entered into a mode of being which is in part the suppression of deep primal anxiety. In the second model, conversion may have provided a means of resolving the absence of a father figure in early childhood, a situation which has produced a lack of control over the world both internally and externally. Such models for understanding conversion should not suggest that the experiences are less than real, or that it is not God meeting people with particular psychological histories. Other models for describing the experience of Christian conversion no doubt exist, and caution should be taken not to make too many claims for any particular model. Nevertheless, it can be seen that among at least some of those experiencing a classical Christian conversion there may well be a mindset which is simultaneously fearful and rigid.

Harriet Harris notes, in her discussion of fundamentalist ideas, how much conservative writers are suspicious of the subjective in biblical interpretation. An insistence on truth being objective and literal may strike the observer as indicating a deep-seated fear of the subjective, precisely because their faith is so deeply enmeshed in it. A claim that the understanding of the Bible needs to be totally objective and unsullied by subjective assumptions may in fact conceal a cluster of subjective elements. A noted conservative scholar, James Packer, believes that 'evangelicals are bound as servants of God and disciples of Christ to oppose Subjectivism wherever they find it'. Such subjectivism is contrasted with the 'submissive spirit' of evangelicals. Thus there is seen to be a dividing line within Christianity between those who have the necessary humility to subject 'their own judgement wholly to Scripture', and those who 'subject Scripture in part to their own judgement'. The subjection to scripture may, according to the models, be simply an act of transference to a needed authority figure who was absent at an early stage in the child's life.

The weakness of the position that always argues for the objective truth of the Christian message in scripture is that it will fail to give due account for the subjective elements of faith that are a necessary part of the Christian life. If everything depends on a scientific knowledge of the 'saving events' of Christianity, then the idea of faith becomes redundant. Critics of conservative ideas of understanding the Bible, such as James Barr, point out that the important thing is that 'the Bible has emerged from these past events as an interpretation of them in faith... the authority of the Bible derives from the saving content of these events and the faith that responded to it, and not from the accuracy of its historical reporting'. As was seen in the last chapter, an obsession with the factual accuracy of scripture means that one's faith starts to depend on one's position on a number of obscure and not very edifying positions. It takes a considerable amount of energy to argue for the unity of Isaiah, the historicism of Jonah or the Pauline authorship of the epistles to Timothy. If it is here that the battle lines are drawn for defending the truth or falsity of one's faith, then one wonders whether any energy is left for defending the reasonableness of one's encounter with a gracious forgiving God in the person of Christ. While it is important to recognize that Christianity depends on the acceptance of certain 'facts' about the existence of Christ, it could be argued that far more crucial is the relationship with him that is established over a process of time. The position of difference between conservative Christians and their opponents is, perhaps, to be found in the interpretation of the word 'faith'. Is faith mainly to be understood as a confident belief that a proposition is true as a result of choosing the evidence that says it is true, or is it a passionate commitment to a person whose existence has been testified for 2,000 years and who is encountered in prayer, the sacraments and in the pages of scripture? John Barton argues that faith existed before the 'facts' about Jesus were written down, and could in principle survive without it.

From what has been said it should not be thought that personal religion among Christians who are fundamentalist in their way of expressing their faith is not important. Alongside a passionate attachment to the factual accuracy of the biblical record is a strong expectation of personal experience which will confirm the truth of the biblical text. This tendency is particularly strong among Christians who would describe themselves as charismatic. The charismatic tendency, which was looked at in the previous chapter, while in theory normally committed to doctrines of inerrancy will in practice give a precedence to the experiences that have been discovered in the course of their church life. The approach of apologists like John Wimber, who regard 'signs and wonders' as providing some sort of proof of God's power and reality which is immediate and accessible, has taken this emphasis on the importance of the interior personal side of faith to a new height. Although John Wimber would wish to claim an orthodox conservative position with regard to scripture, the content of his teaching has not been without numerous critics from within the evangelical world.

The church as a family system

In studying the way in which fundamentalist modes of thinking are sometimes experienced as abusive or harmful by individuals, I have found one particular model helpful as a way of understanding how the church or local Christian community seems to function. Considering the way a human family operates gives, I believe, a good insight into the way the local church nurtures its members either well or badly. It has already been noted how both father and mother play distinct and vital roles in helping the child to achieve some kind of psychological integration in the long process from babyhood to maturity. In a human family, both parents have a shared role which is to love, protect, nourish and value the child until he or she is able to achieve independent functioning. The notion of the 'good-enough' parent has already been mentioned as a shorthand expression for the parent who succeeds in the task of producing mentally and physically healthy children. As a contrast to 'good-enough' parenting there is a potentially damaging form of nurture known as 'conditional love'. This is a love that is offered only when the child fulfils the expectations of the parent, and behaves in a way that is judged to be correct. Good-enough parenting, by contrast, is marked by the unconditional love that every child needs for healthy development during growth. The exercise of conditional love produces a controlling, threatening and unpredictable environment. The child may achieve some sort of maturity within this latter regime, but it is likely to be at the expense of a sense of freedom, spontaneity and joy. Instead there may be fear, guilt and an inability to trust. The deepest individuality of the child may never be uncovered and for the rest of life he or she will be known as dull, conformist and without joy.

This family model, I believe, is applicable to church

congregations. The task of the good-enough parent, represented by the minister and leadership, is to provide an environment in which the parenting of God is made a reality to all members. That parenting, also called fatherhood, will offer forgiveness, unconditional love, acceptance and guidance through difficult times as well as good. It is in this way that the notion of the church as 'family' is a positive and wholesome one enabling the individual Christian member to move slowly along a path towards their own maturity and an experience of life in all its fullness. There will also be the sense of fair play, accountability and open communication that is asked of human families. While there may be in a church a family 'culture' which makes it distinct in relation to other families, that culture should not create enmity with others; it should merely be a celebration of the richness and diversity of human life. The majority of churches would aim to provide such an experience for their members and this fact should be acknowledged and honoured .

The family in which 'conditional parenting' is offered seems to describe the church life contained in most of the stories in this book. In these stories, the pattern which seems to emerge is that members of the congregation are offered 'belonging' on condition that they conform to the rules offered by the leadership. These rules are not just about behaviour, but also about beliefs and attitudes. In return for obedience the individual within the congregation is offered assurance that he or she is saved, and also enjoys the promise of eternal life with God. Thus the individual is allowed to feel safe, a sensation that they may only have enjoyed before as a very small child, and which has been lost in the harsh realities of adult life. But the membership of the church that creates this sense of safety is conditional; at any moment that promise can be withdrawn, and the individual left to fend for themselves outside the warmth of the family in a spiritual and social wilderness. If membership of a human family were granted on the same conditions, we would rightly be outraged and demand that society showed its disapproval on behalf of the children manipulated in this way. The 'conditional' church is able to perpetuate tight and effective control over its members because for many people caught up in such situations, the need to belong is so very strong. Most of the individuals in this book describe less-than-satisfactory childhoods, and thus their need for the parenting offered by the church would be the more acute.

The family model is then a useful one to make sense of what sometimes goes severely wrong in the dynamics of church life. Whether it takes place in a human family or in a church family, conditional parenting will often be experienced as abusive and the cause of anxiety and fear. It is too readily assumed that the moment an individual becomes an adult they are somehow free from the possibility of being abused in this way. The fact, however, as will be seen, that the church is offering ultimate love, forgiveness and salvation means that many people become highly dependent on the institution and its leaders, since to ignore or defy them means stepping out into an abyss of nothingness and despair. As suggested in the section above, which referred to the work of Melanie Klein, many people may carry the imprint of a memory of being abandoned by their mothers which has been resurrected by hearing the language of hell and damnation. The one who holds the key to avoiding re-entering that abyss has power indeed, and certain individuals do not readily cross or antagonize such people.

I would not, however, claim that all churches which conform to the conditional model of parenting are inevitably abusive. It might be suggested that the church and its leadership have assumed too much power over the membership, but that the power is not necessarily being used inappropriately or abusively. Nevertheless, considerable dangers still remain and a 'conditional' church is always liable to slip over into the kind of abusive style described in this study. Any church which deals in absolutes of belief and practice will be in danger of damaging its members, since such absolutes do not allow the possibility of dialogue, which is at the heart of open accountable systems of church life. Conditional styles of church life will have behind them the possibility of using sanctions, sanctions that have the capacity to put real fear into the hearts and minds of individuals who accept their power.

A further way in which family theory seems to be relevant to the stories recounted in this book is the way that churches which use conditional parenting seem to have some interest in maintaining a state of dependency in the members of the congregation that they serve. That at any rate seems to be the pattern reflected in the accounts. A parent keeping a child in a permanent state of dependency is not being actually cruel or abusive, but nevertheless the parenting can be seen as meeting parental needs rather than those of the child. A motive for keeping a child or a congregation in a state of dependency is power. To have people looking up to you and depending on your words and actions to feed them is highly gratifying for a parent or a leader. It also becomes addictive, and not a few of the leaders in the churches examined seem to have become dependent themselves on the power that they possess. Sometimes the power was exercised to gratify the ego of the leader; sometimes it was exercised with restraint and responsibility. In one extreme case it was acted out in sexual violence. Just as parents are required to temper their power over their children with love, so leaders are required to use their power over their flocks with restraint and with a dedication to serve their highest good. The abuse of power within a religious context is particularly damaging, since the victim has already surrendered much of their power in coming to the church and its leaders, and so is extremely defenceless and vulnerable to any power abuse that may be exercised against them.

Another way that the model of a human family seems to be paralleled in church life is in the difficulty that abused members have in breaking free. Just as an abused child will often have great difficulty in readjusting to a new set of relationships outside the family when finally the break comes, so a member of an abusive church will find leaving and starting again in a new church extremely difficult. The task of finding a new spiritual home will never be easy when so much has been invested emotionally and spiritually in the previous one. Trust may have been broken, relationships may have been betrayed, and these things are hard to rebuild. Another word to describe the feelings at breaking away from a human family or a church family is bereavement. Bereavement, as all faced by this common experience know, is not overcome quickly or easily. It needs time and sympathetic support for new ways of coping to be discovered. While the bereavement that comes to all of us through the death of a loved one is understood and well researched, little recognition and understanding is given to those who have ended long-standing associations with church communities because of some kind of abusive behaviour by those in authority. During the time I have been studying this whole area, I have become aware of a great many individuals who have suffered in this way, their numbers pointing to this as a substantial, but unrecognized, issue of church life. How such people can be helped is one of the questions being posed by this whole study. But it is clear that no strategies for helping such people can be found until their existence is recognized. At present there is little sign of this.

In summary, the theory of the way that families function is another useful model in seeking to identify and understand both good and bad practice in the context of congregational life. While this book, due to its subject matter, focuses on the bad end of congregational dynamics, it needs to be borne in mind that many, if not the majority of, churches try to meet both the emotional as well as the spiritual needs of their members without any suggestion of harm or humiliation being perpetrated against them. This study on abusive church families has only become necessary as the result of an apparent wall of silence over the whole issue. A generation ago a similar secrecy prevailed in the issue of violence towards women and children within human families, and the sexual mistreatment of children placed in some children's homes. The naming of abuse is the first step in putting in place the means to prevent its occurrence.

The guru and his disciple – a further model of religious dependence

The model that depicts a member of a Christian congregation functioning as a dependent child before a wise parent, represented by the minister or priest, is not unknown in other religious traditions. A comparable institution within Hindu and other Eastern spiritual traditions is that of the guru or holy man and his disciple. A book that analyses this relationship in a striking way that is illuminating to the current theme is one written by Joel Kramer and Diana Alstad, *The Guru Papers*. Many people might be tempted to regard the guru relationship as comparable to that of the spiritual director within Catholicism, but Kramer and Alstad give a starkly different perspective on the whole issue. Their description, however, seems to be reflecting the situation in the United States where attempts have been made, as elsewhere, to transplant elements of Hindu and other Eastern spiritual practices into a Western environment. Their negative evaluation of the way that the guru relationship operates both in theory and practice in the United States should perhaps be taken as a comment on Eastern spiritual traditions attempting to find a home among individuals brought up in the West, rather than a general appraisal of Eastern religion. Nevertheless, this study of the authoritarian relationship between guru and disciple, as it has developed in the West, can be examined with profit, since it would seem to give a further model through which to consider the way that religious authority operates.

In the book, the description of what draws an individual to

a guru begins with a consideration of the way the world is perceived by the baby. According to Kramer and Alstad, the baby is at the centre of the universe. When the baby cries, he or she has a sense of control as people come to meet its needs; 'the universe around it moves.' Most infants have a memory of being in this good place of 'basic well-being, fundamental security and also of power'. Any individual, especially those for whom later life is unfulfilling, can long to return to this place, one of power, free from conflict and 'where a benign, all-powerful intelligence is taking care of things'. Spirituality for such a person may be paradoxically not a movement of growth, but 'a return to the known'.

The Guru Papers makes the striking claim that spiritual surrender to a guru figure in one's life is 'perhaps the easiest way to simulate that bygone state of innocence'. The guru presents himself not as a figure of tentative searching, but as a powerful, 'realized' and complete human being who has achieved the search for meaning and truth. Because the guru capable of attracting disciples has to be seen as a reliable source of enlightenment, and thus in some way infallible, there will be enormous pressure on him to conform to this model. There will almost inevitably be a certain dishonesty in such posturing, as it will require him to deny the part of himself which Christians would describe as 'fallen' humanity. A guru cannot, for example, afford to own his self-interest, his desire or any fear in himself. In order to attract disciples, he must claim in some way to be above such human attachments.

On the part of the disciple, there will be an expectation that he or she will surrender their will to their master. There will also be a letting go of attachments to the material world, in addition to the part of the personality I would describe as the ego. In their book, Kramer and Alstad make clear that the act of surrender by the disciple is only possible by letting into the personality an equivalent degree of external control by another. The reward for this abandonment of internal control is access to the spiritual experiences that the guru is believed to be able to mediate because of his enlightened state. All attachments in the disciple are thought to interfere with the ability to share this spiritual enlightenment. The one attachment that the disciple is not freed from, the authors note, is the inbuilt conditioning 'to look for an authority that one can trust more than oneself'. Thus a collusive relationship is established which appears to suit both parties. The disciple is attached to having the guru as his centre, while the guru is 'attached to the power of being others' centre' even though he is supposed to be above any form of attachment.

The price of such spiritual surrender is, according to *The Guru Papers*, very high. The numerous scandals in the West surrounding Eastern holy men and gurus show just how rarely, if at all, the guru figure is able to rise above attachments of various kinds. Examples of sexual, material and power abuse abound in the literature. Attachment to any of these things on the part of the guru should theoretically be impossible. Perhaps the weakness of the institution of guru/disciple is the way that both sides want to believe in the possibility of infallible knowledge and a state of detached enlightenment. A more realistic understanding of human nature suggests that such a state will probably never be achieved. To pretend to have achieved a state of sinlessness and total detachment is going to be, according to Christian theology, a state of self-deceit and delusion. Nevertheless, it has been suggested that there are powerful human dynamics in all of us, reaching right back to infancy, which want to surrender to an all-knowing, all-powerful individual who will remove us from the need to live out of our own relative powerlessness.

The action of surrender or devotion to a living guru is a common form of religious practice in the East and (I would claim) in the Christian West. Why, in view of the hazards of power abuse that I have hinted at, does it remain so relatively popular in Western societies? The first immediate benefit of devotion to the guru is the creation of an apparent community, as well as a sharing of experience with other disciples of the guru. The personal boundaries that have been breached through the initial discipling process make one transparent and open to those who have a similar devotion. This capacity for intimate bonding with the group does not, however, survive beyond the time of membership. Members of the guru's entourage do not, in other words, have a greater capacity for love in a Christian sense. The bonding they experience could be described better as a mutual clinging. Secondly, there will also be the possibility of reconnecting with the conflict-free innocence of infancy. Obedience to the guru also achieves a sense of having overcome one's self-centredness, although this may be a re-enactment and re-experiencing of the conditioning of childhood when goodness was equated with instant obedience to parental authority.

The strength given to the disciple through attachment to the guru reflects a similar power given by church leaders who act in a parental role towards their members. Both offer a kind of parental protection as well as the solidarity of the group. This is in stark contrast to the relative powerlessness of the individual. To leave these behind means, on the part of the disciple, the risk of returning to a state of independent functioning which is extremely painful. It is far better to be the dependent child within the family, or with an all-knowing and infallible religious guru who has taken over at the centre of one's personality. The dynamics that hold the individual in place within both types of group are very similar.

The Guru Papers contains a great deal of material about the psychology involved in the particular and distinctive relationship between spiritual master and disciple. Much of it could be read with profit by those who seek to understand the phenomena surrounding any situation in which, for example, religious devotion and sexual scandal are in some way intertwined. Also, the capacity of religious power and authority to be blind to the issues of transference on the part of disciples or followers is of great interest and importance.

Enough, however, has been shared of the book to indicate another model to help to understand the attractiveness of the fundamentalist mindset. It has already been indicated that participation in a church where there is teaching on the infallibility of scripture will often tie people strongly to the expounders of that scripture rather than to the unmediated text. In other words, individuals may come to believe in the doctrine of an infallibility of scripture because they have invested considerable devotion in the leaders who teach the idea.

The leadership may also often present themselves as powerful religious figures with heroic and saintly personae. This will sometimes lead individual church or sect members to adopt a relationship of profoundly unhealthy personal veneration towards these heroes. In another cultural setting they might be described as 'groupies'. Such devotion is sometimes rewarded by making the disciple feel close to the power that is apparently exhibited by the religious leader or guru, whether in terms of shared spiritual experiences or privileged knowledge. But the cost of this closeness to spiritual power and enlightenment is often too high. The readiness to surrender personal power, reasoning faculties and material attachments may mean that the disciple becomes an empty vessel, except when close to his master. What appears to be a position of great privilege and exaltation may be in fact a regression to a state of personal and spiritual impoverishment. Such a deep-seated desire to revisit the experience of the infant who has no responsibilities, only a contented, self-satisfied security, will eventually give way to a recognition that the personality has been severely depleted through this process.

The Guru Papers resonates strongly with this study as it is suggestive of the fact that a demand for infallibility in a book or a person may be rooted in a deep psychological need far more than in a profound grasp of the nature of God. In theory, access to a set of infallible scriptures should render any kind of doubt or struggle in life redundant. The book has the answer; there is no need to worry or doubt. Some Christians succeed in convincing themselves that such a life is indeed possible. The rest, struggling with life in all its ambiguities and uncertainties, are surely closer to reality. Just as Jesus faced up to every aspect of human life, both in its glory and its utter degradation, so should Christians recognize that this is a path which is closer to the true human adventure to which God calls them.

Conclusion

This chapter has sought to indicate various models which may help in understanding the phenomenon of fundamentalist Christianity within today's society from the point of view of psychology and experience. Fundamentalist Christianity seeks to present itself as based on an objective and scientific apprehension of truth, yet it has been suggested that it finds itself often rooted in fear and a sense of anxiety. That anxiety frequently traces itself back to the childhood experience of being parented less than adequately. In that memory there may be a deeply imprinted fear of being abandoned and left to face the world without support. Alternatively, life at the earliest period may have represented the only time of personal stability, and experience after that may have seemed impoverished compared with that original awareness. Thus some individuals are susceptible to the influence of anyone who can assist them in returning to that primordial experience.

It has been claimed that in the need to find certainties in their expression of faith, fundamentalist Christians may be seeking to overcome the uncertainties of their young life or the ambiguities of adult existence. Scientific truth, with its promise of precision and dependability, gives fundamentalist

Christians the apparent reliability and certainty that their life lacks or may always have lacked.

Nevertheless, as has been seen, projecting onto scripture the values of 'fact' and scientific accuracy often has the effect of destroying the character of the writing that is found there. Confusion between sign and symbol in scripture forces the reader to ignore many of the literary forms to be found there in favour of literal description and fact, and makes the Bible into a quite different book. Instead of the wonder and suggestion of symbolic writing evoking the mystery and presence of God and his activity on Earth, the Bible is presented as a textbook which promises new life and salvation and needs only to be 'believed' to become effective in the life of the believer. A more adequate model for a relationship with the Bible would describe scripture as an object of great beauty, engaging people's minds, vision and longing. While Christians can glimpse God through the Bible, they can never possess him or have final precise knowledge of him. They can only journey towards him using the path, direction and knowledge revealed by Jesus. That process never ends for the individual, nor does the church ever complete the task of describing and articulating in words what God wants people to know of himself. That journey goes on as long as life endures.

The power that Jesus understands and exhibits may challenge, but it never threatens or intimidates.

Chapter Nine

Jesus and Power

In order to discover the attitude of Jesus to all that has been described so far in this book, it is necessary to turn to the New Testament. There is no better starting point for unveiling the historical figure of first-century Palestine.

The major historical sources for the life of Jesus are the synoptic gospels, Matthew, Mark and Luke, but it has been known by scholars for decades that it is not valid simply to quote the words attributed to Jesus as if he actually spoke them. Although such a statement is extremely disturbing to a Christian reared on notions of biblical accuracy and reliability, the situation as regards discovering a historical person behind the gospel writings has, in many ways, improved in the last thirty years. From a low point of utter scepticism following the school of Rudolf Bultmann in the 1940s and 1950s, scholarly consensus has moved back to a belief that it is possible to sketch out a distinctive personality and teaching for Jesus behind the gospel accounts. The problem for scholars has been the realization that the gospels have been overlaid with material which has a setting in the teaching and life of the early church, rather than in the life of Jesus. No distinction was made between the teaching of the risen Jesus that was given to the church, as it gathered to remember and continue his work, and the words of the earthly Jesus of Nazareth. Although people today are reared on the idea of the importance of precise historical memory and factual accuracy, this was not the case for the early Christians. Every section of the gospels can be shown to have a setting in the particular concerns of church life, rather than in any interest in recalling details of Jesus' life for their own sake. This is not the same thing as saying, as will be shown, that there are no accurate historical recollections of the words or actions of Jesus, but that all such recollections have been made to serve the purpose of the church and its need to articulate its message and theology.

This distinction is seen in Paul's account of the last supper in 1 Corinthians 11. Clearly Paul was not present at that event, but he claims to have received the tradition of celebrating it 'from the Lord'. Scholars have traced how the Passover supper of Jesus became the eucharist of the early Christians, and even though the detail of this process is lost, it is clear that subtle changes of emphasis did occur. The only way to account for such a development is in the light of the claim that no distinction was made between the words of the risen Lord to his church and the historical memories of the actual words of Jesus of Nazareth. There is an indication that this same process is at work in Acts, when Luke writes of Ananias saying to Paul, 'The God of our fathers appointed you... to see the Righteous One and to hear his very voice, because you are to be his witness...' (Acts 22:14f.).

The task of recovering authentic echoes of the historical man Jesus beneath the layers of early church interpretation is made possible through comparison of the things attributed to

Jesus and the ideas and practices known to belong to early Judaism or the early church. If some saying attributed to Jesus has no obvious context in the practice or thought of his contemporaries, then it is reasonable to suppose that it preserves the historical memory of something Jesus actually said. Although this process, called 'the criterion of dissimilarity', might be thought to be fairly reductionist of the gospel accounts, it does in fact yield a rich harvest, particularly in the way that it allows the parables, as they are in the Bible, to be seen as close to the words of the historical figure of Jesus. The freshness of the ideas and the radical element of challenge in them allow us, according to the consensus of scholarly opinion, to regard the telling of parables as an authentic part of the mission of the historical Jesus.

It has also been clearly demonstrated, particularly through the work of Joachim Jeremias, that the written versions of the parables have usually passed through a process of development. The distinctive ways in which the parables are recorded in each of the synoptic gospels can be seen to reflect the different theological needs of the writers, rather than inaccurate copying or recollection. A detailed study of the way that the versions differ from one another shows how a tradition was being developed. It is possible to work out which version is the least developed and thus arrive at the earliest and most primitive. This version will give, if not the actual words of Jesus, at least something that is not far from the historical figure.

All this has been written by way of introduction to indicate that I do not propose to plunder indiscriminately the gospel accounts of Jesus to construct a figure that will 'prove' a personality which is agreeable to the purposes of this book. I do, however, believe that the initially shadowy figure of the historical Jesus of Nazareth does emerge, through the work of the scholars, into the light of day with a considerable clarity and coherence. It is that Jesus who will, as far as possible, stand before us and be questioned about the themes that have been raised by this book.

Jesus and the kingdom

Any attempted reconstruction of the original teaching and ministry of Jesus has to make sense of his central motif, the kingdom of God. This single theme is essential in giving meaning to the miracles, the calls to discipleship and the welcoming of the outcast into fellowship, as well as being the focus of Jesus' ethical and parabolic teaching. A question immediately arises as to the meaning of the kingdom. In trying to get some clear idea of how to understand the expression, modern ideas and ways of thinking face their first barrier. We tend to think in terms of abstracts and ideals, while the Jew of Jesus' time knew only concrete realities. For Jesus and the Old Testament tradition behind him, the kingdom of God described the rule and sovereignty of God, and there would be experienced, during this reign, his power and mighty deeds. At a late stage in the Old Testament, the notion of kingdom comes to be associated with a final intervention by God, one that will transform or change the world decisively and bring redemption for his people. In Christian understanding, the word 'kingdom' is firmly embedded in the Lord's prayer. When Jesus uses the term, it seems to have two distinct aspects. The first is the idea of

God breaking through into human history and experience, and the second is his proclamation that the kingdom is a state in which the redeemed dwell.

Using the criteria mentioned in the first section, a particular verse from Luke has been generally regarded by scholars as recalling some genuine words of Jesus: 'But if it is by the finger of God that I drive out the devils, then be sure the kingdom of God has already come upon you' (Luke 11:20). The passage enables it to be seen that certain events in the ministry of Jesus are viewed as demonstrating God acting in the present, in this case in a situation of conflict against evil. The experience of one individual has become the focus of God's activity, rather than the kingdom being in some generalized event involving everyone. This interpretation is further confirmed by words of Jesus in Luke 17:21: 'for in fact the kingdom of God is among you'. The natural meaning of these words implies that God is active in the experience of individuals, and Jesus is both an agent of this activity and one who draws the attention of those who will listen to this event.

The teaching about the kingdom gives coherence to all of Jesus' sayings and actions. It certainly represents a key to understanding the point of the parables. All the parables, when stripped of later accretions, present, in a remarkably vivid way, the idea of God's active intervention in human life with the corresponding need for a response and decision on the part of the person faced with it. God moves towards his people, and he is to be received with joy and with a sense of confidence that he has both the present and the future at his command. Above all the movement of God provides forgiveness and reconciliation for those who turn to receive it.

Beyond the parables there is one crucial tradition about Jesus' life which was beyond the capacity of the early church to invent, and which can be seen as an outworking and proclamation of the kingdom. This was the way that he, contrary to Jewish custom and law, kept table fellowship with 'tax-gatherers and sinners' (Luke 5:30). Of all the actions that Jesus carried out in his life, this went the furthest in offending and alienating the Jewish leaders. To proclaim the kingdom in the context of such meals must have seemed a total blasphemy and was itself sufficient to account for Jesus being handed over for crucifixion. Jesus lived at a time of heightened nationalistic sentiment, with the tension between Jew and Gentile at its most acute. For the Jew the kingdom was a future ground of hope, the ultimate vindication of the Jewish nation by God, who was going to come and reward Israel for its faithfulness to the Law. Jesus came along and claimed that they were wrong in their understanding of the outsiders, that God's kingdom was aimed at them as well as all who would receive it. The veracity of these meals is attested not only by the improbability of their having been invented, but also by some words attacking Jesus recorded in Matthew 11:19: 'a glutton and a drinker, a friend of tax-gatherers and sinners!' These words, which apparently have echoes of Aramaic poetry, can be seen to represent a very early strand of tradition about Jesus. The words 'glutton' and 'drinker' would appear to reflect the quality of joy that surrounded the meals and hospitality that Jesus shared with this group.

I have now sketched out the beginnings of a coherent picture of the kind of impact that Jesus made on his contemporaries, the outlines of his teaching and activity. He was a man who believed that the kingdom of God, the sphere of his direct activity in the world, could be known and experienced by all who opened themselves to it. That movement of God towards his people was revealed in the forgiveness, love and healing that individuals knew through their association with Jesus. The kingdom was at odds with evil, and at times its impact resulted in conflict, but on other occasions it was received in a spirit of joy and freedom. Jesus himself was possessed of a radical awareness of the way that this apprehension of the kingdom cut through certain conventions, laws and regulations set up by human religious institutions. It was new wine, threatening and challenging the old wineskins of custom and convention. Thus, in spite of all the problems outlined at the beginning of reconstructing any knowledge of the historical Jesus of Nazareth, there is apparently enough material which is consistent in itself to use as a kind of yardstick to evaluate other recorded actions and sayings. For the next section of this chapter I want to look at the statements about power that are recorded in the gospels, and look particularly to see whether they cohere with the picture of Jesus that has so far emerged.

Jesus' sayings about power

In his gospel, Mark records a radically challenging statement about power, which Christians have ever since found difficult to internalize within their thinking and their institutions: 'You know that in the world... the recognized rulers lord it over their subjects... That is not the way with you' (Mark 10:42–43). Clearly for Jesus the authority of God as experienced within the kingdom is not like that. The power that Jesus understands and exhibits may challenge, but it never threatens or intimidates. There may be burdens and heavy responsibilities which fall to human beings who accept the kingdom of God, but the response called for in return, summed up in the word 'repentance', seems to imply both freedom and conviction. The same freedom marks all Jesus' associations with individuals. He mixed with people of all classes and walks of life, without heeding the criticism that in doing so he was disobeying the Jewish law. It was a freedom exercised for the sake of freeing others. The choice of eating with those beyond the law had, as its aim, their inclusion within the sphere of God's gracious acceptance and love. It is, in short, a freedom of service. All the miracle stories can be seen as acts of freeing those who were oppressed and enslaved by sickness of whatever kind. For Jesus, God's power was active, liberating those it touched, and Jesus himself was a servant of that power.

There is one crucial section, recorded in two of the synoptic gospels, which shows that Jesus discovered the freedom of God's power to be not without cost. This is the story of the temptations. The temptations are not to be read as edifying or moralizing stories to help Christians who themselves face temptation. The temptations seem to be actual accounts of Jesus' struggle to understand how power was to be used in his ministry. Each of the temptations represents a question about the use of power. The first, as recorded in Matthew 4:3–4, concerns the possibility of using power to create food miraculously. No doubt such power would relieve human need, but it would also focus the expectations of those who received such food well away from the message that he had to share. Seen as a wonder-worker and one able to meet physical needs, it would have been hard, if not impossible, to be also seen as the embodiment of love which sought to challenge and draw people to God.

The same point applies to the next temptation, for which the devil sets Jesus on the pinnacle of the Temple (Matthew 4:5–7). Could God's purposes ever be served by such a dramatic demonstration of power? Should the use of miracles designed merely to impress people be contemplated? Would people follow a leader whose appeal lay in the possession of power? The same questions need to be asked of many Christians today who exercise power and influence through a 'signs and wonders' ministry. Are those who admire them really attracted to their message, or are they impressed by their power, following them so that they can obtain some of it through closeness to its apparent catalyst?

The final temptation of Jesus was to exercise power politically, after being shown 'all the kingdoms of the world in their glory' (Matthew 4:8). Such an exercise of power could force human beings to follow a particular way, rather than choose it freely. Jesus faced these temptations, these possible ways to exercise power, and rejected them all. The way, in fact, that Jesus chose to exhibit power for the rest of his ministry was a way that risked him losing everything. By allowing his hearers and followers freedom to choose, he also gave them freedom to reject. He was the sower, casting his seed with no guarantee that it would reach the good soil and take root and grow. By setting up no power structures in his lifetime, the whole of his teaching and insights about God risked being dissipated and allowed to be like water running into thirsty sand. The temptations, the ways that could have facilitated a structured memory of what he stood for and taught, were rejected in favour of freedom without power and love without coercion or imposition.

Jesus' denunciation of tyranny and hypocrisy

The proclamation of the kingdom by Jesus resulted, as has been seen, in a situation of conflict. In the first place, that kingdom reality came face to face with mysterious sources of evil power that were perceived to be at work in the lives of the sick and diseased. These can be described collectively as the demonic. In the second place, Jesus' forthright proclamation of freedom and the new reality of God's forgiveness came into head-on collision with the powers of human authority that sought to control access to God's favour. Not only do the gospels record details of arguments and controversies over the keeping of the law, but Jesus is also recorded as denouncing the power structures of his time, which he apparently believed to be working against the kingdom and all that it represented. These denunciations reflect passion and anger on the part of Jesus, feelings apparently far stronger than any he may have had about the sins he encountered in the ordinary people he met. In short, Jesus seems to have been more affected by power abuse than any other human failing, presumably because he recognized it as doing far more damage than the other sins of his time.

While there is much in the gospels about the way the traditions of the scribes and the Pharisees had masked the will of God, the hostility of Jesus is also focussed on the rich and powerful. It does not seem that possession of riches was in itself an evil; rather the wealth of an individual was sometimes seen by Jesus to be the result of exploitation of others, and in addition it led to indifference and lack of compassion towards the vast underclass of the day. Zacchaeus, in Luke 19, had cheated and exploited other people in pursuit of wealth, but through his determination to restore the money to the cheated and fulfil his obligations to the poor, he ceased to be a sinner in Jesus' eyes. It might be imagined that Zacchaeus was still a relatively wealthy man, even after all these obligations had been met, but 'salvation' had been obtained because the pursuit of money no longer dominated his life. Something far more important now replaced it. The comments by Jesus about the worship of 'mammon' touch on the central issue. Was wealth, like power, to be the goal of people's lives, or were they able to accept the will of God and his kingdom as the central focus of their existence? The kingdom of God would always find itself in contrast and, indeed, opposition to attitudes which either directly or indirectly involved exploitation of or power abuse towards other people.

For many people reared on children's portraits of Jesus as the gentle and kind friend of all, it still comes as something of a shock to be reminded that he was capable of human anger. The story of the driving out of the money-changers from the Temple implies that Jesus was passionate about preventing the dishonouring of God that he saw taking place within the sacred precincts. But the same passionate anger is recorded in the denunciations of the scribes and Pharisees set out in Matthew 23 and Luke 11. The anger is particularly focussed on their use of the law to oppress people. This is in addition to their vanity and hypocrisy. In Luke's account the scribes are singled out for the way they 'load men with intolerable burdens, and will not put a single finger to the load'. They are also accused of approving of the killing of the prophets, and denying knowledge to the people by controlling their access to it. The experts on the law thus stand accused of manipulating and controlling other people through their very expertise. Finally, the scribes and Pharisees are condemned for doing all that they can to convert people to their way of thinking, and in the process making the proselyte 'twice as fit for hell as you are yourselves'.

The passionate accusation against the official practitioners of the Jewish faith is not only that they have failed to understand its true spirit for themselves, but that they have used their privileged access to the law to set themselves above and apart from the ordinary people, oppressing them and denying them access to the true word and will of God. It is this that arouses the special condemnation and anger of Jesus. Such implacable opposition to the power-brokers of the Jewish faith would almost certainly have put Jesus in the position of a notable public enemy. The privileges of the powerful were being attacked in a way that could not be tolerated.

Jesus' attack against the religious establishment of his day was met with resistance. The synoptic gospels all describe a multitude of plots and conspiracies against him, culminating in the betrayal, trial and crucifixion. Those who are said to have plotted against him, the scribes, Pharisees, Sadducees and Herodians, all held positions of influence in that society, and all were threatened by Jesus' condemnation of established religious power structures. It can be seen that Jesus criticized all such structures on behalf of and in defence of their victims, the poor, the outcasts and those alienated from God because the religious system had denied them access. There is a keen sense that Jesus strongly identified with all these 'sinners', and that his love for them, and desire for them and indeed all humankind to be part of the kingdom, was the dominant motif of his work on Earth. It was the driving force of his human existence and indeed the expression of God's will for his life. With the awareness of God at work in him and in his ministry, Jesus was able to look forward to an eschatological breaking through of God's kingdom. It is hard to know exactly what meaning Jesus gave to his own death, but clearly he did see some meaning in it. I believe there may well have been an identification with the innocence of the servant described in Isaiah 53. Jesus may well have been convinced that he was the one 'who had made himself as a sacrifice for sin' so that he may 'vindicate many, himself bearing the penalty of their guilt'.

Conclusion

An account of Jesus has been set out which attempts to reconstruct historically some aspects of his life and his attitude to power. There does appear to be in the synoptic gospels a coherent picture of Jesus having a radical attitude to issues of power and oppression. His passionate attack on those who abused power suggests that the right use of power was an important if not central part of his teaching. The God of Jesus was a God who invited human beings to be part of his kingdom, and there was never any attempt to force individuals to do or accept anything which would compromise their freedom and their full humanity.

The often-quoted emphasis on love as a key element of gospel teaching resonates with this understanding of power. As all human beings know, love worthy of the name can never be forced in an individual. If there is fear or compulsion involved in a relationship, it can be concluded that love is absent or severely compromised. Love, as Paul reminds readers in the magnificent passage from 1 Corinthians 13, is 'patient… kind and envies no one… never selfish, not quick to take offence'. Although Paul does sometimes stray into somewhat forceful coercive language, it is clear that in this passage at any rate he has closely identified with the spirit of Jesus that has been revealed in the gospel accounts. In all Jesus' dealings with individuals in the gospels, one never detects power games on his part towards the vulnerable, but only compassion and a longing to give back to them the dignity and power that they have lost or been denied. The outbursts of anger that Jesus displayed were directed towards those who caused the weak and vulnerable to stumble.

As the end of this book approaches, it remains to comment on the fact that if Jesus were alive today, and facing the situations that have been set out in earlier chapters, then he would without a doubt have taken the side of the victims of power abuse against their abusers. Whether thinking of the children in the Christian school being humiliated through physical punishment, Kathleen's exposure to battering through fashionable diagnoses, or Rita's continuing humiliation by patriarchal churches during her search for healing, the spirit of Jesus identified in this chapter is never encountered. What have been seen in the stories are the very things that Jesus used so much passion in condemning. Among other things, there has been the use of religion to humiliate individuals, the restricting of free, open understanding of the scriptures in favour of an approved party line and the imposing of heavy burdens of conformity and belief, so that the individual can belong to the favoured group of those who are to be saved. Above all, there has been the pervasiveness of fear creeping into churches and groups, a fear that is destructive of the very spontaneity and freedom that seems to have been so much a feature of Christ's ministry. Few churches or institutions are able to provide such an environment of freedom and creativity, but while those difficulties are recognized, there can be little excuse for churches or institutions which carry his name abusing power in a manner that runs totally counter to Jesus' example and spirit.

This shadow of ministry is, I believe, the exact opposite of service; it is the use of position and power to obtain emotional gratification.

Chapter Ten

Summing Up

If I had to use one word to sum up the features of the churches that have harmed and undermined the individuals who have appeared in this book, it would be 'control'. Each one of the fellowships or churches commented on has claimed a high degree of control over its membership, and has dictated in detail the content of its belief system and what is acceptable in every area of its life. It has been postulated that a Christianity of control is a religion that appeals to people who have, in some area of their life, lost control, whether through external circumstances or through unresolved psychological need. It has also been claimed that for some people a particular area of vulnerability is found in their past experience of family life. Whether as the result of an absent father or inadequate parenting of some kind, they have become particularly attracted to the promise of an accepting family, offering them all that their blood families failed to provide in terms of guidance, acceptance and love. The church has, for them, become a place of safety, of predictability, instead of the chaos that threatens to well up in them from their insecure past or from the outside world. In a fascinating article in a book called *Fundamentalism and*

Gender, Karen Brown locates one particular area of chaos in the breakdown of Enlightenment society in the West. Many of the promises of greater control that Enlightenment philosophy promised over nature, in terms of technological progress and steady evolution of society, have not been fulfilled. Instead, fearful Christians look out at a society threatened by an ever-growing tide of lawlessness and lack of predictability. The fear engendered by this new unpredictability breeds a strong conservatism both in politics and religion. In extreme cases, conservative Christians abandon the world and head for the hills to await the final collapse of society, bolstered by their guns and their millennial fantasies.

If, as I would claim, the need to exercise tight control within the church arises out of psychological rather than theological factors, then those who seek to challenge fundamentalist religion will need to be aware that any head-on confrontation is unlikely to be successful. Throughout this book I have mostly tried to avoid arguing with the position of fundamentalist Christians by, for example, quoting counterbalancing texts; rather I have simply pointed out that particular patterns of belief can have consequences that cause human suffering. If I am right in seeing that the position of 'Bible-believing' Christians as frequently linked to issues of human psychology, then it would be unwise to seek to debate with it. Reason and psychological passion do not make for equal debating partners. The passion from the other side would overwhelm my position, and quickly show up my weak and unskilled abilities in the area of marshalling biblical texts in my defence. Debates that are conducted by quoting biblical texts to prove a point are, in any case, of questionable merit as the society values represented by the Old Testament are often of little guidance for the ethical issues of today. It is worth remarking how little encouragement there is from conservative interpreters to pore over the details of the society reflected by the book of Leviticus. Christians are also not to enquire too deeply into the behaviour of Israelite soldiers after they had conquered their enemies. God, as understood by some Old Testament writers, seems at times to have willed nothing but total destruction for Israel's enemies (e.g. Joshua 10:28 and 11:10–11), and such texts came as a solace to Christian armies such as the crusaders in their murderous rampage through the Near East in the Middle Ages. Text-quoting from scripture on its own will seldom result in a conclusive, unassailable position which cannot be counter-quoted from another part of scripture. It is this fact that indicates the use of the Bible to discover the realities of the Christian faith has to arise out of a far more sophisticated method than simply quoting a favoured text or verse.

If the church as a whole is to have a counterbalancing position about the nature of Christian truth to the one that uses Christian teaching and doctrine in a way that oppresses people, then it needs to present it in an oblique way rather than head-on. I have yet to work out fully how this might be done, but it would have to begin with an affirmation of those values that have been identified as a feature of Christ's teaching in the gospels. In the place of humiliation and shame should be the emphasis on forgiveness and the assertion of individual worth. In the place of exploiting the vulnerable, should be the affirmation of Christ's protest on behalf of the weak and marginalized. Jesus' attitude towards children would become the feature of Christian families, rather than appeals to some of the values of the book of Proverbs. Above all, the exercise of power would need to be handled with enormous care and sensitivity, so that no one who came into the orbit of the church's life ever felt bruised or battered by this encounter.

The formation of church leadership

The previous paragraph contains very broad brush strokes about the shape of a church that could challenge the culture of control that exists in many fundamentalist churches today. It remains to move from vague generalities to spelling out more precisely how a real difference could be made in the atmosphere of many churches, by looking at the issue of forming and training the leadership. Although this study has focussed on the issue of church leadership in charismatic and fundamentalist settings, power abuse does, in fact, exist as a real problem for churches of all kinds. If I have given the impression that power issues are only to be found in one specific culture, then I must repeat that I do not believe this to be so. The reason for the particular problem in charismatic and fundamentalist settings is that when power abuse occurs it is supported by a particular powerful system of theology and scriptural backing, and this makes it more difficult to resist and counter. Where it happens in other non-fundamentalist settings, it will be propped up by other theological, social and psychological sanctions, which may be equally effective and abusive.

The previous chapter focussed on Jesus and the

temptations that he experienced in the desert. It was suggested that what were reported as the temptations of the devil were in fact an exploration of the various options for exercising power in his ministry. He rejected them all in favour of a quite different way of using power, and this led to the cross. Another way of describing the temptations is that in them, Jesus was meeting his 'shadow'. This concept of the shadow, which was coined first by Carl Jung, is one that has been found by many to be very useful in describing the hidden, unacknowledged part of our personality. We meet our shadow in the things we feel passionate about when criticizing other people. When we hate the man of violence, it may be that we have not owned up to our own internal violence. To talk about the shadow of Jesus may seem unduly presumptuous, but clearly in the story there do seem to be real possible alternative options for Jesus' ministry, ones that would have given an expression to his calling, even if in an incomplete form. Above all, the 'shadow ministry', in any one of its three forms, would have allowed Jesus to avoid the cross and receive the acclamation of many. Clearly Jesus had to penetrate deeper into his awareness of God and transcend that shadow. In Jungian terms he had to know it and befriend it before he could move beyond it to his true vocation.

In speaking about the shadow of Jesus, I also want to introduce the idea of the shadow of Christian ministry. Most ministers within the church will speak about the concept of vocation, the idea that ministry is something that they have found in some way to have been chosen for them. They have allowed themselves to cooperate with that call and have offered themselves for Christian ministry. Most ministers will see their ministry in terms of service and being available for the needs of others, as well as teaching and forming Christian disciples. All will have internalized, at some point in their training, the picture of Jesus washing the feet of his disciples, and the judgement scene in Matthew 25 in which the righteous are seen as those who have fed the hungry, welcomed the stranger and visited those in prison. A model for ministry is clear, but there is also a need to face up to what I shall call the shadow of ministry. This is, I believe, the exact opposite of service; it is the use of position and power to obtain emotional gratification. Unfortunately congregations of whatever kind may often want to cooperate with the shadow rather with the ideal of ministry. It is easier to have a vicar or a minister who controls you, and tells you what to do and to believe, than to have one who surrenders his power for an authority of service and humility.

Many of the ministers in the stories have quite given up any pretence of being the servants of their communities. They have allowed themselves to act out the shadow of their ministry, aided and abetted by congregations who, for reasons of personal need, want a powerful and controlling figure in charge. It is difficult from the outside always to assess what precisely is going on in such a collusion between minister and people, but it has been suggested that both sides, though apparently content with the arrangement, may be surrendering any chance of spiritual and emotional maturing. As far as the minister is concerned, once this particular pattern of being in control has been established, it is hard to see how any change can ever easily take place. Such a way of relating to the flock becomes habitual. The acting out of the shadow of ministry, with its apparent emotional rewards, removes the minister further and further from the pattern of Christ. Authoritarianism then becomes a fixed psychological pattern. Situations where such a style impedes ministry, such as particular pastoral settings of caring for the vulnerable, are not able to be handled. A pattern of relating has been established which cannot easily be broken.

If it is difficult to break the pattern of authoritarian behaviour in clergy, what can be done? For a start, power issues could be far more openly acknowledged in the training colleges for clergy and ministers. In Jungian terms, ordinands need to be taught to enter their own personal wilderness, meet their personal shadow and befriend it. Like Jesus, they have to own up to their temptation to exercise power wrongly before it can be transcended and avoided. Ordinands and trainee ministers need to realize that it is not surprising to have within the psyche such a mixed-up motivation, but training should help them to identify it and not allow it to be acted out. In setting out these suggestions, I realize that the task will be all the harder in churches and institutions which have allowed inappropriate power to be codified in theological systems and patterns of ministry. That is the tragedy of the shepherding movement. Apart from its very earliest manifestations in Argentina, the theology of the movement set in stone for an entire generation harmful patterns of interrelating in the church, and it is extremely difficult to extirpate such deeply embedded ideas. Some churches will need a massive revolution to rediscover Jesus' understanding of power, while others have retained structures which make such a shift not too difficult to imagine.

This book is then a plea for a radical review of the way that power is exercised in the church. This is not just about the way the clergy and ministers do their job, but the way the laity encourage and collude in harmful structures. The hope in all this is that the Bible itself has a great deal to say about what is appropriate and helpful. Words like 'fellowship', 'communion' and 'love' are all in the New Testament to be constantly rediscovered and reinterpreted for each generation, so that congregations and fellowships can find the spirit of Christ in them. Power abuse, though found in churches of all traditions, is not inevitable as Christians relearn their traditions in an atmosphere of tolerance, acceptance and openness.

Helping the victims of religious abuse

What about the victims? During the nine months I have been writing this book, I have been brought face to face with further victims of Christian abuse. I have no idea how big the problem is in Britain, but perhaps this book, in naming it as an issue, will bring much more of it to light. I want to offer some final thoughts on how such people can be supported and helped. First of all they must be listened to and believed. Having spent many hours with the victims in this book, I know first-hand how much they feel they will not be believed. The story of Kathleen was particularly tragic. Not only was her relationship with her family almost destroyed, but her own voice was almost silenced. She lacked the confidence to name what had been done to her because she still carried a deference to the 'people in authority', whom she felt knew more than she did. When individuals have internalized such attitudes, a great deal of patience is needed to encourage them to tell their story.

Victims of Christian abuse will need to find a safe place to tell their story. The tragedy is that in Britain there is little enough recognition of the existence of any problem, let alone any organized group of men and women to help the victims recover. I am, however, optimistic enough to believe that there are many clergy and other wise Christians called to some kind of ministry all over the world, who, during the process of training for ministry, have successfully owned and transcended the shadow of power and its enjoyment. Probably they will be found in very ordinary parishes and churches. They will have long since abandoned the ambitious part of the shadow of power. There will be no urgency in them to look for larger, more responsible posts or larger, more complex churches. They are content to serve God in a humble capacity, away from the clamour of wider recognition and fame. Whether or not ambition is an inevitable part of this shadow of power can only be known by those who experience it. I would only comment that some ambition I have observed in the church certainly seems to participate in the shadow of power.

These men and women will recognize the particular manifestation of suffering and distress that this book has tried to describe, and will be able to allow the individual to find their voice once more, to relearn their sense of appropriate boundaries. They will rediscover what belongs to them and to their relationship with God, and what may reasonably be shared with others. Many vulnerable people will have had their inner boundaries invaded in the course of 'ministry', so that the core of their being has been undermined. The minister needs to assist in the task of giving them back their 'power', so that they can make real decisions once more. Above all the victim needs to experience appropriate love, a love that honours their uniqueness and their dignity. The love of God, which Christians talk about so freely, is a love that does not judge a person in terms of giftedness, wealth or ability; it is one that values and simultaneously builds up the core of the individual's unique being.

The helpers of the abused will need to have a particular theological outlook which will help them to move forward in their thinking. One cannot stipulate exactly what theological insights are important to possess, but clearly a theology which is flexible in its expression is required. The picture that comes to me to describe the wrong kind of theology is that of the suit of armour. If a belief system is used to protect identity then it is never going to be useful in helping another person who needs to disentangle themselves from abusive patterns of understanding. The kind of theological outlook I would hope for would, when dealing with vulnerable individuals, be sparse with words. As I have commented earlier in this book, fundamentalist Christianity is often fearful in its manner of expression, and frequently words are used in vast quantities to cover up that sense of insecurity. The defence of particular propositions about Christ and the Bible elicits a great deal of text-quoting and fiery rhetoric. If these doctrines are in any way undermined, the whole edifice is believed to come crashing down. The minister to the abused Christian cannot afford to have this kind of faith. Although they will believe many of the same things as the conservative Christian, they will be less anxious to encompass their beliefs in numerous words and propositions. They might go so far as to claim that there are no statements that contain the essence of the faith. They may point to it, but they do not contain it. A flexible Christian will know within themselves something of the reality of God and Christ, and their theological work will have enabled them to relate the orthodox formulae to the realities of which they speak. There is, however, never to be a final identification between the words and the realities to which they point. The task of knowing God in Christ is a never-ending one. There is no sudden breakthrough of 'arriving' in knowledge of God, nor is there a perfect language with which to express and articulate it. An individual may move closer and closer, but they can never, this side of the grave, say that they have achieved it. In the words of a father of the church, Gregory of Nyssa, there is a movement from glory to glory into the infinity of the divine reality.

The victim of a fundamentalist mindset is likely to have been taught two closely dependent ideas. The first is that salvation depends on accepting a series of propositions based on the teaching of the Bible, and the second is that the particular church he or she belongs to has a firm grasp of what this teaching is. The idea that truth is containable in a verbal statement is one that has already been questioned in the previous paragraph. The implicit idea that there is a certainty to be had by following the example of the leaders of a particular church should also be questioned. The victim of the fundamentalist mindset needs to have pointed out to him the improbability that God, in his dealings with humankind over 2,000 years since the arrival of Christ, should have chosen one particular church or network of churches in the whole world with which to entrust the full substance of his self-revelation. There is a profound arrogance at work here, something which is simultaneously absurd and unrealistic. If the understanding of what truth is is tempered with a certain realism, it will soon be recognized that even if part of the truth is known, it is unlikely to be the last word on the subject or a complete statement of what it is.

One word that is much bandied about in fundamentalist circles, alongside 'truth', is 'certainty'. From what has already been said it is clear that 'certainty' in the modern sense is something that should neither be sought, nor expected in the Christian life. The word 'certainty' is one that emerges from the scientific and mathematical sphere. Certainty is sought and obtained when one has successfully conducted an experiment or proved a mathematical theorem. Outside mathematics and certain branches of science, certainty is not something that is found very often. In much experimental science, work is carried out on the basis of an hypothesis or hunch. Translating the work of the experimental scientist into Christian terms, Christians act on the basis of faith. Faith is in fact the ground of an individual's decision-making in most areas of life, from choosing a marriage partner to deciding where to live. Trust is based on what is seen already and knowing deep within that such a person or place is going to be right in the future. There is no certainty given when embarking on marriage, and neither should an individual expect it on becoming a Christian. The absence of certainty in this strict sense is not the absence of any kind of reassurance or rational ground for commitment. I can almost hear my fundamentalist interlocutor responding that without certainty, there are no grounds for confidence in my salvation. To him I would reply that if I have to make life-important decisions in every other area of my life on the basis of faith, why should my Christian life be any different?

The helper of the abused Christian will need to teach a new and more biblical understanding of faith. Faith is not accepting, on the authority of someone else, a series of formulae concerned with the nature of God and Jesus Christ and believing them to be finally true. Faith is the ability to open oneself to see in a new way the reality of God reaching towards humankind through the ministry and words of Christ. The word, in its original Greek meaning, has the idea of reliability and trustworthiness. When people open themselves to God, they affirm that they believe him to be reliable and worthy of exploration. It is only as time passes that they begin to identify with the various formulae of the Christian church and the experience of the biblical record. At the beginning it is all strange and new to them and certainly what they find to be 'true' at that stage is unlikely to be closely identifiable with the highly developed formulae of Christian doctrine. Many abused Christians will need a 'holiday' from doctrine as they may still be suffering from the effects of having it imposed on them in an aggressive way. It may be more important to discover what is really believed than what ought to be believed. I feel certain that God will understand that some Christians need a longer time to rediscover the faith in a more highly articulated form.

In chapter eight, I spoke about the work of Reuben Alves and his description of the conversion experience. The convert met Christ who was able to release him or her from the profound sense of loss or abandonment that had been encountered in his or her life. I mentioned that immediately after conversion, the church community may move in to interpret the experience in the language of Christian orthodoxy. In the process of helping a Christian who has come through such an experience, and then moved on into a controlling Christian community, one would seek to take them back to that original experience. He or she would be encouraged to explore it without having to use the language of orthodoxy and 'correct' Christian expressions to talk about it. There then could be a time of integration of that experience, and the victim could be offered the chance to explore a variety of Christian 'cultures' through which to express his or her faith.

Speaking personally for a moment, I find that no single expression of the Christian faith is adequate to contain what I believe. I find I need constantly to examine different types of biblical interpretation, as well as wander across different denominational emphases to express my understanding of what faith is about. One classic expression of Christianity to which I return frequently is that of Eastern Orthodoxy. It is not that I find there a total presentation of what I believe about God, but I do find valuable resources of language and expression that help me in trying to hold on to the total mystery of God. Alongside its tendency to be highly dogmatic in its formulae, it also retains a mystical language of the unknowability of God, which helps me to express what I want to say. The concepts in what is known technically as 'apophatic' theology are of enormous help in breaking free from what seems to be the banal and trivializing language about God which sometimes appears in the discourse of popular piety. Apophaticism, in essence, is a way of talking about God in terms of what he is not. It allows God to rise above all human words and all human concepts, refusing to allow him to be contained in human 'certainties' and in human conceptual formulae.

Conclusion

The reader has travelled a long journey with me in exploring and hopefully understanding a disturbing aspect within the life of the church – Christian abuse. For many Christians, being hermetically sealed off from the cultures I have described, the problem does not exist. Ironically it is those outside the churches who will often know more about the incidence of Christian abuse, as the popular press finds stories of people being 'demonized' or abused in some way by Christians undeniably attractive for their purposes. So, while 'respectable' Christianity is trying to serve the world through its institutional life and its prophetic witness to the values of society, abusive Christianity is simultaneously discrediting the whole church by its actions. Few people outside the church take the trouble to distinguish between the two manifestations and the good is condemned with the bad. The problem, as I have repeated many times, is not just about the moral lapses of individuals, but the potential within certain ideologies and belief systems to devalue and oppress individuals. In particular, I claim that a Bible which is presented to be without error or contradiction is a dangerous and possibly harmful weapon in the hands of fallible and corruptible human beings. People need, in any doctrine of biblical authority, to be protected from the unconscious choices produced by the 'shadow' of men and women within ministry. I have not in this study offered a new alternative doctrine of biblical authority. That has not been my aim, though clearly those who may have been negatively affected by the ideas surrounding the teaching of an inerrant scripture will need to find, with the help of trustworthy Christians, a new way to use the resources contained in the Bible. Whatever that new approach to the Bible consists of precisely, I trust and pray that that teaching will release them to discover the glorious freedom of the children of God – how they can in Christ know what they are meant to become, both in this world and in the next.

Notes on the Chapters

This book has been written without footnotes as it does not aspire to any kind of scholarly status within the pastoral or theological literature. Nevertheless, as the bibliography will indicate, it is based on a great deal of reading, as well as actual observation of the workings of conservative Christianity over several years. This participation and the listening to personal accounts of individuals caught up in the belief system have, of course, shaped the precise areas of study and descriptions that are made in this book. For those interested I offer below some notes on the individual chapters, indicating the main external sources for the factual material used to interpret my accounts, as well as to help me to form judgements about their meaning.

Chapter One

This chapter (and to some extent the whole book) is largely written against the background of a book by K. Ritter and C. O'Neill, which seeks to place Catholic Christianity and Fundamentalist Christianity within the context of family theory, *Righteous Religion*. This book helped me to see the issues of John and Rachel against the model of a church operating as a dysfunctional family. Another book that has greatly influenced this chapter is Philip Greven's *Spare the Child*. This accounts for the possibly disproportionate amount of space given to the ideas about Protestant child-rearing and biblical beliefs. Few could read Greven's work and not be moved by his thesis, and this book did more than anything to fuel my interest in the whole subject of abuse within a Christian context. More space could have been given to discussion of actual Christian schools. The literature available is all American and my brief remarks are based on *God's Choice*, by A. Peskin. Another book consulted about the content of the curriculum is that by A.J. Menendez, *Visions of Reality*. The comments on the Word of Faith churches are taken, for this part of the book, mainly from the remarkably absorbing book by Steve Brouwer and others, *Exporting the American Gospel*. This book explores the wider political and social effects of American fundamentalist ideas.

Chapter Two

Kathleen's story is, as the text indicates, to be understood against the background of a wide variety of Christian counselling styles that have dominated the charismatic scene over the last twenty years. One very striking book consulted, which gives the basis for some of the 'fashions' of counselling ideas over this time period is that by J.S. Victor, *Satanic Panic*. This sets out the interest in the demonic in an historical context. Another book on the topic of 'false memories' which had a considerable impact on me was by R. Ofshe and E. Watters, *Making Monsters*. Much American material exists on the World Wide Web on this theme, since the social impact of the 'panic' has been far more widespread in the United States than in Britain, with a greater need to counteract it. The material on the 'need to be right' came from the interesting book by R.B. Cialdini, *Influence, Science and Practice*, and from parts of J.M. Hull's book, *What Prevents*

Christian Adults from Learning? As stated in the text I have found less published source material than I would have liked about the principles of Christian counselling styles, though the literature on the demonic as a cause of distress among Christians is extensive. The book by Kenneth McAll, *Healing the Family Tree*, needs to be read by anyone who wants to understand one part of the preoccupation of Kathleen's counsellors. Kathleen's story could, in many ways, be read as a case study of the paranoia that existed in Christian and social-work contexts in the early 1990s, and Jean La Fontaine's *Speak of the Devil* is an excellent overview of the whole rather sad story.

Chapter Three

Teresa's story in many ways is a continuation of the same belief systems covered by the previous chapter. The issue in the story is how a set of beliefs about the demonic becomes translated in practice into an actual parish situation. The discussion of Peter Horrobin's ideas is not only a critique of the theology, but also it expresses an anxiety as to how the teaching of a book becomes appropriated by individual readers. That is a problem the literature (which is considerable) never seems to address. Andrew Walker's essay in *Charismatic Renewal*, edited by Tom Smail, is the source of the historical material in the chapter. Further historical source material is found in the notes to chapter seven.

Chapter Four

My reading on the issue of homosexuality in the church is not extensive, and I have relied mainly on Michael Vasey's book,

Strangers and Friends, and one from a conservative perspective, B. Edwards' *Homosexuality*. The material about the Lambeth conference was readily obtainable from the World Wide Web. This gave me access not only to the day-to-day reports of the conference, but also to a number of commentaries. The website run by Reform gave access to the other conferences within the Anglican Church which have discussed the issue over the past few years.

Chapter Five

There is an extensive literature appearing on the subject of sexual abuse within the context of the church. A recent, but particularly wise, book is one by P. Parkinson, *Child Sexual Abuse and the Churches*. I received guidance in the matter of post-traumatic stress from a book by J.L. Herman, *Trauma and Recovery*. This set out what would have been an appropriate response towards Rita and her experience. In the chapter I also revert back to the influence of *Righteous Religion*, mentioned in chapter one, as a way of understanding Rita's continuing attraction to abusive churches. The section on the biblical and social control of women is heavily indebted to a book edited by C.C. Kroeger and J.R. Beck, *Women, Abuse and the Bible*. Many of the quotations in this section are those made by Kroeger and Beck from other sources. James Poling's important book, *The Abuse of Power*, is the main source for the final section, but I have also added material gleaned from Marty Raphael's book, *Spiritual Vampires*.

Chapter Six

I am indebted to the book, *Why Waco?*, by J. Tabor and E.V. Gallagher, for much of the material in the first two sections of this chapter. The material on Darby and Scofield is in all the standard histories of fundamentalism, including G.M. Marsden's *Fundamentalism and American Culture* and M.A. Noll's *The Scandal of the Evangelical Mind*. I have also made use of a variety of books dealing with the theme of the millennium, such as R. Kyle's *Awaiting the Millennium* and D. Thompson's *The End of Time*. The material about Christian response to the Jews is largely drawn from D.A. Rausch's *Fundamentalist Evangelicals and Anti-Semitism,* but K.C. Boone's *The Bible Tells Them So* also contains material on this theme.

Chapter Seven

This chapter has many sources, but in the end I created my own definitions. I am much indebted to the space given by Martyn Percy, in *Power and the Church*, Harriet Harris, in *Fundamentalism and Evangelicals*, K.C. Boone, in *The Bible Tells Them So* and G.M. Marsden in his seminal writings to this discussion, but ultimately I found it important not to depend on any one of their definitions. The definitions that are offered are based on observations of the way that fundamentalist churches operate, as much as on the literature that exists on the subject. The problem of how to use a word that is felt by many to be insulting is one that will not lend itself to an easy solution.

My motives for writing about the charismatic movement in the way I do come from my own participation in it, but I am greatly indebted to D. McConnel's book, *The Promise of Health and Wealth*, for shedding light on the background of this movement in one of its manifestations. The material about the shepherding movement and its collapse was taken from M.A. Chrnalogar's book, *Twisted Scriptures*. Her account has all the feel of sober reporting, but I have not verified this material in any other source. The material on the interpretation of the Bible is mainly taken from James Barr's books, *Fundamentalism* and *Escaping from Fundamentalism*, and John Barton's *People of the Book?* I have also gained much from the wise discussion of J.D.G. Dunn in *The Living Word*. The influence of the other key book, Harriet Harris's *Fundamentalism and Evangelicals*, is also gratefully acknowledged.

Chapter Eight

Material for the section on signs and symbols was obtained mainly from T. Fawcett's book, *The Symbolic Language of Religion*. It is as far as I know unsurpassed for clarity and enlightenment on this subject. The material on Melanie Klein came from a conversation with a psycho-dynamic counsellor who put me in touch with I. Salzberger-Wittenberg's book, *Psycho-Analytic Insight and Relationships*. Reuben Alves's book, *Protestantism and Repression*, has been a long-time favourite, and Alves's model for understanding the conversion process is highly illuminating. I believe I have been faithful to the arguments of C. Ullman, presented in *The Transformed Self*, though, as with the book about Klein, I was attempting to reproduce material from a discipline a long way from my own areas of study. The conclusions in the final paragraph at the end of this section are my own. The section 'Conversion and Faith' also contains my own reflections against the background of some observations from Harriet Harris's book.

Most of what is said about the church as a family system is taken from the book mentioned above, *Righteous Religion* by K. Ritter and C. O'Neill. I have used some of my interview material to reflect on the issues that this book raises. *The Guru Papers*, by J. Kramer and D. Alstad, and its influence on the final section of the chapter is, I hope, adequately acknowledged.

Chapter Nine

The material on Jesus is a reproduction of that which I have used in talks and absorbed over many years, so I am not aware of all the sources I have used. One book that influenced me greatly as a theological student was Norman Perrin's *Rediscovering the Teaching of Jesus* and I reread his account in preparation for this chapter. Walter Wink's books on the 'Powers' have all been read in the past few years, but only one, *Engaging the Powers*, has fed directly into this chapter. *Jesus the Liberator* by J. Sobrino was also a considerable help and influence in getting my ideas sorted out for what I wanted to say.

Chapter Ten

Apart from references to other works in the first section, I have allowed myself the luxury of writing this chapter without consulting any books directly. I am aware of only one book, *Meeting the Shadow* by C. Zweig and J. Abrams, that has fed into this chapter directly. The rest of the writing is a direct personal reflection on the material of the book and has to be read and either accepted or rejected in this vein.

Bibliography

The reader is offered here a list of those books that have been read or consulted during the course of this study. Not all of them are of equal value. I have taken the liberty of marking with an asterisk the forty-plus books that I have found the most useful. Clearly the list could have contained many others, but the task of consulting books on this theme, many of which are published in the United States, has not been without its problems. The books listed below, most of which are in my possession, will provide the reader with some help in going further in understanding the issue of fundamentalism and its abuse.

All quotations from scripture are taken from the New English Bible copyright © 1961, 1970 by Oxford University Press and Cambridge University Press.

Adams, J.E., *Competent to Counsel*, Baker, 1970.

Adorno, T.W., et al., *The Authoritarian Personality*, Harper and Bros, 1950.

Allport, G.W., *The Nature of Prejudice*, Anchor Books, 1958.

Alves, R.A., *Protestantism and Repression*, SCM, 1979.*

Ammerman, N.T., *Bible Believers: Fundamentalists in the Modern World*, Rutgers University Press, 1987.

Arterburn, S., and Felton, J., *Toxic Faith: Understanding and Overcoming Religious Addiction*, Oliver Nelson, 1991.

Ashton, J., *Set Free: How to Break Spiritual Bonds*, LBA, 1992.

Babinski, E., *Leaving the Fold: Testimonies of Former Fundamentalists*, Prometheus, 1995.

Barker, E., *New Religious Movements*, HMSO, 1992.

Barkum, M. (ed.), *Millennialism and Violence*, Frank Cass, 1996.

Barr, J., *Escaping from Fundamentalism*, SCM, 1981*.

Barr, J., *Fundamentalism*, SCM, 1977.*

Barr, J., *Holy Scripture, Canon, Authority, Criticism*, Westminster Press, 1983.

Barton, J., *People of the Book? The Authority of the Bible in Christianity*, SPCK, 1988.*

Bawer, S., *Stealing Jesus: How Fundamentalism Betrays Christianity*, Crown, 1997.*

Beale, D.O., *In Pursuit of Purity: American Fundamentalism Since 1850*, Unusual Publications, 1986.

Beasley-Murray, P., *Power for God's Sake: Power and Abuse in the Local Church*, Paternoster, 1998.*

Bebbington, D.W., *Evangelicalism in Modern Britain: A History from the 1730s to the 1980s*, Routledge, 1993.

Bendroth, M., *Fundamentalism and Gender, 1875 to the Present*, Yale, 1993.

Blamires, H., *The Christian Mind*, SPCK, 1963.

Blue, K., *Healing Spiritual Abuse*, Intervarsity Press, 1993.

Boone, K.C., *The Bible Tells Them So: The Discourse of Protestant Fundamentalism*, SCM, 1989.*

Borg, M.J., *Jesus, A New Vision, Spirit, Culture, and the Life of Discipleship*, HarperCollins, 1987.

Boyer, P., *When Time Shall Be No More: Prophecy Belief in Modern American Culture*, Harvard, 1992.*

Brouwer, S., et al., *Exporting the American Gospel: Global Christian Fundamentalism*, Routledge, 1996.*

Bruce, S., *Pray TV: Televangelism in America*, Routledge, 1990.

Burgess, S.M., et al. (eds), Dictionary of Pentecostal and Charismatic Movements, Zondervan, 1988.

Camp, G.S., *Selling Fear: Conspiracy Theories and End-Times Paranoia*, Baker, 1997.

Carroll, R.P., *Wolf in the Sheepfold: The Bible as Problematic for Theology*, SCM, 1997.

Chrnalogar, M.A., *Twisted Scriptures: A Path to Freedom from Abusive Churches*, Control Techniques Inc., 1998.*

Cialdini, R.B., *Influence, Science and Practice*, HarperCollins, 1993.*

Clifford, P., *A Brief History of End Time*, Lion, 1997.

Cotton, I., *The Hallelujah Revolution: The Rise of the New Christians*, Warner Books, 1996.

Davis, S.T., *The Debate about the Bible: Inerrancy Versus Infallibility*, Westminster Press, 1977.

Dillistone, F.W. (ed.), *Myth and Symbol*, SPCK, 1966.

Dominian, J., *Authority: A Christian Interpretation of the Psychological Evolution of Authority*, DLT, 1981.

Dunn, J.D.G., *Jesus' Call to Discipleship*, Cambridge, 1992.

Dunn, J.D.G., *The Living Word*, SCM, 1987.*

Edwards, B. (ed.), *Homosexuality: The Straight Agenda*, Day One Publications, 1998.

Elliott, P., *Brotherhoods of Fear: A History of Violent Organizations*, Blanford, 1998.

Ellis, M.H., *Unholy Alliance: Religion and Atrocity in Our Time*, SCM, 1997.

Enroth, R.M., *Churches That Abuse*, Zondervan, 1992.

Erickson, M.J., *The Evangelical Left: Encountering Postconservative Evangelical Theology*, Baker, 1997.

Erikson, E.H., *Childhood and Society*, Norton, 1950.

Erikson, E.H., *Insight and Responsibility*, Norton, 1964.

Erikson, K.T., *Wayward Puritans: A Study in the Sociology of Deviance*, Macmillan, 1986.

Fawcett, T., *The Symbolic Language of Religion*, SCM, 1970.*

Fife, J., *The Power to Heal Now: Charismatic Healing Ministries and the Sexual Abuse Survivor*, unpublished M. Phil thesis, Manchester, 1998.

Fosdick, H.E., *The Modern Use of the Bible*, SCM, 1924.

French, H.W., *A Study of Religious Fanaticism and Responses to It: Adversary Identity*, Edwin Mellan Press, 1990.*

Fuller, R.C., *Naming the Antichrist: The History of an American Obsession*, Oxford, 1996.

Geisler, N. (ed.), *Inerrancy*, Zondervan, 1980.

Gilbert, R.A., *Casting the First Stone: The Hypocrisy of Religious Fundamentalism and its Threat to Society*, Element, 1993.

Green, M., and Townsend, A., *Hidden Treasure: A Journey Towards Healing from Sexual Abuse*, DLT, 1994.

Greven, P., *Spare the Child: The Religious Roots of Punishment and the Psychological Impact of Physical Abuse*, Vintage Books, 1992.*

Guinness, O., *Fit Bodies, Fat Minds: Why Evangelicals Don't Think and What to Do About It*, Hodder, 1995.

Habgood, J., *Confessions of a Conservative Liberal*, SPCK, 1988.

Halsell, G., *Prophecy and Politics: Militant Evangelists on the Road to Nuclear War*, Laurence Hill, 1986.

Hammond, F., and I.M., *Pigs in the Parlour: A Practical Guide to Deliverance*, New Wine Press, 1992.

Hanegraaf, H., *Christianity in Crisis*, Word Books, 1993.

Hanegraaf, H., *Counterfeit Revival*, Word Publishing, 1997.*

Harris, H.A., *Fundamentalism and Evangelicals*, Oxford, 1998.*

Harris, J.L., and Milam, M.J., *Serpents in the Manger: Overcoming Abusive Christianity*, Barricade Books, 1994.

Hassan, S., *Combating Cult Mind Control*, Park Street Press, 1990.

Hawley, J.S.H. (ed.), *Fundamentalism and Gender*, Oxford, 1994.

Hebert, G., *Fundamentalism and the Church of God*, SCM, 1957.

Herman, J.L., *Trauma and Recovery: The Aftermath of Violence from Domestic Abuse to Political Terror*, Basic Books, 1992.

Hinshelwood, R., et al., *Melanie Klein for Beginners*, Icon Books, 1997.

Hoffer, E., *The True Believer: Thoughts on the Nature of Mass Movements*, Harper and Row, 1989.

Hofstadter, R., *Anti-Intellectualism in American Life*, Jonathan Cape, 1964.*

Hollenweger, W.J., *Pentecostalism: Origins and Developments Worldwide*, Hollenweger, W.J., *The Pentecostals*, SCM, 1972.

Hendrickson, 1997.

Horrobin, P., *Healing Through Deliverance: The Practical Ministry*, Sovereign, 1995.*

Horton, M.S. (ed.), *Power Religion: The Selling Out of the Evangelical Church?*, Moody, 1992.

Houlden, J.L., *Explorations in Theology 3*, SCM, 1978.

Howard, R., *Charismania: When Christian Fundamentalism Goes Wrong*, Mowbray, 1997.*

Hugman, R., *Power in Caring Professions*, Macmillan, 1991.

Hull, J.M., *What Prevents Christian Adults from Learning?*, SCM, 1985.

Hunter, J.D., *Culture Wars: The Struggle to Define America*, Basic Books, 1991.

Jacobs, M. (ed.), *Faith or Fear? A Reader in Pastoral Counselling*, DLT, 1987.

Johnson, D., and VanVonderen, J., *The Subtle Power of Spiritual Abuse*, Bethany House, 1991.

Jorstad, E., *The Politics of Doomsday: Fundamentalists of the Far Right*, Abingdon, 1970.

Kaplan, L., *Fundamentalism in Comparative Perspective*, Massachusetts, 1992.

Kepel, G., *The Revenge of God*, Polity Press, 1994.

Kilpatrick, W.K., *Psychological Seduction*, Arthur James, 1983.

Kramer, J., and Alstad, D., *The Guru Papers: Masks of Authoritarian Power*, Berkeley, 1993.*

Kroeger, C.C., and Beck, J.R., *Women, Abuse and the Bible: How Scripture Can Be Used to Hurt or Heal*, Paternoster, 1998.*

Kuitert, H.M., *I Have My Doubts: How to Become a Christian Without Being a Fundamentalist*, SCM, 1993.

Kung, H., and Moltmann, J. (eds), *Fundamentalism as an Ecumenical Challenge*, SCM, 1996.

Kyle, R., *Awaiting the Millennium*, IVP, 1998.

La Fontaine, J.S., *Speak of the Devil: Tales of Satanic Abuse in Contemporary England*, Cambridge, 1998.*

Ladd, G.E., *The Blessed Hope: A Biblical Study of the Second Advent and the Rapture*, Eerdmans, 1956.

LaHaye, T., *The Battle for the Mind*, Revell, 1980.

Lake, F., *Clinical Theology*, DLT, 1966.

Lasley, J., *The Threat of Radical Fundamentalism*, Nisgo Publications, 1990.

Lindhom, C., *Charisma*, Blackwell, 1991.*

Lindsey, H., *The Late Great Planet Earth*, Bantam Books, 1973.

Lines, D., *Christianity is Larger Than Fundamentalism*, Pentland, 1995.

Logan, K., *Satanism and the Occult*, Kingsway, 1994.

Ludeman, G., *The Unholy in Holy Scripture: The Dark Side of the Bible*, SCM, 1997.

Mackay, C., *Extraordinary Delusions and the Madness of Crowds*, 1841 and 1995.

Mackey, J.P., *Power and Christian Ethics*, Cambridge, 1994.

Marsden, G.M., *Fundamentalism and American Culture: The Shaping of Twentieth-Century Evangelicalism, 1870–1925*, Oxford, 1980.*

Marsden, G.M., *Reforming Fundamentalism*, Eerdmans, 1995.

Marsden, G.M., *Understanding Fundamentalism and Evangelicalism*, Eerdmans, 1991.

Marty, M.E., and Appleby, R.S., *Fundamentalism Observed*, Chicago, 1991.

Marty, M.E., and Appleby, R.S., *The Glory and the Power: The Fundamentalist Challenge to the Modern World*, Beacon, 1992.

McAll, K., *Healing the Family Tree*, Sheldon Press, 1982.

McConnel, D., *The Promise of Health and Wealth: A Historical and Biblical Analysis of the Modern Faith Movement*, Hodder and Stoughton, 1990.*

McGrath, A.E., *A Passion for Truth: The Intellectual Coherence of Evangelicalism*, Apollos, 1996.

Menendez, A.J., *Visions of Reality: What Fundamentalist Schools Teach*, Prometheus Books, 1993.

Methvin, E.H., *The Rise of Radicalism: The Social Psychology of Messianic Extremism*, Arlington House, 1973.

Middlemiss, D., *Interpreting Charismatic Experience*, SCM, 1996.

Miles, A., *Setting the Captives Free*, Prometheus Books, 1990.

Miller, A., *For Your Own Good: Hidden Cruelty in Child-rearing and the Roots of Violence*, New York, 1984.*

Miller, D.E., *The Case for Liberal Christianity*, SCM, 1981.

Moore, R.L., *Selling God: American Religion in the Marketplace of Culture*, Oxford, 1994.

Moscovici, S., *The Age of the Crowd: A Historical Treatise on Mass Psychology*, Cambridge, 1985.

Nathan, P., *The Psychology of Fascism*, Faber and Faber, 1943.

Nelson, R., *The Making and the Unmaking of an Evangelical Mind: The Case of Edward Carnell*, Cambridge, 1987.

Noll, M.A., *The Scandal of the Evangelical Mind*, IVP, 1994.

Ofshe, R., and Watters, E., *Making Monsters: False Memories, Psychotherapy and Sexual Hysteria*, André Deutsch, 1995.*

Ortiz, J.C., *Disciple*, Lakeland, 1976.*

Osborn, L., and Walker, A., *Harmful Religion: An Exploration of Religious Abuse*, SPCK, 1997.*

Parkinson, P., *Child Sexual Abuse and the Churches*, Hodder and Stoughton, 1997.

Parsons, S., *The Challenge of Christian Healing*, SPCK, 1986.

Parsons, S., *Searching for Healing: Making Sense of the Many Paths to Wholeness*, Lion, 1995.

Payne, R., *The Corrupt Society*, Praeger, 1975.

Percy, M., *Power and the Church: Ecclesiology in an Age of Transition*, Cassell, 1998.

Percy, M., *Words, Wonders and Power: Understanding Contemporary Christian Fundamentalism and Revivalism*, SPCK, 1996.*

Perrin, N., *Rediscovering the Teaching of Jesus*, SCM, 1967.*

Perry, M. (ed.), *Deliverance, Psychic Disturbance and Occult Involvement*, SPCK, 1996.

Perry, M.J., *Love and Power: The Role of Religion and Morality in American Politics*, Oxford, 1991.

Peskin, A., *God's Choice: The Total World of a Fundamentalist Christian School*, Chicago, 1988.*

Pfister, O., *Christianity and Fear*, London, 1948.

Poling, J.N., *The Abuse of Power: A Theological Problem*, Abingdon Press, 1991.*

Rambo, L., *Understanding Religious Conversion*, Yale, 1993.*

Raphael, M., *Spiritual Vampires*, The Message Company, 1996.

Rausch, D.A., *Fundamentalist Evangelicals and Anti-Semitism*, Trinity Press, 1993.

Reed, B., *The Dynamics of Religion: Process and Movement in Christian Churches*, DLT, 1978.

Ritter, K., and O'Neill, C., *Righteous Religion: Unmasking the Illusions of Fundamentalism and Authoritarian Catholicism*, Haworth Press, 1996.*

Rokeach, M., *The Open and Closed Mind*, Basic Books, 1960.

Rubin, J.H., *Religious Melancholy and Protestant Experience in America*, Oxford, 1994.*

Rutter, P., *Sex in the Forbidden Zone: When Men in Power Betray Women's Trust*, Tarcher, 1989.

Salzberger-Wittenberg, I., *Psycho-Analytic Insight and Relationships: A Kleinian Approach*, Routledge, 1970.

Saxbee, J., *Liberal Evangelism: A Flexible Response to the Decade*, SPCK, 1994.

Schapiro, L., *Totalitarianism*, MacMillan, 1983.

Schelflin, A.W., and Opton, E.W., *Mind Manipulators*, Paddington Press, 1978.

Schultze, Q.J., *Televangelism and American Culture*, Baker, 1991.

Scott, D., *Everyman Revived: The Common Sense of Michael Polanyi*, Book Guild, 1985.

Shaw, G., *The Cost of Authority*, SCM, 1983.

Shupe, A. (ed.), *Wolves Within the Fold: Religious Leadership and Abuses of Power*, Rutgers University Press, 1998.

Sinason, V. (ed.), *Treating Survivors of Satanist Abuse*, Routledge, 1994.

Smail, T., et al., *Charismatic Renewal*, SPCK, 1995.*

Sobrino, J., *Jesus the Liberator: A Historical Reading of Jesus of Nazareth*, Burns and Oates, 1994.

Soskice, J.M., *Metaphor and Religious Language*, Oxford, 1987.

Spong, J.S., *Liberating the Gospels*, HarperCollins, 1996.

Spong, J.S., *Rescuing the Bible from Fundamentalism*, HarperSanFrancisco, 1991.

Strozier, C.B., *Apocalyse: On the Psychology of Fundamentalism in America*, Beacon, 1994.*

Szasz, T., *The Manufacture of Madness*, RKP, 1971.

Tabor, J., and Gallagher, E.V., *Why Waco? Cults and the Battle for Religious Freedom in America*, University of California Press, 1995.*

Thompson, D., *The End of Time*, Vintage, 1999.

Tomlinson, D., *The Post-Evangelical*, Triangle, 1995.*

Townsend, A., *Faith Without Pretending*, Hodder, 1990.

Ullman, C., *The Transformed Self: The Psychology of Religious Conversion*, Plenum Press, 1989.*

Vasey, M., *Strangers and Friends: A New Exploration of Homosexuality and the Bible*, Hodder and Stoughton, 1995.

Victor, J.S., *Satanic Panic: The Creation of a Contemporary Legend*, Open Court, 1993.*

Walker, A., *Restoring the Kingdom*, Eagle, 1998.

Widdas, J., and Mockford, P., *Lightning From Heaven*, Kingsway, 1993.

Wilcox, C., *Onward Christian Soldiers: The Religious Right in American Politics*, Westview, 1996.

Wills, G., *Under God: Religion and American Politics*, Simon and Schuster, 1990.

Wink, W., *Engaging the Powers*, Fortress Press, 1992.*

Wookey, S., *When a Church Becomes a Cult*, Hodder and Stoughton, 1996.

Young, P.D., *God's Bullies: Native Reflections on Preachers and Politics*, Holt, Rinehart and Winston, 1982.

Zweig, C., and Abrams, J., *Meeting the Shadow: The Hidden Power of the Dark Side of Human Nature*, Putnam, 1991.*

List of Bible References

Index